STUMBLING OVER TRUTH

STUMBLING OVER TRUTH

THE INSIDE STORY OF THE 'SEXED UP' DOSSIER, HUTTON AND THE BBC

KEVIN MARSH

Biteback Publishing

First published in Great Britain in 2012 by
Biteback Publishing Ltd
Westminster Tower
3 Albert Embankment
London SE1 7SP
Copyright © Kevin Marsh 2012

ISBN 978-1-84954-152-7

10 9 8 7 6 5 4 3 2 1

A CIP catalogue record for this book is available from the
British Library.

Set in Sabon

Printed and bound in Great Britain by
CPI Group (UK) Ltd, Croydon CR0 4YY

To my father, John, who never knew

CONTENTS

PREFACE

This is not a book anyone could ever have wanted to write.

At its centre is the death of a good man. Dr David Kelly. A wise, gentle, brave man, universally respected and honoured by his country for his loyalty and dedication.

A man who made the mistake of telling the truth to journalists about a government that had become better at creating the truth than recognising it.

This book is about that and the lengths to which New Labour was prepared to go to 'create the truth'. It's about Lord Hutton's failure to recognise that for what it was, how he failed justice and failed us all.

And how, unforgivably, he failed Dr Kelly.

ACKNOWLEDGEMENTS

My thanks to Melissa, Jack and Ellen, who read my manuscripts and made many corrections, though any errors that remain are mine alone. To Iain Dale and Sam Carter at Biteback; Iain for encouraging me to take on the project in the first place and Sam for his wise advice throughout.

Thanks to former BBC colleagues and bosses John Humphrys, Steve Mitchell, Mark Damazer, Richard Sambrook and others for their help in recalling events of the time; Nick Jones for a memory that reaches even further back; and especially to Gordon Corera for his insights into the workings of MI6 and his advice on intelligence matters.

Thanks, too, to the people I won't name here who were on the inside in Downing Street, the Foreign Office and elsewhere at the time the government's September 2002 dossier was being written. They know the contribution they made and I hope I've represented them fairly.

Finally, thanks to a group of people I don't know and have never met. The tireless researchers and journalists who've trawled through thousands of documents hidden in dark corners or revealed under the Freedom of Information Act. I share none of the conspiracy theories some propose – but I'm immensely grateful for their spadework.

BBC DRAMATIS PERSONAE

JENNY ABRAMSKY: Managing Director, Radio (later Audio and Music) and former *Today* editor

GAVIN ALLEN: *Today* assistant editor, later deputy editor, was on duty the morning Andrew Gilligan's story was broadcast and received the first complaint from Downing Street

HELEN BOADEN: Controller of Radio 4, later Head of News

MARK BYFORD: acting Director General following Greg Dyke's resignation

ANDREW CALDECOTT QC: the BBC's counsel at the Hutton Inquiry

MARK DAMAZER: Deputy Head of News during the row with Downing Street, wrote most of the replies to Alastair Campbell and masterminded the BBC's case at the Hutton Inquiry

GAVYN DAVIES: Chairman of the BBC Board of Governors

GREG DYKE: BBC Director General

GEORGE ENTWISTLE: *Newsnight* editor who, in 2012, became BBC Director General

ANDREW GILLIGAN: the *Today* reporter who met Dr David Kelly and reported his allegations on the morning of 29 May 2003

MIRANDA HOLT: *Today* assistant editor, on duty the afternoon that Andrew Gilligan first offered his story about the September 2002 dossier

JOHN HUMPHRYS: *Today* presenter

ROD LIDDLE: *Today* editor 1998–2002

STEVE MITCHELL: Head of Radio News, my immediate boss

RICHARD SAMBROOK: Head of News

SUSAN WATTS: *Newsnight* science reporter who spoke to Dr Kelly and recorded one of her conversations with him

STEPHEN WHITTLE: Controller of Editorial Policy, wrote the first briefing note for Director General Greg Dyke on Andrew Gilligan's story

Men occasionally stumble over the truth, but most of them pick themselves up and hurry off as if nothing ever happened.

Sir Winston Churchill

CHAPTER ONE

LORD HUTTON REPORTS

I consider that the editorial system which the BBC permitted was defective in that Mr Gilligan was allowed to broadcast his report at 6.07 a.m. without editors having seen a script of what he was going to say and having considered whether it should be approved.

Lord Hutton, 28 January 2004

It was lunchtime one day in late January and Lord Hutton was about to speak. Live on TV. Giving the conclusions of his inquiry 'Into the Circumstances Surrounding the Death of Dr David Kelly'. His judgment on the biggest row ever between Downing Street and the BBC. The row over the government's September 2002 dossier, *Iraq's Weapons of Mass Destruction*. The row that had ended with the death of a good man.

I was anxious. It was a shapeless anxiety that came from the schoolboy in me. The boy in a school cap always willing to please. Who'd always had to get everything right. Who hated criticism.

I expected Lord Hutton would criticise me. I was the editor who'd set in train the events that had ended with Dr Kelly's death on the edge of an Oxfordshire wood. I'd made the decision to put Andrew Gilligan on air on the *Today* programme on 29 May 2003. I'd given him the OK to report Dr Kelly's allegations that the September dossier had been 'transformed … at Downing Street's behest'. I'd checked his notes and script. If I'd said 'no' instead of 'yes' at any stage, none of this would have happened. The row with Downing Street wouldn't have happened, not over this, anyway. And a man wouldn't have died.

I'd been at the centre of it all yet Lord Hutton hadn't called me to give evidence. He hadn't heard why I'd made any of those decisions. The BBC hadn't put me in the witness box either and much of what had been said in evidence was factually wrong, assumption or guesswork. Witnesses had pored over documents I'd written, speculating on what they meant. Yet Lord Hutton never asked me directly.

Our journalism hadn't come out of it well. Andrew Gilligan in his evidence had admitted mistakes in one of his broadcasts – an early morning interview, or 'two-way', with *Today* presenter John Humphrys. The infamous 6.07 two-way. Some of those mistakes he'd already acknowledged, to the BBC internal team. Others, though, came as a surprise to me and to my bosses, especially the BBC Director General, Greg Dyke. They were mistakes he'd never conceded during the row with Downing Street. But the BBC had gone further and 'admitted' to Hutton mistakes and errors that no one had made, all of which made our journalism look shoddy.

So, yes, there was going to be criticism and I didn't imagine it would be comfortable.

• • •

I'd decided to watch Lord Hutton's televised statement in the glass box that passed for my office. It was one of a 'suite' of similarly sized glass boxes set against an outside wall of the news factory where *Today*, *World at One*, *PM*, *Broadcasting House* and *The World Tonight* are made. I rarely worked there, using it mostly for editorial conferences. I preferred to be out on the main newsdesk. I'd always worked that way. It's quiet inside the glass box. But it's no place to hide. It's just another stage where, as *Today* editor, you play out your life in plain sight.

Lord Hutton's report would be our main story tomorrow. Yet again. The row with Downing Street, or more precisely with Alastair Campbell, had never dropped far down our or anyone else's news agenda. There'd be an orgy of opinion and comment in the hours after Hutton published his conclusions. I needed to focus to think of any angles there'd be left for the morning.

There was a small TV screen on the desk beside my computer. Like something in a school physics lab. It was already on. I think it was always on. Tuned to BBC News 24, as the News Channel was called then. A reporter was standing in a street somewhere outside a building he couldn't get into, delivering vacant speculation moments ahead of the real thing.

In spite of the schoolboy anxiety over the certainty of criticism, I didn't really know the form that criticism would take. There'd been a clue with an apparent leak on the front page of that morning's *Sun*, but there was no way of knowing whether it was accurate and many reasons to think it wasn't.

The paper's political editor, Trevor Kavanagh, had splashed an exclusive 'HUTTON REPORT LEAKED'. He had four gobbets: 'Blair cleared of using sneaky ploy to name Dr Kelly'; 'Hoon off the hook ... but mild rap for MoD'; 'Kelly WRONG to meet BBC ... and felt in disgrace'; 'BBC "at fault"... Gilligan's story was "unfounded"'.

The first two seemed highly unlikely. The evidence was clear: a government press office had confirmed to journalists that Dr Kelly had spoken to Gilligan, allowing the inference that he was the source. Alastair Campbell was convinced that if it were known that he was Gilligan's source, it would 'fuck' him, as he'd put it in his diary.[†] There was no doubt that Dr Kelly had felt 'in disgrace', or something like that. But it was hard to

---

† In his diary for 4 July 2003, Campbell wrote: 'G. H. [Geoff Hoon, the Secretary of State for Defence] and I agreed it would fuck Gilligan if that [Dr Kelly] was his source.'

see how Gilligan's story was 'unfounded'. He'd made a dog's breakfast of that 6.07 two-way, but not the other broadcasts he'd done that day. And the story he'd offered, the story he'd intended to broadcast, was very well founded.

Kavanagh had appeared on the programme that morning. And of course he'd refused to say where he'd got his 'leak' from. But he did insist it was someone who 'had nothing to gain financially or politically, no axe to grind, no vested interest'. And he denied outright it was Downing Street or Alastair Campbell.

A week earlier, exactly seven days before Hutton finally delivered his report, I was in Davos at the World Economic Forum. That five-day party in the snow for the world's most powerful 2,000 people. I was never sure why I was invited. There, in a quiet corner of the Arabella Sheraton, the BBC's Head of News, Richard Sambrook, and I had shared our anxieties and expectations. Richard had been one of the main players throughout the row with Campbell.

We both wondered whether Hutton had understood the difference between journalism and the world he knew, the law. Whether he'd understood how newsrooms worked, how political offices like Downing Street worked. Sambrook was sure he'd share out the pain. He would hurt us, that was certain. He couldn't ignore the string of mistakes we'd admitted. But he had to have realised that Dr Kelly had been acting in the public interest when he'd blown the whistle on the dossier. That the concerns he'd shared with a number of journalists were genuine, his allegations well founded. And surely he'd understood we had a duty to report them and to defend the BBC's independence when Campbell challenged us. He'd heard the concerns of Dr Kelly's former friends and colleagues, intelligence analysts who'd worked on the information that went into the dossier. He'd even heard Dr Kelly voice those concerns himself in a taped conversation with a reporter. He couldn't ignore that.

Government witnesses had been minimalist. Evasive, even. Yet we'd all seen the Downing Street emails urging stronger and stronger language in the dossier. So strong, eventually, that some of the experts thought the intelligence couldn't support it. We'd all seen the emails that had changed the language and the meaning after intelligence chiefs had signed it off. There couldn't be any doubt it had been 'sexed up ... at the behest of Downing Street'.

There could be no doubt either, we thought, that Alastair Campbell and the MoD had played a cynical game to reveal Dr Kelly as Gilligan's source. A game that, according to the UK's leading expert on suicides, had driven Dr Kelly over the edge through 'dismay at being exposed' and 'publicly disgraced'.

I thought it was unlikely that Hutton could stray too far from the conclusions of the MPs on the Foreign Affairs Select Committee. They'd also gone over the September dossier. They'd questioned Gilligan, Campbell and Dr Kelly. They'd looked closely at the so-called '45-minute claim', the claim in the dossier that Saddam's WMD could be deployed within 45 minutes of an order to do so. Dr Kelly had told Gilligan that the claim was single sourced and that the experts in intelligence thought it didn't refer to WMD at all. Some thought it was wrong and had said so. Yet it had been included in the dossier as if it were an unqualified fact. The 'classic' example, according to Dr Kelly, of the dossier's 'transformation' at Downing Street's hands.

The MPs had concluded that 'the 45-minute claim did not warrant the prominence given to it in the dossier, because it was based on intelligence from a single, uncorroborated source'. And that the language in the dossier was 'in places more assertive than that traditionally used in intelligence documents' and 'contained undue emphases for a document of its kind'. Parliamentary language for 'the dossier had been sexed up'.

While Richard Sambrook and I were sharing these thoughts deep in the Swiss Alps, back in the UK, BBC1's *Panorama* was doing a much more critical job for an audience of millions. The programme, called *A Fight to the Death*, was written and presented by the BBC's toughest and most independent minded investigative reporter, John Ware, best known for his fearless and relentless pursuit of the Omagh bombers. 'Only the BBC could submit itself to this kind of public self-loathing', one paper said when it reviewed the programme. That's true. Only at the BBC could one of its star reporters, the kind of figure many people trusted more than the corporation itself, give his bosses a good kicking and be praised for it.

Ware had interviewed both Sambrook and me for his programme. But in true BBC style, no one outside the *Panorama* team – indeed, no one outside the edit suite where it was being put together – was allowed to know what was in the final cut. Or the final script. Especially not Sambrook and me. And, even more especially, not Greg Dyke.

Out in Switzerland, I knew I wouldn't be able to watch the programme live. So I'd asked Ware to email me his script. He did so. But only after the programme had gone out. His judgements were tough. He concluded that Dr Kelly had shared with Gilligan real concerns inside the intelligence community about the government's September 2002 dossier. The dossier, according to those concerns, had included dodgy intelligence stripped of its essential qualifications in order to make the case for war. The 45-minute claim, for example. He charted, too, the game of 'Russian roulette' that No. 10 and the MoD devised and put into play to 'out' Dr Kelly.

But, Ware reported, Gilligan had screwed up. In that early morning two-way, he'd attributed to his source, Dr Kelly, inferences that were his own. Dr Kelly hadn't told Gilligan that the government 'probably knew' the 45-minute claim 'was wrong … before it decided to put it in'. That was Gilligan's inference. He'd screwed up, too, during the subsequent row with Downing Street when he'd revealed Dr Kelly as another journalist's source. That had happened in an email to an MP.

Ware was tough on me, Sambrook and Dyke, too. We'd all defended Gilligan based on his personal assurances, he argued, while knowing that his language could be loose and inaccurate and his methods less than perfect.

Now, though, the speculation was over. Lord Hutton was about to start speaking. I took an A4 pad and drew a line down the middle making two columns. One side, conclusions that went for us; the other, those that went against us. Within minutes it was clear I would need only the one column.

After the ritual openings, Hutton got to the meat of it. The question at the centre of the whole affair was this: was the intelligence 'of sufficient strength and reliability', as Hutton put it, to justify the government's assessments and language in its dossier? Dr Kelly's allegation was that some in the intelligence community thought it was not.

Lord Hutton reminded us that there had been 'controversy and debate ... because of the failure, up to the time of writing this report, to find weapons of mass destruction in Iraq'. That failure suggested the allegations Gilligan had reported were well founded. But Hutton summarily closed the argument down: 'a question of such wide import, which would involve the consideration of a wide range of evidence, is not one which falls within my terms of reference.'

I looked up from the TV screen. Through the glass walls I could see the *Today* team. Some were bemused and shaking their heads. Over on the far side, sitting away from the rest on an empty bank of desks, John Humphrys grimaced. He wasn't normally in the office at this time of day. But I'd called him in to watch the statement and join in the editorial conference afterwards.

Hutton moved on and was speaking now about 'the major controversy which arose following Mr Andrew Gilligan's broadcasts on the BBC *Today* programme on 29 May 2003 and which closely involved Dr Kelly'. At the centre of that, the 45-minute claim. Some of those at the sharp end of intelligence had made it clear they thought the intelligence was wrong. Dr Kelly himself couldn't think of any munitions system in Iraq that it could apply to. The analysts thought it shouldn't have been in the dossier at all, but if it had to be, it should have been heavily qualified.

Hutton swept the question aside. 'The issue whether, if approved by the Joint Intelligence Committee and believed by the Government to be reliable, the intelligence contained in the dossier was nevertheless unreliable, is a separate issue which I consider does not fall within my terms of reference.' I wasn't sure I'd understood. But it seemed to be a swerve around yet another important question. This had never been about intelligence that turned out to be unreliable after the event. It was about intelligence some experts had told their bosses was unreliable before it went into the dossier. It hardly mattered. He'd decided that the question of whether anyone 'probably knew it was wrong before they decided to put it in' was out of his remit. So was another question: whether the 45 minutes claim applied to weapons of mass destruction or merely to battlefield weapons. 'A consideration of this distinction does not fall within my terms of reference...'

There was a pattern. Lord Hutton hadn't considered any shortcomings in the intelligence. And yet it was the way Dr Kelly understood those shortcomings to have been overlooked or overridden that had, apparently, motivated him to speak to journalists. They were at the centre of 'the circumstances surrounding the death of Dr David Kelly'.[†]

Nor did it end there. The BBC had insisted at Lord Hutton's

---

† Lord Hutton set out his terms of reference as '"urgently to conduct an investigation into the circumstances surrounding the death of Dr Kelly". In my opinion these terms of reference required me to consider the circumstances preceding and leading up to the death of Dr Kelly insofar as (1) they might have had an effect on his state of mind and influenced his actions preceding and leading up to his death or (2) they might have influenced the actions of others which affected Dr Kelly preceding and leading up to his death.'

inquiry that Gilligan had been reporting the allegations of a credible source. He wasn't making the allegations himself. That line of argument was based on a relatively new development in media law, the so-called 'Reynolds Defence'. Crudely, that meant careful and responsible reporting on a matter of urgent public interest was protected by law even if the facts reported in good faith turned out to be untrue.

Hutton had no time for it. Gilligan had, he said, made 'very grave allegations in relation to a subject of great importance ... false accusations of fact impugning the integrity of others ... should not be made...' That wasn't quite right. Then this: 'I consider that the editorial system which the BBC permitted was defective in that Mr Gilligan was allowed to broadcast his report at 6.07 a.m. without editors having seen a script of what he was going to say and having considered whether it should be approved.'

That wasn't true. I *had* considered what he intended to say and had approved it but Gilligan hadn't followed the script. Because Lord Hutton hadn't called me to give evidence, he didn't know that. He'd taken absence of evidence as evidence of absence. It stung and I found it hard to listen to the rest of what he had to say.

Once he'd finished, the TV screens screwed to the *Today* newsroom walls filled with a predictable crowd. Friends and enemies. Reporters and pundits who'd been following the inquiry. Some were already dismissing it as a whitewash.

I came out of the glass box. People stood up. No one spoke. A courier arrived with a pile of hard copies of Hutton's report. I signalled him to drop them on the *Today* newsdesk. Still no one spoke. Someone came over and picked up one of the copies. Others followed. Looking stunned. Hurt. Depressed. All energy gone. Someone broke the silence. 'What was that all about?' and 'Was that as bad as it sounded?' It was as bad as it sounded.

I called a listless huddle but almost straight away the TV

screens flicked over to the chamber of the House of Commons. The Prime Minister was about to make his statement to MPs. The chamber was full. The team went back to their seats to watch. I leant against the pillar at one end of the newsdesk.

Blair's delivery was quiet. Businesslike. More in sorrow than in anger, he listed the ten points where Hutton's findings could not have been more favourable. He quoted Hutton's misreading of the law: 'false accusations of fact impugning the integrity of others … should not be made'. And added: 'Let those who made them now withdraw them.' He didn't call for heads to roll. He didn't have to. He didn't even have to rely on his own MPs on the benches behind him.

Robert Jackson, a Tory and Dr Kelly's constituency MP: 'the BBC has admitted that Mr Gilligan's broadcast was wrong … and Lord Hutton has concluded that the BBC did not exercise proper editorial control … if Mr Gilligan had not felt encouraged to make the gravest allegations as a matter of routine, my constituent Dr Kelly would still be alive today.' None of that was true, but that didn't seem to matter much now.

Another Tory, Sir Patrick Cormack, wanted scalps too: 'those who have charge of our public service broadcasting should really consider their position.' As did the charmlessly eccentric Labour veteran, Gerald Kaufman: 'the BBC broadcast a lie … Richard Sambrook withheld from the Board of Governors information showing it to be a lie … Kevin Marsh and John Humphrys endorsed and built on the lie.' He wanted 'these people … cleared out and a new regime appointed'.

And so it went on. I'd had enough and called another huddle. Interrupted again, this time by Alastair Campbell. No longer on the Downing Street payroll, he'd had to find somewhere to make whatever statement he felt fit. He could have settled for putting out a short written statement via the Press Association. Bizarrely, he didn't. Instead, with that failure of self-awareness to which spin doctors are prone, he chose the most operatically inappropriate backdrop possible. The foot of the ornate staircase in what was then the HQ of the Foreign Press Association on Carlton House Terrace. The heart of London clubland and a former home of William Ewart Gladstone.

There was no orchestra but there was gilt and chandeliers and plush. It was *Tosca*. He was Scarpia. '*E avanti a lui tremava tutta Roma*' – 'before him all Rome used to tremble' – Tosca sings over Scarpia's impotent, lifeless corpse. That made me laugh.

He was cool and controlled at first. But it didn't last. He lashed out at me, at Gilligan, at Sambrook, Dyke and the BBC chairman Gavyn Davies. We'd waged a 'vicious campaign' to paint him and Tony Blair as 'liars'. I think he'd really come to believe that. 'The Prime Minister told the truth, the government told the truth, I told the truth – the BBC, from the chairman on down, did not.' In a faux-innocent aside he observed that if Hutton had reported similarly against the government, there would have been 'several resignations at several levels'. I smiled at that, too. Same old Campbell. It meant he could never be accused of calling for resignations. But everyone knew what it amounted to.

I called the team into the conference room. This time we wouldn't be interrupted. We had to get on with business. Maybe not as usual, but business nonetheless. Deciding who to invite onto tomorrow's programme. There was hardly anyone left, though, who hadn't already spoken.

Outside, a freak electric storm crackled. Snow began to fall. Through the windows that faced onto the outside, I watched sudden sharp gusts of wind chuck the thick, heavy flakes around. Like solid chunks of fog.

I was only half listening to the conference. Producers and editors argued the merits of inviting Campbell, Blair, Scarlett onto the show. Would Hutton talk? Someone asked. What should we do with Gilligan? How could we approach Dr Kelly's family? I hardly cared. I was watching the snow settle outside. Watching it cover the patches of oil. A crisp bag. A

Styrofoam cup. A curl of dog shit. By the time the conference was over, a couple of inches covered everything that was ugly under a spotless white blanket.

We broke. People went back to their desks to make phone calls. I needed to catch up with what had been happening on the other side of London, in Broadcasting House, where the governors were meeting. News had come through that Gavyn Davies had gone. That he hoped his resignation would be the only one. Then, there'd been a rumour that Greg Dyke had gone, too. Then, that he hadn't gone but would soon. Then, that he was safe. Then, that he'd stormed out of a meeting with the hawks on the Board of Governors. The only real thing anyone had to go on was his statement. That accepted Lord Hutton's conclusions as far as he had to. 'At no stage in the last eight months have we accused the Prime Minister of lying and we have said this publicly on several occasions.' They were wasted words. Hutton had taken us through the looking-glass to a place where truth was falsehood and falsehood truth. Guilt innocence and innocence guilt.

At about half past six, the news factory grew quiet. It does that every day at that time. The other programme teams have done their work for the day and have gone home or to the BBC club. It's a melancholy time. Just half a dozen *Today* producers are left, sitting around the newsdesk. Some have been there for eight or ten hours and have another two or three to go before they hand over to the night team. Distant lights go off. The heating powers down to its night-time setting. The canteens wind down until there are only omelettes and chips.

I got a call to go up to the fifth floor – or 'The Fifth Floor' – where Richard Sambrook had his suite of offices. He was on his way back from Broadcasting House. When I got up there, there were half a dozen or so news executives, including Mark Damazer, Sambrook's deputy and the brains behind the BBC's defences throughout the row and the inquiry. We all stood around. Saying little. I felt awkward. Someone found a carton of orange juice.

Sambrook arrived. He avoided eye contact with everyone. Sat down in a bundle in the chair behind his desk, his coat still on. Distracted. He hadn't slept for three days and it showed.

'I'll have to resign...' No one spoke. He was close to tears. 'I'll have to resign. How can I stand up and talk about BBC values after all of this...' He paused. Then somehow found news-chief mode again. Told everyone that they'd done their best. We asked what Dyke was going to do. He said he wasn't sure. It was all pretty tense. There was 'stuff' going on. He said he hoped no one else would have to go.

We mooched around for a while, sipping water and orange juice. But there was little to be said. It was awkward. I left and went back down to the *Today* newsroom. I was angry. For a decade, I'd seen it as my job to get underneath the 'truths' that the New Labour media machine, led by Campbell, had created for the media. It had become personal. Campbell had accused me of bias and obsession to lobby journalists. Once, he'd even tried to torpedo my career.[†] But he'd never succeeded. He'd never landed even a glancing blow.

Until this.

Back downstairs, I walked over to the day editor's desk. He asked if I was OK. I snorted. 'Yeah. I'm OK. But he's let the fuckers win.'

• • •

The next twelve hours were miserable. My mood was uniformly black, not helped by some of the morning press. *The Sun* said Hutton had 'exposed the culture of sloppiness, incompetence and arrogance that infects [the BBC] ... Mr Dyke and the head of news, Richard Sambrook, cannot be allowed to keep their jobs'. Its stablemate, *The Times*, cheered Gavyn Davies's

---

† See, for example, Alastair Campbell's diaries, volume 2, pp. 234, 236, 337, 567, 590, 614.

resignation but wanted more. His going was no more than a 'symbolic act ... the BBC is interested in ceremonial and not cultural change'.

But there was support too. The *Daily Mail*'s judgement that we'd 'got far more right than wrong' damned with faint praise. *The Independent* had really gone for it, though, clearing its front page but for the one word: WHITEWASH. The former BBC chairman Sir Christopher Bland judged Hutton had shown a 'curious imbalance'. Establishment code for bias. Lord Rees-Mogg dismissed it as 'quite simply, a bad bit of work'.

With the chairman of governors, Gavyn Davies, gone, the deputy chairman was in charge at the BBC. That was Lord Ryder. As plain Richard Ryder he'd been Tory chief whip under John Major, in charge of party discipline during the Maastricht rebellion, when Eurosceptics and Euroloathers cost Major his parliamentary majority and helped make the Tories unelectable. He'd been appointed for political balance and became the key player in what most outsiders saw as the governors' overreaction to Hutton.

It just happened that the governors were due to hold a routine monthly meeting on the day that Lord Hutton reported. It might have been a good idea to postpone it, but they didn't. Instead, they met locked away in Broadcasting House, isolated from reaction in the real world. They even refused to see the barrister who'd been the BBC's counsel at the Hutton Inquiry, Andrew Caldecott QC. He'd rushed over to their meeting to explain how Lord Hutton had got the law wrong. They left him sitting outside. After several hours he gave up and went back to his chambers.

By all accounts, it seems it was Lord Ryder who decided that Greg Dyke must go. Most of the other governors had no appetite for another sacrifice and it was certain that Dyke would fight. But Ryder had an ally in another governor – Dame Pauline Neville-Jones, a former chairman of the Joint Intelligence Committee.

I knew Dame Pauline reasonably well in those days. She was brusque. Sharp witted and sharp tongued. And though she'd spent a large chunk of her life in a world defined by mendacity and deception, paradoxically she'd always seemed pretty straight to me. Amongst other things, she'd fed my doubts about the September dossier, a couple of months after its publication, when we chatted at a BBC Christmas party.

Lord Ryder and Dame Pauline gave Dyke an ultimatum. Resign or be sacked. At first, he decided to go. Then decided no. He'd force them to sack him. He slept on it. Then decided he would resign, but would make it clear what he thought. Twenty-four hours after Hutton had reported, Dyke confirmed he'd gone with an email to 'All Staff'.

> The management of the BBC was heavily criticised in the Hutton Report and as the Director General I am responsible for the management. I accept that the BBC made errors of judgement and I've sadly come to the conclusion that it will be hard to draw a line under the whole affair while I am still here. We need closure. We need closure to protect the future of the BBC, not for you or me but for the benefit of everyone out there.

The next few hours were an extraordinary kaleidoscope of all that's best and all that's worst about the BBC. Minutes after his email landed in our inboxes, Dyke was live on TV in the middle of an extraordinary ruck outside Broadcasting House. Reporters, camera crews, BBC staff, Dyke's team. And probably a few lunchtime shoppers too, on their way to Oxford Street. The defiance was elating. But if the ruck around Dyke outside Broadcasting House was the BBC's inner strength on show, what happened next was its opposite.

By now, everyone could see the public mood was starting to run heavily in favour of the BBC and against Hutton, Campbell and the government. A rumour spread that Ryder and the acting Director General, Mark Byford, were about to appear live on TV. What they said next would tell us how the BBC planned to play it from now on.

I switched one of our TV screens from News 24, which was running and re-running pictures of Dyke outside Broadcasting House, to the internal BBC feed that was coming directly from the cameras being set up to carry Ryder's and Byford's statements. It was an unfortunate picture. At first, the camera position was too high and too softly focused. The lighting was poor. The image almost monochrome. And as they walked into shot, they seemed flushed, rushed and uncertain.

'The BBC', Ryder said, 'must now move forward in the wake of Lord Hutton's report, which highlighted serious defects in the Corporation's processes and procedures ... on behalf of the BBC I have no hesitation in apologising unreservedly for our errors and to the individuals whose reputations were affected by them.'

I was not happy. I had to leave the *Today* newsroom to go for a walk to calm down. On my way out, I passed close by James Cox, *The World This Weekend* presenter. He looked up from the game of solitaire he was playing on his PC and delivered in a grand and deliberate voice one of his favourite lines: 'a shiver entered the chamber looking for a spine to run up.' I'd heard it many times before. It was a well-used political insult. Cox had used it, too, in more scripts and interviews than was reasonable. But it still made me laugh.

Lord Ryder's apology made Campbell laugh, too: 'I would like to thank Richard Ryder for the apology that has been delivered by him on behalf of the BBC and for the fact that these allegations have now been withdrawn,' he told Radio 5 Live. It was typical Campbell. Ryder hadn't withdrawn a thing but Campbell knew that if he repeated it often enough it would become 'true'.

That evening, I took my copy of Hutton's report home and read it cover to cover. I needed to know it thoroughly. The detail was even grimmer than first I'd thought. There were errors of fact, assumptions and speculation, contradictions and omissions.

By the weekend, the press was mostly favourable to us, though almost all of it took Lord Hutton's conclusions as its 'factual' starting point. That was annoying. Acting DG Mark Byford appeared on the Saturday morning edition of *Today*, repeating his apology and saying the BBC broadcast too many 'exclusives'. He followed that with an interview on *Breakfast with Frost*, repeating the apology once again: 'We wanted to apologise for the errors that we made. If we apologised for them unequivocally I'll do that today for you as well.' It rankled.

As well as the apologies, Byford had also announced an internal inquiry intended to 'learn lessons' – what became known as 'The Process'. It was easy to see his thinking. Easy, too, to see it was flawed. He and Ryder had already told the world that they, on behalf of the BBC, accepted Hutton's conclusions in full. They'd apologised 'unequivocally' for any and every 'error' and 'mistake' that gave rise to those conclusions, though without specifying what they thought they were.

That was the flaw. Hutton had criticised me and my 'editorial system' as 'defective' but without hearing any evidence from me. 'The Process' would have to hear it. And I was confident that, when it had, the BBC would have to say publicly that Hutton was wrong.

They would have to hear, as Hutton hadn't, how I'd considered Gilligan's story and how I'd checked it against what else I knew and what my own, very senior, sources were telling me; how I'd assessed his source in line with the BBC guidelines and judged him to be credible, authoritative and reportable; how I'd checked over Gilligan's 'notes', insisted he write a script of what he was intending to say and then checked over that script before he went on air; how I'd offered the government the right of reply and how they'd taken it with a ministerial response that had confirmed one key allegation.

If people then wanted to criticise me for making the wrong calls, so be it. But it seemed to me that could only be fair if they'd first heard exactly what I'd done and why I'd done it.

To condemn me without a hearing, as Hutton had, seemed a long way from justice.

CHAPTER TWO

NEW LABOUR AND 'CREATING THE TRUTH'

ὅταν γὰρ ἡδύς τις λόγοις φρονῶν κακῶς
πείθῃ τὸ πλῆθος, τῇ πόλει κακὸν μέγα.
*When one with honeyed words but evil mind persuades the
mob, great woes befall the state.*

Euripides, Orestes

The roots of the row between Alastair Campbell and the BBC over the September 2002 dossier reach back almost a decade.

From the moment Tony Blair descended on Campbell at his holiday villa in Flassan, Provence in August 1994, and offered him the job of his media chief, a long attritional war with the BBC was inevitable. So was some sort of climactic, terminal clash. In one vital respect, Campbell was unlike any previous Labour media chief, or the media chief of any political party. The others wanted influence. He needed control. And he could never control the BBC. It was a failure that, as he recorded throughout his diaries, frustrated him 'til the end.

Lord Hutton took no account of Alastair Campbell's track record with the BBC. His 'form'. No doubt, for a judge, that was the right thing to do. Everyone deserves a fair hearing. But Campbell's 'form' was an important factor in my decision to put Dr Kelly's allegations on air.

When Andrew Gilligan presented me with his notes and script, I asked myself, amongst other things, 'is it likely these allegations are true? Was it possible, probable or likely that Campbell had 'sexed up' the September 2002 dossier? Perhaps if Campbell and New Labour hadn't routinely 'created the truth' for the whole of the previous decade, just as Gilligan's source was alleging now, I might have looked at the story differently.

From the summer of 1994, I'd had to struggle every day with the New Labour media machine. It had been energy sapping. But if I'd ever been tempted to give up, Peter Mandelson's notorious interview with Katharine Viner of *The Guardian* in August 1997 would have persuaded me otherwise. That was the interview, quoted often, in which he said: 'If you're accusing me of getting the truth across about what the Government has decided to do, that I'm putting the very best face or gloss on the Government's policies, that I'm trying to avoid gaffes or setbacks and that I'm trying to create the truth – if that's news management, I plead guilty.'

That phrase 'create the truth' was chilling, though it did no more than confirm what we'd all come to believe about the New Labour mindset. That they thought 'truth' was something for them to 'create' and shape. But I didn't want any politician or party apparatchik 'creating the truth' for me or for my millions of listeners. It was wrong and, I believed, bad for our democracy. And I said so. On air. Repeatedly.

Campbell's response was often, so it seemed to me, over the top. Those closer to him, the journalists in the parliamentary lobby, have described elsewhere his bullying behaviour and contempt for those who fell out of his favour. Tony Blair himself described how Campbell was 'mercurial', 'difficult', prone to 'erupt with damaging consequences' and not conforming to 'predictable modes of behaviour'.

It's difficult to convey just how wearying a decade of daily scraps with the New Labour media operation and with Campbell actually were. But the reality was a constant daily effort to get behind their 'created truth'. Spotting the deceptions and sleights of hand. Repelling the daily barrage of derision and insults. Eventually trusting nothing they said.

That 'truth creation' developed and grew in audacity day by day. Eventually, anyone reporting politics in those years had to choose whether to be sucked in or keep their distance. I chose distance and, as I saw it, independence. That meant I didn't 'enjoy' the close-quarter combat that the journalists in the parliamentary lobby had with Campbell. I was never in the lobby and never wanted to be. I like, respect and admire many current and former lobby journalists. They're some of the cleverest people I know and some of the best journalists we have. But I've always had reservations about the institution and have always believed it played an important part in alienating ordinary voters from Westminster politics. It played an important part, too, in enabling Downing Street to 'create the truth'.

Since I was not a member of that brotherhood, I had no interest in keeping their secrets. And it was usually when I put in front of an audience much wider than Westminster insiders the realities of this 'truth creation' that I got most attention from Campbell.

So yes, his form mattered to me.

• • •

I'd been editor of *The World at One* for a little over a year when Tony Blair hired Alastair Campbell as his media chief. I'd joined *WATO*, as we called it, as a young producer back in June 1980 and had learnt all that I knew about politics, political interviewing and political reporting in its cramped, nicotine-daubed offices. I'd never wanted to work anywhere else and, but for a year at ITN, never had.

WATO was in good shape when I took over from Roger Mosey when he moved on to *Today* in spring 1993. I'd been editor of its sister programme, *PM*, and the two of us had built a strong team full of good people who really knew what they were doing. We were also in the middle of an extraordinary political story that was being worked out in our studios. The Tories were knocking lumps out of each other over the EU. And when they weren't doing that, they were pocketing envelopes full of cash or taking off their trousers inappropriately. It was the era of 'The Bastards' and 'flapping white coats'. The 'whipless wonders', 'back me or sack me', 'sleaze' and 'cash for questions'.

It was visceral politics. Real and it mattered. And whatever secret plots and treachery there were in the dark, they were nothing compared to the plots and treachery out there in the open, every day in the TV and radio studios and in the press.

Before I took up the job, though, Mosey landed a problem in my lap. He'd persuaded James Naughtie, who was then *WATO*'s main presenter, to go with him to *Today*. That wasn't great news, though it did force a rethink about how to take *WATO* to the next stage. There'd been a simplicity, clarity and logic to the format that had served us for many years: big-name presenter (Hardcastle, Day, Naughtie), five or six interviews, each introduced by a short script setting out the facts and introducing the interview. That was fine as far as it went. But it could rarely move beyond adversarial journalism, 'devil's advocacy', confronting any argument or judgement with its opposite. I thought we could do better than that.

Politics were no longer simply adversarial. The country had become a complicated place. More complicated than just opposition and government. Employer and union. Capital and labour. Of course, listeners still liked the verbal combat, especially if their chosen villain was getting a kicking. But more and more of them were writing to me to ask: 'yes, but what's the truth?' Or 'what does it all mean?'

This was all fine for the medium and long term. The short term brought a more practical problem. I had to find a replacement for Naughtie sharpish. There was no stand-out candidate so I was resigned to pressing on with some kind of serviceable option. What I had no way of knowing was that the 'serviceable option' would turn out to be the best possible option. And that it would begin a decade-long relationship with the finest presenter I ever worked with.

Nick Clarke was the regular presenter of the Sunday edition of the programme, *The World This Weekend,* or *TW2* as we called it. When Naughtie had been away, Clarke had been the first choice stand-in for the weekday programme. Behind him, James Cox would fill in on *TW2.* I knew neither of them well but I did know that Clarke was BBC through and through. He'd been the industry specialist and occasional presenter on *Newsnight* but had fallen out with TV in general and a new editor on *Newsnight* in particular. I knew there was nothing flash about him. And that he was unfailingly polite, both on air and, more importantly, to even the most junior researcher.

I knew, too, that he was painfully fastidious, particularly in hotels and restaurants. A trait that drove producers round the bend when they were out on the road with him. He once sent a seafood dish back because it had one fewer prawn than the same dish on an adjoining table. And he was a careful chooser of wine, though sadly the cellars in the kind of restaurants we could afford on BBC expenses rarely met his expectations.

He showed the same fastidiousness in his journalism. He demanded accuracy and needed to understand the fine detail of any story. He was also more interested than was healthy in obscure political stories in faraway places of which we knew little and cared less. My first impression of him was that these two characteristics meant his *TW2* interviews could be arcane and underwhelming.

James Cox was a contrast. Though English through and through, he was an expert on Scottish politics and admirer of all things Scottish. He liked to shock, often dropping an incendiary aside into an interview. He once chucked the 'N' word into a live on-air discussion about race for no reason other than to startle his guests, the audience and BBC News executives. His scripts were always masterpieces of overwriting. Ironically, I hope. He adored the English language and was almost as much of a pedant as I. He knew his classics, too. His computer screensaver was a quote from *The Aeneid*: *'Forsan et haec olim meminisse iuvabit'* – 'perhaps one day it will be a joy to have remembered even these things.'

When Naughtie departed, there was no reason not to put Clarke full-time into the *WATO* chair and Cox into the *TW2* seat. Both took their chances. Both made the programmes their own. I never had to think about presentation again.

What I didn't know in the summer of 1993 was that a bug had set up home on one of my heart valves. I started to notice pains in my calves while muscles in my arms and hands randomly stiffened. I started to get short of breath and by the winter, I felt like shit most days and my GP was puzzled.

Then one day in January, I felt in my right leg the most pain I'd ever known. I went into hospital. They kept me in. Told my wife I had lung cancer and arranged for more tests. It wasn't lung cancer. According to the cardiologist who eventually diagnosed what I really had, it was 'worse than cancer'. It was endocarditis. A killer. The bugs sit on your heart valve producing poisonous stuff charmingly called 'vegetation' that breaks off and, untreated, infects your brain or another major organ.

In my case the 'vegetation' had got stuck behind my knee. I needed two operations. One to save – or sacrifice – the leg. The other to take out and replace the heart valve. The surgeons were good and I was lucky. I kept my leg and my heart didn't give out or spray any more 'vegetation' around. Now, a plastic ball in a metal cage clicks noisily in my chest, a constant reminder of the thin line between being and not being.

I was out of things for five months in all. While I was away, a brilliant young journalist called Martin Fewell had to take charge of *WATO*. Fewell had joined us just a couple of years earlier from BBC Southampton. I'd promoted him quickly on the strength of his intellect and resourcefulness. But also because he had oodles of that indefinable quality, charisma. I'd made him my deputy at *WATO* and we'd talked, with Nick Clarke, about those new ideas for a different way of doing things. Whatever pace I intended for that became irrelevant. Within just a few weeks, I was in hospital and he was on his own, making real that new, sharper, borderline investigative *WATO*. He was also plunged into all the other stuff that occupies you as an editor: bedding in presenters, keeping on top of the money, people, complaints.

In those five months, Fewell and Clarke laid all the foundations for *WATO*'s most successful decade. They were a perfect partnership; Fewell was decisive, quick witted and would spot the tiniest glitch or inconsistency in a political argument. He had a formidable memory, too, and seemed able to remember at will what any politician had said in all his or her previous interviews. Nick Clarke's great skills were twofold; first, he had a way of bringing real clarity to the most complex political stories, leading listeners carefully through all they needed to know while at the same time chucking out the conventional wisdoms and distractions that always encrusted them. Second, his interviewing was always designed to reveal. He would politely strip obfuscations away, trying to get to a 'truth'. On paper, it was a simple technique. In reality, it became more and more complex and difficult once New Labour had decided that we, and the rest of the media, were obliged to report only the 'truths' it had 'created' for us.

When I returned to *WATO* in June 1994, I wondered whether it was a good idea even to try to do any kind of work again, let alone run a BBC programme. I found it hard to persuade myself that any of the things that drive editors mattered at all – I was glad enough to see the sun come up each morning. So what if it was Jean-Luc Dehaene or Jacques Santer who succeeded Jacques Delors as EU Commission President? Or what Peter Lilley thought of it? And what difference would it

make to any of us if it was Gordon Brown or Tony Blair who
won their private, mutual eye-gouging contest to succeed John
Smith as Labour leader?

Especially since I knew for sure now that some things
mattered more than politics and journalism.

• • •

Throughout the 1990s, *WATO* and *Today* were the stages
on which the Tories played out their tragedy's complex plots.
Europe, 'Back to Basics', sleaze, impotence in the Balkans,
missed opportunities in Northern Ireland. All combined with
their new-found fondness for stabbing each other in the chest.

There were obvious resonances with the Labour Party of the
1980s. Settling scores and fighting sectarian battles were much
more important than looking like a government. By the mid-
1990s, it was clear to everyone that they'd made themselves
unelectable by economic incompetence over the ERM and failing to learn Labour's lessons of the 1980s. Unity mattered. So
did a coherent story.

Blair, Mandelson and Campbell had learnt those lessons.
And had set about changing not just the Labour Party but our
politics. It wasn't just the lurch to the right, turning Labour
into New Labour, breaking the power of the unions, ditching
Clause IV, miming to Kenneth Clarke's macroeconomic tunes
and outflanking Michael Howard's social conservatism on
the right. Nor was it just about a new, iron-fisted leadership
that crushed disunity and petty squabbling. Nor professional,
effective media management. It was all of those things but
more than the simple sum of them.

It began with a superficial calculus. Open debate + real
ideological difference x argument = time spent in opposition.
The paradox at the heart of open, democratic politics. The less
democratic a party became, the more likely it was to spend
time in government. The key, they decided, was to hollow out

the party. Gather power at the centre; close down real debate; excise ideology; muzzle, disown or undermine anyone who wanted to carry on the argument. And then find a new way to tell the New Labour story, not settling for the traditional way of making that story persuasive. But, as Mandelson so frankly put it in 1997, by 'creating the truth'.

Blair's to-do list after he'd been crowned John Smith's successor at the end of July 1994 was long, but close to the top of it was finding someone who could master the media and especially the Murdoch press. Its hostility, even its contrariness, could still stand between him and Downing Street. He saw how Peter Mandelson had failed at the job for Kinnock, in spite of the reputation he'd created for himself as master of the dark arts. It was easy to see how and why he'd failed. Whatever his talents as a back-room strategist and manipulator, he was a very easy person to dislike. And many in the media disliked him.

I first met him at the 1988 Labour Party conference in Blackpool. I was having breakfast with Charles Clarke, who was then Kinnock's Chief of Staff. Mandelson joined us and, for some reason, decided that morning to play the aesthete, drawing out his words as if they had a significance and meaning we couldn't quite catch. Clarke seemed annoyed and impatient. Mandelson was putting his back up just as much as he was mine. But Mandelson himself showed no sign of recognising it.

That lack of self-awareness was his biggest flaw. While he stayed behind the scenes as Kinnock's stage director, he was effective. It was usually more entertaining to watch Mandelson than Kinnock at a photocall, speech or event. He'd stand behind the forest of cameras, watching the image on the TV screens making covert hand signals. Move a little closer to Glenys. Lift your chin. Look to the right. Calm down.

But the more he moved into the foreground, especially after he became MP for Hartlepool in 1992, the less of an asset he became and the less he seemed to realise it. Though his Labour roots were deep, he hadn't a single mannerism or turn of phrase that looked or sounded Labour. He invited mockery.

I was guilty of mocking him once after he'd made an election speech about 'trust'. A speech so pompous it was impossible to listen and keep a straight face. Something about it suggested Kaa's song in *Jungle Book* – the s-s-s-s-serpent's s-s-s-s-s-song that goes-s-s-s-s: 'Trust in me, just in me ... Shut your eyes and trust in me ... You can sleep safe and sound ... Knowing I am around...' So the report I broadcast intercut clips of his speech with lines from the song. He phoned me afterwards and failed to see either the joke or the point.

Blair recognised Mandelson's strategic values. So long as he stayed out of sight. It was Mandelson's scheming – duplicity others would call it – that clinched the leadership for him. But it wasn't the kind of help he wanted anyone to see. Hence the sobriquet 'Bobby' and the other lengths to which he went to keep Mandelson's role secret. When Mark Seddon stood down as editor of *Tribune*, he recalled the occasion when a shadow minister who was supporting Blair's leadership bid called him and threatened to sue if the magazine revealed what was both the truth and an open secret amongst lobby journalists – that Mandelson was driving Blair's campaign. A taste of things to come.

I don't think many of us on the outside could have predicted that Alastair Campbell would have been Blair's choice. He was a well-enough-known political journalist, though tainted by his connections with Robert Maxwell. He'd been a close friend of and advocate for Neil Kinnock but seemed to have few sympathies for politics as a profession or politicians as a breed. He was a vocal critic of the monarchy, the establishment, any interest he judged vested. And while he was a regular newspaper reviewer on BBC TV, he would call us 'weak', 'privileged' and 'full of Tories'.

Campbell's approach to his old colleagues in the lobby was robust. He seemed to enjoy showing contempt for them and offered access and exclusives to those who behaved, withdrawing favours from those who didn't. He'd bully or mock those who questioned the 'created truth'. Blair, even in the early days, was more circumspect. He was more inclined to do deals. The biggest one of all with Murdoch, bringing *The Sun* onside and, in due course though never explicitly, *The Times*. And he winced at Campbell's full-on aggression: 'We can't be at war with them all the time,' he was quoted as saying. 'We're going to have to work with these guys again at some point.' One newspaper editor agreed, calling Campbell 'the most pointlessly combative person in human history'. But those editors who found favour were guaranteed an inexhaustible supply of 'Blair' articles ghost-written by Campbell and former *Daily Mirror* journalist David Bradshaw.

In opposition, Campbell and Blair found it easy to achieve the control they needed. So easy that it worked as a catalyst in an alchemical reaction that was already underway in New Labour. Blair and those around him realised that political communication was much more than just putting the best gloss on things. The words didn't have to follow the politics. The words *were* the politics.

The narrative, the 'truth' you created was more important than any reality. It *was* the reality.

• • •

I think it was Blair's first full conference speech as leader, at Blackpool in 1994 that really alarmed me. Made me think that here was something different.

All political speeches have an element of fantasy to them. All of them make claims about past, present and future that are carefully chosen, carefully honed and carefully framed. Few, though, in my experience had ever strayed to the outer edge of truth as often as that conference speech. Few had so often stepped over it.

'Crime has more than doubled...' Arguable, but misleading. It had doubled since 1979. But it had been falling since 1992 and fast.

Or, 'spending is up and growth, over the last fifteen years, is down...' I couldn't work out how that could be true. Spending as a proportion of GDP was falling. And the phrase 'growth over the last fifteen years is down' doesn't mean anything, unless it was a claim that the economy was smaller in 1994 than it had been in 1979 which was patently false.

And so on. Maybe I was being hypercritical. Maybe I was in a bad mood and the speech was just standard political hyperbole after all. It didn't feel like it, though. I couldn't remember any political speech where there'd been so many claims that were so diffcult to sustain.

Few remember those parts of his speech now because it was the speech in which he ditched what had been the cornerstone of the Labour Party since 1918. Clause IV. Sydney and Beatrice Webb's legacy to the party that stated its purpose was: 'To secure for the workers by hand or by brain the full fruits of their industry and the most equitable distribution thereof that may be possible upon the basis of the common ownership of the means of production, distribution and exchange, and the best obtainable system of popular administration and control of each industry or service.'

That, not the flirtation with mendacity, was the big story of the day. Trailed before, spun afterwards, it was audacious. The death of Old Labour, the birth of New. But the words were weasel. In spite of the exhortation 'let us say what we mean and mean what we say', Blair didn't quite manage to say what he meant. 'It is time we had a clear, up-to-date statement of the objects and objectives of our party. John Prescott and I, as leader and deputy leader of our party, will propose such a statement to the NEC.' It was impossible to know what he really meant without the background briefing round the back of the stage. That's where the narrative, the 'truth', was being created. Not on the stage, out in the open, in front of his party conference.

But there was a wrinkle. My old friend and BBC political correspondent Nick Jones had been trawling MPs and union leaders, as was his manner. And he'd discovered that the deputy leader, John Prescott, was unenthusiastic about ditching Clause IV. Apparently, he'd been won over only in the final week before the conference. Once Blair's standing ovation had died down, Jones went live on TV to report that Prescott was 'only on board a week ago and did advise against it'.

Campbell cornered Jones as he came off air and laid into him. He bawled that Prescott had supported ditching Clause IV 'every step of the way'. He demanded an instant correction. Jones reported the denial while Campbell himself went on air to dismiss the story as 'a complete load of nonsense'. Jones was shaken but insisted his original story was true. He went back to his sources to check. Every one of them assured him that what he'd said was correct.

Years later, Prescott himself confirmed it to the political journalist Colin Brown in his biography of the former deputy leader, *Fighting Talk*.[†]

• • •

Still, I might have been wrong. It was possible this wasn't a new departure in our politics.

I thought about it. Fewell, Clarke and I talked about it. But it was New Labour's draft manifesto, produced in 1996 and called *New Labour, New Life for Britain* that dispelled any doubts.

---

† Prescott's account given to Colin Brown for *Fighting Talk* was detailed, setting out how Blair's speech on Clause IV was settled only the night before it was delivered. Campbell had phoned Prescott on the morning of the speech to agree the final text.

This was a Potemkin document for a Potemkin party. It never went near a party conference or anywhere it could be realistically challenged. It went out, instead, to all party members. That sounds democratic but it was, in fact, a mass mailshot with no return coupon. There could be no detailed line-by-line scrutiny. It could be voted down in theory only.

That was just as well. Its passage on the economy, for example, was pure fantasy. By 1996, Britain was emerging pretty rapidly from recession. It wasn't a golden age but it was undeniably a recovery. And while *New Labour, New Life for Britain* was entitled to attack the Thatcher/Major record on the economy, it wasn't entitled to create its own facts. But it did.

It claimed that the UK's growth had trailed its main competitors; that we'd fallen to eighteenth in the league table of national incomes; that wages had fallen and people were having to 'work harder to stay still'; and that Tory governments had created fewer new jobs than any similar country.

On *WATO* we tried and failed to substantiate any of these claims. Reporting the economy was something we did as a matter of routine. None of the claims in the draft manifesto seemed familiar. But we checked. And checked again. And as far as we could find, UK growth was second only to Japan between 1979 and 1996; we were fifth in the league table of national incomes; real wages had, on average, increased almost 20 per cent; and a larger proportion of the UK population was in work than in the three countries at the heart of the EU: Germany, France and Italy. The 'facts' in the draft manifesto were misleading. So we said so. It wasn't the last time I had to put on air allegations that the government had included questionable 'facts' to lend a political document a persuasiveness and authority it never had.

As far as Campbell was concerned, there was only one explanation. I was a Tory. We were all Tories. It was nothing to do with trying to get behind the 'created truth'. But by the time the real manifesto was published, the spurious claims had gone. They'd been subsumed into the meaningless statement that: 'We have experienced the slowest average growth rate of any similar period since the second world war...'

New Labour 'truths' couldn't afford to be over-complicated. I learnt that about six months before the 1997 election when I had dinner with Blair's Chief of Staff, Jonathan Powell. We'd failed to keep in touch over the twenty years or so since we'd worked on *Isis*, the Oxford University magazine, together. I'd been muddling along in the BBC while Powell had built a successful career as a diplomat.

Powell told me the New Labour election strategy would be to focus on four or five very specific pledges. Something on schools, something on law and order, something on the NHS, something on the economy. That turned into the famous 'Five Election Pledges', printed on a card and waved repeatedly throughout the campaign.

Brevity wasn't the only thing about the pledges. They were also light on meaning and ambition. Cutting class sizes for the under sevens; halving the time from arrest to sentencing for young offenders; cutting 100,000 patients off NHS waiting lists; and a windfall tax to take 250,000 under-25-year-olds off the dole via the 'New Deal'. They made good, if superficial, headlines and were readily achievable.

It was the fifth pledge, on the economy, that brought us into most conflict with the New Labour war room in Millbank, the tower block on the Thames a little along from the Palace of Westminster where the party had its HQ. That pledge read: 'We will set tough rules for government spending and borrowing and ensure low inflation and strengthen the economy so that interest rates are as low as possible to make all families better off.'

Those 'tough rules', of course, were Tory Chancellor Ken Clarke's. The manifesto could have called them 'Tory rules'. But it didn't. There was no mention of the other major change to the way the economy would be managed, either. Subletting interest rates and monetary policy to an 'independent' Bank of England. A policy, incidentally, that made a nonsense of the pledge to keep interest rates 'as low as possible'. If rates were to be in the gift of the Bank, shadow Chancellor Gordon Brown could make no meaningful promise about them. He must have known this was wrong before he decided to put it in the manifesto.

We spent a lot of airtime unpicking the language. Low interest rates didn't make all families better off, for example. Only those swimming in debt and with no savings. Older people, like *WATO*'s 2 million listeners, with little debt and living on index-linked pensions and the interest on their savings, would be worse off. And then there was the deception of the Golden Rule, a commitment to balance the books over the economic cycle. An end to tax and spend, an end to boom and bust, Brown boasted. That was nonsense too. In crude terms, an 'economic cycle' can be pulled, pushed, squeezed and stretched to be whatever a Chancellor of the Exchequer says it is. Brown's attack dog, Charlie Whelan, called us 'illiterate wankers' when we questioned what the pledge really meant. Years later, Brown was forced to tinker with the start and end of an economic cycle to make his figures add up.

We got daily flak and abuse but my reasoning was straightforward and I wasn't going to take a step back. If New Labour was to form the next government – and it was certain that they would – people had to know exactly what they were voting for. And exactly how New Labour were trying to shape what it was that they knew.

But the heat over the 'Five Pledges' was only part of it.

• • •

When Major called the 1997 election, he left time for a long six-week campaign. Hoping something would turn up. Exiting the ERM, sex and sleaze scandals and the party's addiction to self-harm over Europe made the Tories unelectable, in spite of the improving economy.

Nevertheless, New Labour fought the campaign as if they could lose. And that, they believed, meant as much aggression as possible towards non-compliant journalists and news organisations. The BBC and especially *WATO* was never going to be compliant.

They delivered most of that aggression via their rapid rebuttal unit, a team of people in the Millbank war room who monitored every word written and broadcast – especially broadcast – during the campaign. If they heard something that wasn't consistent with their carefully created narrative of the day, they'd bombard us with 'corrections' and 'rebuttals'.

It was a powerful weapon. Not because it forced us to tell their story uncritically. It never did. As far as I could tell it was counter-productive. Except for this. When they turned it on the BBC, it suffocated programme editors in a bog of BBC bureaucracy.

The New Labour war room knew that every 'rebuttal', however unfounded or trivial, triggered an instant investigation that stole our time and sapped our will to live. In Birt's BBC, the assumption was that any and every complaint was justified until proven otherwise. And even if you could show immediately it was factually wrong, an investigation kicked in. Notes, scripts, evidence would be summoned. Separate teams from the DG's office, the Head of News's office and Editorial Policy would scour it all. There were no shortcuts.

Every programme I made during the campaign involved me either in a row before or a 'rebuttal' afterwards. Most, more than one of each. But every one was vexatious, designed to make me and other BBC editors reluctant to question and challenge the New Labour 'truths'. The message was: 'make your life easier, swallow what we tell you whole.' Birt never accepted this was the rapid rebuttal unit's real purpose. But it made a farce of accountability. The only losers were the licence-fee payers who footed the bill and those members of the public whose genuine complaints were swamped by New Labour's posturing. In any event, not one 'rebuttal' fired at me was upheld in the whole campaign.

The staffers in the Millbank war room were committed to the cause. They had to be. Many of them had learnt campaigning in the US, attached to or just watching the Clinton campaign. Politics as marketing. It was their job to keep candidates on message, ration media access to senior party figures, organise the events that wheeled out celebs, monitor the media and fire off those rapid rebuttals.

One of the most effective Millbank warriors was Tim Allan. Blair had hired him as his advisor while he was still shadow Home Secretary, the era of 'tough on crime, tough on the causes of crime'. Allan's style and outlook were similar to Blair's and a contrast with Campbell's, whose deputy he eventually became. He was not aggressive by nature, rarely lost control and seemed to like journalists, including BBC journalists. He preferred reason to rant. But his role in what was possibly the most arcane election row ever speaks volumes about New Labour's need to control rather than merely influence the news agenda. It was a row over the date that Parliament was prorogued. To most voters and journalists, it was totally baffling.

The prorogation is the date on which Parliament is dissolved and MPs retire or go back to their constituencies as mere candidates. Normally, it's a matter of no interest or importance whatsoever to anyone other than the MPs themselves. In 1997, though, Major had a dilemma. What to do with a 'sleaze' report that the Parliamentary Commissioner for Standards, Sir Gordon Downey, was writing.

Sir Gordon had been investigating 'cash for questions', an affair that had enveloped two former Tory ministers and several backbenchers, since the autumn of 1996 and, by the spring of 1997, his report was thought to be almost ready. The problem was that if Parliament were prorogued, Sir Gordon would have no one to deliver his report to until after the election. And that would look like a cover-up. If prorogation were delayed, if it could be delayed, and the report published, it would finish whatever sliver of hope Major believed he still had of winning.

'Cash for questions' had begun in July 1994 when two *Sunday Times* reporters posed as lobbyists and persuaded two Conservative MPs, Graham Riddick and David Tredinnick, to take money in return for putting down parliamentary questions. And though one of the MPs, Graham Riddick, had immediate second thoughts and sent the cheque back, Parliament suspended both MPs once the *Sunday Times* story appeared.

Then, in October that year, *The Guardian* published allegations that two Conservative ministers, Neil Hamilton and Tim Smith, had taken money from the Harrods owner Mohamed Al Fayed, via lobbyist Ian Greer, to ask parliamentary questions on his behalf. Two thousand pounds per question according to the source of *The Guardian*'s story ... who was, as it happened, Mr Al Fayed himself 'acting in the public interest'.

Tim Smith resigned, admitting he hadn't made a proper declaration in the register of MPs' interests. Neil Hamilton also resigned but sued *The Guardian*, as did the lobbyist, Ian Greer. They both claimed the newspaper couldn't stand up its story. Shortly before the action was due in court, Al Fayed produced more witnesses and allegations and in the face of those allegations the two men dropped their action.

But it got worse for Major. A Cabinet minister, the Chief Secretary to the Treasury Jonathan Aitken, was also linked to Al Fayed. A parliamentary inquiry cleared him but the following year *The Guardian* and ITV's *World in Action* revealed details of secret and lucrative deals he'd made with Saudi princes. Aitken sued: 'If it falls to me to start a fight to cut out the cancer of bent and twisted journalism in our country with the simple sword of truth and the trusty shield of British fair

play, so be it. I am ready for the fight. The fight against falsehood and those who peddle it. My fight begins today.'

He lost that fight. Perjured himself along the way. And ended
up in prison.

For New Labour, it couldn't have been better. It was sleaze. It
was cover-up. Major could do nothing to dispel those impressions. All Blair had to do was stand by, looking 'purer than
pure' and statesmanlike.

Sir Gordon had warned that he wouldn't rush writing his
report 'to meet an electoral timetable'. That would be 'against
the interests of natural justice,' he said. But towards the end
of that first week of the campaign, he produced an 'interim
report' that exonerated fifteen of those he was investigating.
While that cleared the air for them, it focused attention on
the others, including the two former ministers, Hamilton and
Smith. Major aimed a jibe directly at Alastair Campbell and the
New Labour media operation: 'based on what has happened
on earlier occasions, parts of the substance of the report might
leak in a prejudicial way before the matter is fairly concluded.
That would not be in the interests of the House or of
natural justice.'

But few now seemed to care much about natural justice. *The
Guardian*, which had exposed Tory sleaze time and again over
several years, had been campaigning for full publication. At
the end of that first week, it got a great scoop. A partial leak of
the unpublished report.

'SLEAZE: THE EVIDENCE' the front-page banner read. Inside,
verbatim details of what was, in effect, the case for the prosecution against former ministers Neil Hamilton and Tim Smith.
'Lies, a failed libel case, gifts galore.' There were columns of it.
Thousands of words.

It was a great scoop for *The Guardian*, but it made me feel
uneasy. I couldn't see how Hamilton and Smith could possibly
rebut these findings, but media lynchings always felt wrong
to me. And neither Hamilton's nor Smith's defence, however

weak, was part of the leak. Plus, I suspected that the source was someone on the New Labour campaign team.

The scoop posed tough questions for Major. Had he made Tim Smith a minister knowing he'd already admitted to taking money from Al Fayed? And did Major let Smith continue as a minister after he knew he'd taken yet more money from the Harrods owner? Major wasn't prepared to come onto the programme to answer. But the deputy Prime Minister, Michael Heseltine, was.

About half an hour before air time, Tim Allan called me from the New Labour war room offering two pages of transcripts of some of the evidence in the Tim Smith case, 'on lobby terms ... to help with the interview' with Heseltine. I'd no reason to distrust Allan but was permanently on my guard. I said 'OK' and a few minutes later, the two pages arrived on the fax machine. I looked over them quickly. At first reading, they seemed to contain material that hadn't been in *The Guardian* that morning. New material. A fresh leak.

If that were true, it suggested it was the New Labour campaign team that was leaking this stuff. And that would mean Blair's 'purer than pure/more in sorrow than in anger' façade was exactly that. A façade. And a cynical one at that. I called over to Jon Sopel, the BBC political correspondent who happened to be in the office, preparing to present *PM* that evening. He'd been at the New Labour campaign press conference that morning. I asked him if he'd read *The Guardian* stories in any detail. Sort of, he said. So what about this? I asked. And shoved the fax in front of him, telling him where it had come from. That figured, Sopel said. War room staffers had been handing round what he thought were transcripts of *The Guardian*'s scoop at the morning news conference.

We had to work fast. Comparing the contents of the Allan fax with the thousands of words in *The Guardian*. We had to be certain it was a fresh leak. That was always going to be difficult.

Sian Williams, now one of the best-known presenters on TV, was the output editor in charge of the show that day. I told her what was happening. And to carry on making the programme with what she had unless I told her otherwise. Leading on the interview with Heseltine.

Less than ten minutes to go. Jon and I still couldn't be certain one way or the other. The phone rang. It was Tim Allan again. Was the material any use? Were we going to use it? I gambled. To see what a bit of pressure would do.

Yes, we'll be using it, I said. But to say you're the source of the leak. We're going to accuse you of dirty tricks. And then ask Hezza, live, what he thinks.

Everything depended on his reaction.

'You're wrong,' he said. 'If you do that you'll finish me.' He sounded small. I imagined his lip quivering. But it wasn't the answer I needed. It told me nothing.

'I swear to you, you're wrong. You'll be making a big mistake. And you'll finish me.'

I looked across at Jon who was still reading. He shook his head and shrugged. Still no smoking gun.

Williams was on my shoulder. Minutes to go before air. She mouthed: 'Yes? No?' Nick Clarke was standing half in the office, half in the studio corridor. If he was going to open the programme, he was going to have to go now.

One last gamble. I pretended to read the headline I was going to use – that New Labour had leaked the cash for questions report.

Sian heard. Gave a big thumbs up to Nick who turned to sprint into the studio. I grabbed her shoulder. Shook my head. Pointed to the phone's mouthpiece.

'Look. You're wrong. There's nothing new in what I sent you. It's all in *The Guardian* already. I just wanted to make sure you'd seen the best bits.' I looked over to Jon. He shook his head. I ran into the studio. The pips had started. I pressed the key to talk into Nick's headphones. 'Go with Heseltine.'

Nick gave the thumbs up. 'The World at One...' he began. Calm. Unflustered. As if nothing had happened.

Sopel and I never did get to the bottom of it. We spent a couple of hours after WATO going over the fax, comparing it with the Guardian reports. It wasn't conclusive. And when Sopel asked Robin Cook, on that evening's PM, whether he knew how the evidence had got into The Guardian and whether he condemned the leak, he played the outrage card.

'If you're accusing us of leaking the evidence to The Guardian that's an outrageous claim and you should withdraw it.'

And there was no one better than Robin Cook at moral outrage.

• • •

It had been a rough first week. I'd had to scrap two or three times each day with someone in the New Labour war room. Mostly trivial scraps that came to nothing. But wearing, all the same. And that question still preyed on my mind. Was this something different? It certainly felt like it.

I'd covered four previous election campaigns, three of them as an editor. And, yes, I'd always felt manipulated to some extent. We were all spoon-fed planned events and speeches and photocalls. Our reporters travelled with the leaders at their discretion. There was a lot of chatter on the sidelines, briefings, stories and news lines planted on the quiet. I always tried to go my own way, of course, and got flak from party minders when I did. Mostly, though, Thatcher, Kinnock and Major had been focused on getting a broad image across, fighting bush-fires when they broke out and preventing gaffes. This was different. It was about controlling every detail. Before, during and after. Aggressively. Cynically. If you didn't swallow the New Labour message uncritically, they would try to undermine you. Play on your uncertainties. Take you out of the game if you persisted. It wasn't just me. Nick Clarke felt it, too. So did everyone else on the *WATO* team. At the end of that week, I was genuinely worried. If New Labour was this obsessive and controlling in opposition when the polls said they were cruising to an easy victory, how much more like it would they be in government?

I decided it was even more important now, in this campaign, to tell our millions of listeners just how New Labour went about 'creating the truth'. How they went about ensuring voters heard nothing other than that 'truth'. It was our job to turn our back on their news grid – the spreadsheets that set out in fine detail who was to say what, where and when. It was our job to shine a light on what they weren't saying. Show how 'truth' was a negotiable concept to New Labour.

It took me to the brink of resignation.

• • •

The holes in Gordon Brown's spending plans were obvious to anyone who could do simple arithmetic. There was, in that favourite phrase of journalists and politicians, a 'black hole'. What was less obvious was the way New Labour had embraced Thatcherite privatisation as a way to fill it. 'We will privatise everything the Tories said they were going to sell off' wasn't one of their five pledges. It wasn't even in the manifesto.

At the beginning of April, Brown was finally forced to put a number on the size of the black hole. In a *WATO* interview he conceded it was £1.5 billion. But there was nothing to panic about – a third of it would be filled by privatising the National Air Traffic Control Service, NATS. It was no big deal – the Tories had already said they'd sell NATS. And since Brown had pledged to mime for two years to Ken Clarke's tax and spending plans, they had to go through with the NATS sale or think of something else.

But there was a problem. While Brown and the rest were chucking this particular bit of Old Labour baggage overboard, most party members were still clinging to the handles.

That Tory plan to sell NATS had been a live issue at the Labour party conference in Blackpool the previous October. Just six months before the election. And when the shadow Transport Secretary Andrew Smith had declared 'Our air is not for sale' he'd won the second biggest standing ovation of the week. Unsurprisingly, then, most party activists as well as trade unionists thought that was party policy. NATS wasn't for sale. As the election campaign began, one of the NATS trade unions wrote to the shadow transport team and got what seemed to be a reassuring reply: privatisation had indeed been ruled out.

Except … that wasn't quite right. Margaret Beckett, the shadow Trade Secretary had mumbled a U-turn a month earlier.

On 23 February, in an interview for *On the Record*, she'd said New Labour hadn't ruled out 'considering' privatising NATS. But that's not what the shadow transport team's reply to the union said. The leadership blamed a junior researcher in the shadow Transport office for the confusion, not fully realising that shifting the blame in that way underlined the secretive way they'd ditched the old policy and embraced privatisation. At best, it was a botched attempt at a sly evasion. At worst it was deception.

The one person we, and everyone else, wanted to speak to was Andrew Smith. To find out when he'd been told the policy had changed and why it hadn't been signalled in the manifesto. And what he now thought of that commitment he'd given at the party conference. Getting hold of him was easier said than done. Calls to the New Labour war room got nowhere. 'He's out campaigning.' 'Where?' 'We don't know.' No one had seen him, not even in his Oxford constituency. At least, that's what they told us. Their tactic was to stall. Hang tough. It might take a day or two, but things would move on.

I wasn't going to let that happen. The fact of the policy change as well as the way it had been done told voters a huge amount about their next Prime Minister and the team around him. I couldn't just let it go.

I assigned one of my reporters, Jackie Long, to track Smith down. Each day, we updated the *WATO* audience on our search for him. The Millbank war room complained. Then tried abuse: 'You're up your own arses,' one staffer told one of my young, female researchers. 'You're obsessed with your-selves,' one told me. I was happy to carry on 'til election day if I needed to. Then one evening, after a few days of fruitless searching, I got a phone call at home from a senior BBC News Executive, Peter Bell. He was troubleshooting for the Head of News, Tony Hall, during the election.

I'd known Bell since we'd worked together on *Nationwide*. He as a senior producer, me as a trainee. We went separate routes, he into TV news management, me into radio. Then, under one of Birt's theological reforms, he became in some way I never fully understood one of my many bosses.

He asked what I was planning to do on the following day's *WATO*. I said I didn't know. That was true. I'd opted out of the election planning grid – both New Labour's and the BBC's – and had no idea what I'd end up putting in a programme more than twelve hours away. I did know that New Labour were planning to wheel out some business celebs to support the 'New Deal'. And we'd carry on pursuing Smith. But apart from that, I hadn't a clue.

Are you planning to do any more on NATS? Bell wanted to know. I said we'd give another update on the search for Smith. We might even find him. That would be good, I said. With a hint of an upward, interrogative inflection.

Maybe you should give it a rest tomorrow, he thought. Maybe not, I thought back.

Why not give the 'New Deal' the time it deserves? he thought.

Are you telling me not to have anything in tomorrow's programme about NATS? Or Smith? Come what may?

I didn't like this at all. I couldn't work out where it was coming from. Bell had never called me at home before. It felt very odd.

If you're ordering me not to cover the NATS story tomorrow, I said, then you can have my resignation.

Bell went quiet. I'll call you back, he said. He did call me back, ten minutes later to clear up the misunderstanding. He wasn't ordering me not to cover NATS or anything else. Just making sure we didn't take our eye off the main agenda.

So if we get that interview with Smith tomorrow, we lead on it? Of course, he said. We didn't speak again during the rest of the campaign.

The irony was, we didn't cover NATS or even the search for Smith the following day. We had a much better story. Brown and New Labour were caught out mis-stating the extent of business support for the 'New Deal'.

At his morning news conference, Brown presented a list of business celebs who, he said, had endorsed his plan to give a £60 a week tax rebate to employers who gave jobs to youngsters under the 'New Deal'. Celebrity endorsements were a standard feature of the New Labour campaign. And in theory, little should ever have gone wrong.

But this particular list cried out for a truth check. Some of the names weren't readily identifiable as New Labour supporters. A group of us worked name by name down the list, calling each and asking whether they'd specifically endorsed Brown's 'New Deal'. One producer scored a direct hit with Nick Scheele, who was then chairman and chief executive of Jaguar Cars. When we called him, he told us he was surprised to hear his name was on the list. He hadn't endorsed the policy at all. Was he prepared to say that on the record, we asked. Yes he was. So Nick Clarke recorded an interview with him and he repeated that he emphatically had not endorsed the £60 a week tax break. 'We need to focus on the issue [of youth unemployment] and I am comfortable with doing that. But whether this scheme is better than any other I really don't know.'

It was as clear cut as could be.

About an hour before we went on air, I got a call from the

Labour Party press chief David Hill, demanding that we pull the interview. We'd breached BBC guidelines by secretly recording Scheele, he claimed. It was a fairly typical New Labour 'pre-buttal', as we were starting to call them. Aggressive. Vehement. Categorical. There was no doubt about this. What Hill didn't know was that the producer editing the interview had kept the section of tape which had Clarke's pre-interview chat with Scheele on it. Including Clarke saying: 'Well, we're now ready to record if you are, Mr Scheele.' 'Yes I am,' he replied. I played it over the phone to Hill. He retreated. Another pointless spat.

The following day, we returned to the NATS story and put together a 'new listeners start here' take-out, disentangling who knew what and when. It was a useful thing to do in its own right but, more importantly, it sent the message to the New Labour war room, and to any of my bosses who wanted to know, that I wasn't going to give up. Then, late that same afternoon, Jackie Long called in. She'd been in Northern Ireland and had somehow found out that Andrew Smith was going to be at an event in Fleetwood, near Blackpool, the following day, 10 April.

Long found a flight and shipped up to find Smith in the middle of a muddy field. A long way from media minders. A long way from the media. Since she'd been on his trail for over a week, she knew every detail of the story inside out. Probably more than Smith. But he'd been briefed well, too, on the line to take.

As their wellington boots squelched in the mud, Long pressed him on why the policy had changed. He echoed Blair: 'this is a Conservative privatisation.' Long wanted to know when he knew the policy had changed. Who told him? When? Where? The more direct her questions, the more evasive Smith became. Smith said it was at the end of February that the policy changed. The date Margaret Beckett gave her interview to *On the Record*. Long jumped in: 'so it was when you saw Margaret Beckett on telly, you saw then that the policy had changed.'

It was the word 'telly' that made the interview.

CHAPTER THREE

THE TROUBLE WITH CAMPBELL

The conscious and intelligent manipulation of the organized habits and opinions of the masses is an important element in democratic society. Those who manipulate this unseen mechanism of society constitute an invisible government which is the true ruling power of our country.

Edward Bernays, *Propaganda*, 1928

It was hard to see what Blair could have done to win a majority of under 150. In the event, it was 179, though that massive majority derived from a share of the vote that was just 1 per cent higher than John Major's had been in 1992. Some of that was down to the swing of the pendulum, some to the Tories' infighting. Major had been reduced to appealing to his own party discontents, pleading with them 'don't bind my hands', when he should have been talking to voters. Mostly, though, New Labour's easy victory was down to the public's total loss of confidence in the Tories' ability to run an economy.

In spite of that, Blair and his new Cabinet seemed to think they'd won the election, not that the Tories had lost it. And they seemed to believe that it was the obsessive control over the narrative, over the 'truth' they'd created, that had won it for them. It became clear very early on that what they believed had worked in opposition would work in government.

Take the control over the new intake of MPs for example. With each new Parliament, the first thing journalists working on political programmes had to do was to find the MPs who were the good talkers. The independent thinkers or those with some expertise from a former life. In May 1997, that was near impossible. New backbenchers seemed fearful. Distant. They wouldn't return calls. Or if they did, they'd read their words off their pagers. In those first few weeks, we'd fix interviews with a new backbencher but then, just before the programme, they'd become unavailable.

The Central Lobby of the Palace of Westminster changed from the noisy, messy, gossipy agora at the centre of our politics to an ornate desert. Not that bumping into an MP or even junior minister would cast much light on what the government was up to. In the new order of things it was the army of New Labour special advisors who really mattered. And I learnt that it was more important to have their mobile phone numbers than it was to be on speaking terms with anyone who'd been elected.

Politics as I'd known it since the dying days of Jim Callaghan was all but closed down. What New Labour had done to their party, they were planning to do to the country.

And that scared me.

•••

I found out pretty soon what life was going to be like with Campbell in No. 10. Within a month of the election, after the EU summit in Amsterdam.

Blair and Campbell had already written the New Labour story on Europe. A fresh start. A break with the Tory past that had veered between scepticism and strident hostility. The reality was, though, that New Labour was hardly more united on Europe than the Tories. Blair was a Europhile by instinct, wanted sterling to join the Euro and believed that it would. Brown, though, was as Eurosceptic as they come. As determined as any of Major's 'bastards' that sterling would never join the Euro. The famous 'five economic tests' which he set out later in the year were tests that sterling could never pass. Not objectively so, at least.

Amsterdam was all about a new EU treaty. The last had been the Maastricht Treaty in 1992. Major had come away from that declaring victory and clutching a sheaf of opt-outs on borders and the Social Chapter as well as the single currency. Eurocrats and continental EU leaders thought it was unsustainable. Now, five years on and with the union striding towards enlargement and the single currency, the new British government might be more amenable.

Blair's Amsterdam story was all about a 'clear sense of direction'. Getting stuck into the arguments and winning them, not walking away. Photocalls emphasised Blair's youth and virility. Contrasting that with the pale, grey, familiar and, in Chancellor Kohl's case, the overweight. There was even a bike race over Amsterdam's canal bridges which, of course, Blair had to win and the Germans had to boycott.

Campbell's briefings at Amsterdam told and retold that 'clear sense of direction' story. Blair was getting stuck in. His wisdom and insight were steering EU leaders to solutions they hadn't been able to see before. On the new treaty, on defence, economic growth and stability, more democracy. But if you stepped back and asked what was actually happening at Amsterdam you saw something different. You saw that Blair had made major concessions whose consequences he never properly explained and which we're seeing played out today.

On *WATO*, we took that step back.

On the Social Chapter, it was hard to disagree with the ideal: 'the promotion of employment, improving living and working conditions, proper social protection, dialogue between management and labour, the development of human resources with a view to lasting high employment and the combating of exclusion'. But what kind of UK legislation did it mean? Blair wouldn't tell us and probably didn't know himself. Yet

he handed authority over vast areas of British social legislation
to the EU.

It was the same with the Common Foreign and Security
Policy that created a High Representative, a step towards an
EU Secretary of State or Foreign Minister. And with the decision to hand more powers to Europol. Whatever 'clear sense
of direction' these signalled, it wasn't one that a majority of
the British people had voted for. Nor was it clear they would
have assented to it if they'd realised what it really meant. The
boring detail, the detail that really mattered, never made it into
Blair's and Campbell's narrative.

There was a lot of talk about the 'red line' on borders, the
one concession Blair didn't make. For the rest, though, Blair
beamed at the cameras as he handed one power after another
to the unelected EU Commission. It wasn't my job to argue one
way or another about the policy. We had plenty of contribu-
tors from all sides to do that. It was my job and *WATO*'s job
to get behind what seemed to me a misleading façade. And
to show exactly how Blair and Campbell had spun the story,
'created the truth' of Amsterdam.

The following week, a handwritten note arrived in the post.
It was on a single A5 sheet of Downing Street notepaper, signed
by Campbell. I'd never had a handwritten note from No. 10
before. And for some reason, it amused me that it had come
through the post and was sandwiched in my in tray between
a 'WHY OH WHY OH WHY....?' letter and another from a
regular correspondent who suffered, sadly, from delusions.

This, too, was a strange letter. It didn't complain as such.
It wasn't even the kind of rebuttal I'd got used to during the
election campaign. Instead, it accused me of what was, in my
eyes, the worst crime possible. That in reporting Amsterdam,
I'd followed 'any old *Daily Mail* guff'.

I wrote an insipid reply. It all seemed a bit childish really.

• • •

It was a few days later that Campbell tried a more 'matey' approach. During one morning's programme prep, the 'batphone' rang. That was a red, old-style GPO-type phone someone had parked in the middle of the *WATO* production desk. A direct line to the outside world in case the BBC phone system went down. I'd never used it. No one had. I didn't think anyone knew the number. It was half-buried in all the debris that accumulates on newsdesks. Old papers. Coffee cups. Scripts. And, for reasons no one knew, a vest.

Nick Clarke and I looked at each other. Puzzled. I nodded to Nick to answer it. He did. Ultra politely, as was his way. He listened for a moment. Then put his hand over the mouth-piece and whispered to me 'Alastair Campbell'. I shrugged. He shrugged. I looked quizzical. He looked quizzical.

'That's very kind of you, Alastair, but I think we can manage.' He put the batphone down.

'He says he sees we're interviewing…' I forget who it was. 'He wants to know if we need any help. With briefing or thoughts about lines of questioning.' I assumed it was some kind of joke and got on with making that day's programme.

Afterwards, I thought more about it. In one sense, it wasn't an unreasonable thing to do. Call a major news programme with an offer of a briefing or help. But it wasn't something any of his predecessors had ever done. It felt like a trap. If cold-calling us with nudges this way and that about the stories we were covering became a habit, we'd soon stop noticing it. And once we stopped noticing it, we'd also stop noticing how he was influencing our output.

I didn't want that. I didn't want Campbell's or Downing Street's voice to be any louder than any other. And I certainly didn't want to get into a position where I was taking dictation from Downing Street, as some journalists had already shown themselves willing to do.

I decided *WATO* would never be drawn in and would keep its distance. I insisted on knowing if Campbell or anyone else at No. 10 cold-called us or tried to influence our reporting or interviews. I also tweaked the way we reported Campbell's lobby briefings, an important part of our programmes. From then on, we made it clear we were reporting a source just like any other, leaving it to listeners to decide how much of it they believed or trusted.

I didn't realise at the time that this was the start of a long-range, attritional artillery battle with Campbell. That was his choice, not mine. We hardly ever met and I certainly didn't want to find myself drawn into his circle. In that first year of the New Labour government, he let his frustration show by repeatedly calling me a 'Tory' whenever *WATO* went off his grid. Or when we found ways of covering stories he'd tried to kill or dug out the New Labour dissident voices he'd tried to silence.

Or just told our listeners the inside story of how the truth was being created.

• • •

In the summer of 1997, Campbell acquired a power that no unelected, unaccountable, party-political appointee should ever have in a democracy. The power to give orders to impartial, apolitical civil servants and to ministers.

Until that summer, government information was carefully and properly separate from party propaganda. There was in theory and, usually, in practice, a wall between the two. It was leant on routinely, not least by one of Campbell's predecessors at No. 10, Bernard Ingham, though he always insisted that he was speaking for the government rather than for Mrs Thatcher. He used to remind critics, too, that he was a civil servant from beginning to end and that he'd served Labour ministers as well as a Conservative Prime Minister. Ingham knew and understood the limits. Blair, on behalf of Campbell, simply swept the limits away.

The Government Information Service (GIS) annoyed and irritated Campbell from day one. It was, he thought, slow and old-fashioned. Unprofessional. The GIS would concede it was old-fashioned in one sense: it wasn't its job to sell the New Labour narrative, to 'create the truth' or sell that 'truth' in the face of contrary facts. Senior government press officers saw their job as an extension of a minister's account-ability to Parliament. It was as unacceptable to put out false, distorted or doctored information or to omit information that was politically uncomfortable as it was for a minister to mislead Parliament.

I'd been dealing with government press officers day in, day out for over fifteen years by the time of Campbell's coup. Some days, I would spend an hour or more talking through a white paper or a set of figures with a GIS press officer, trying to get to the nub of a story. The press officers would answer questions as truthfully as they could and never, as far as I could tell, had any of them ever deliberately misled me or steered me towards an overtly party political perspective. And while they'd plan media campaigns, it wasn't their job to tie everything into a 'grid', obsessively dictating which stories the media must cover and how they must cover them.

Campbell saw their reluctance to mirror the fevered commit-ment of the New Labour party workers in the Millbank war room as foot-dragging ineptitude rather than a moral objec-tion to politicisation. Within a couple of weeks of the election, senior GIS civil servants were telling people like me about the pressure they were under to become more 'political'.

By an Order in Council, an instrument not previously used for such an overtly political purpose, Campbell was given the authority to command civil servants to create and tell the New Labour story. It was too much for those who thought the GIS should be scrupulously apolitical. Within months, an exodus of senior civil servants began.

For *WATO*, it meant we had to get used to the idea of

dealing in tainted government information just as we'd had to deal with tainted information from New Labour when it was in opposition.

The architects of New Labour showed every sign that they actually believed the story they had created about themselves. Soon after the 1997 election, Peter Mandelson, by then Minister Without Portfolio, appeared at a BBC 'seminar' intended to 'help us understand' the new government. We met in the Council Chamber, the asymmetric, vaguely crescent-shaped room stuck between floors at the front of Broadcasting House. Former Directors General stared out from portraits nailed to the wooden panelling. Reith looking stern but dynamic; Hugh Carlton Greene serene and mildly amused.

I remember little of it. Unusually, I took no notes. But two incidents stuck in my mind. The first when Mandelson was lecturing us on New Labour's vision. It was all fairly dull stuff, I remember, and nothing I hadn't heard before. Suddenly, he became poetic. Reached for the kind of flowery language that never worked for him but which he had a habit of using. What we had to realise, he told us, was that the British people had rejected the Tories and had voted 'in huge numbers, to walk in the broad sunlit uplands of New Labour'. I looked up. For any hint on his face that he knew what he was saying was absurd. Risible and, frankly, weird. There was no such hint. He went on. Our duty as the BBC, he said, was to recognise that desire in the British people 'to walk in those broad sunlit uplands'. And that if we didn't recognise that desire in them and reflect it, 'you will not be serving them as you should.'

I put up my hand. He looked annoyed. I apologised for the interruption but wondered how he could claim the British people had this yearning for New Labour's 'broad sunlit uplands' when fewer people voted for Blair in May than had voted for John Major in 1992? It was one of those stats I happened to know. We'd used it on air several times. Major in 1992 had outpolled Blair in 1997 by half a million votes.

'And you only have 43 per cent of the popular vote. One per cent more than Major,' I added. I happened to know that, too. Same reason. Mandelson said nothing. Then he turned away to pick up his thread as if nothing had happened, smiling his gashed pumpkin smile in Lord Reith's direction as if they were equals.

The second incident came at the end. We began to leave, muttering 'waste of bloody time' as was mandatory at BBC meetings when I saw Mandelson seek out Steve Hewlett, then the editor of *Panorama*. There'd been a major row with the programme back in June, just a month after the election, when John Prescott had accidentally left a sheaf of papers in the studio after recording an interview.

Panorama reporter John Ware picked up the papers and found they set out an option the new government was considering to privatise the London Underground. Another Thatcherite turn they hadn't mentioned in the election campaign. Hewlett and Ware decided it might be a good idea to interview Prescott again, though this time round they'd be able to have a conversation that was based on the facts, down there in black and white. Facts the New Labour media machine hadn't allowed out into the public domain. Prescott and Downing Street were unhappy and accused *Panorama* of theft. Then they claimed the papers said nothing Prescott hadn't said in public but none of us could remember him saying anything of the kind.

Mandelson towered over Hewlett and was in full finger-jabbing mode. Lecturing Hewlett on the ethics of leaked or lost documents. *Panorama* should have handed the papers back unread ... just as he would have done, he said. Hewlett, who isn't usually lost for words, found it difficult to know what to say. Or perhaps he was trying to suppress a laugh at the idea that Mandelson had never been complicit in handling leaked, or found, documents and making sure they got into the media. Hewlett walked away: 'You wouldn't have done it to a Tory government,' Mandelson shouted after him. They're paranoid, I thought.

•••

Ever since Franklin D. Roosevelt's 'first hundred days' (his first three months in office in which he saved the world) it's been a journalistic trope to take stock of any new government's 'first hundred days'.

It's completely meaningless. But because UK elections tend to be in the first week of May, the end of the 'first hundred days' usually falls at the start of the political holiday in late July and early August. It gives those political journalists who aren't on holiday something to fill their columns and airtime with. Well planned, it can be eked out for a week or more and, if well done, isn't entirely without merit.

Blair's 'first hundred days' had an added touch of spice which seems extraordinary given Downing Street's obsession with control. Blair and Campbell both intended to race off to the sun as soon as the parliamentary term was done, leaving the 'first hundred days' operation – and running the country for that matter – in the hands of ... well, who exactly?

Peter Mandelson? The Minister Without Portfolio did have a role in presentation so he'd be the natural choice for the 'hundred days' fiesta. But running the country? Or the Deputy Prime Minister, John Prescott? He could probably do the trip-wire/holding the fort job and had the status. But presentation wasn't his strong suit. Nor were the two of them likely to play nicely together. Prescott had dubbed Mandelson 'one of the beautiful people', fully aware of its overtones. And, later that month, named a Chinese Mitten Crab found in the Thames 'Peter'. 'Do you think you'll get on the executive, Peter?' Prescott asked the crab, for the cameras. It was a mocking reference to Mandelson's bid to get elected to the National Executive Committee of New Labour. It was the kind of mischief that was bound to break out if they were left together without a responsible adult. But that's exactly what Blair and Campbell did.

They called the 'first hundred days' event '100 achievements in 100 days'. But as one mischievous journalist pointed out, the list stopped short at day ninety. And failed to mention some of New Labour's more striking achievements. Its first sex scandal, for example. A recent by-election defeat. The whispering campaign against an MP who had committed suicide. It was generally agreed, half seriously, that lists like this should be regulated by some independent body, perhaps called 'Ofgov'.

It was all an amusing diversion and it should have passed off as the substance-free politicking that it was. But it led to my first really serious row with New Labour in government. One that revealed the lengths to which they were prepared to go to defend their 'truth creation'.

On Friday 1 August Campbell was mentally winding down. He'd just had another 'clear the air' chat with Mandelson when the *News of the World* editor called him to tell him the paper had got hold of a set of photographs 'proving' that the Foreign Secretary, Robin Cook, had spent several nights with his secretary, Gaynor Regan, the previous week. If he didn't run them, someone else would. So he was going to, on the coming Sunday.

It was New Labour's first sex scandal. And an unlikely one at that. Campbell had to act quickly. He tracked Cook down to Heathrow where he'd just arrived from Scotland on his way to Boston for a holiday with his wife. He broke the news and told him bluntly 'in pure media terms and in political terms too' what was needed was 'clarity'.

Within minutes, Cook decided that 'clarity' meant leaving his wife, cancelling the holiday and returning to London. It seemed brutal, though we learnt later that Cook's wife, Margaret, knew that her husband and Regan were involved in an affair. Campbell meanwhile went into overdrive. He promised Cook that he'd personally organise the best possible coverage, shaping the 'cleanest' possible story of Cook's decision to dump his wife at the airport and set up home with his secretary.

We heard rumours of the story in the *World This Weekend* office during the Saturday afternoon. But it wasn't until we saw the early edition of the *News of the World* much later that we knew any of the details. It was all pretty tacky, though restrained by the paper's usual standards.

Sex scandals were a problem for the BBC. We didn't like them and generally left them to the tabloids unless there was a resignation or some other real-world consequence. Or until everyone else had reported them and they'd become part of the national conversation. Bulletin editors would take the soft option and leave them to the paper reviews, under the catch-all 'allegations about his private life'.

This one gave us problems, though. New Labour in opposition had benefited hugely from Major's sex scandals while Cook himself had brilliantly exploited the Tories' financial scandals. And Blair had promised us a new kind of politics; 'purer than pure', he'd said, having no truck 'with anything that is improper in any shape or form at all'. You could almost hear how the audience would groan 'politicians ... they're all the same'.

I got a call from Jon Sopel, the BBC's duty political correspondent that weekend. He wanted to talk to me about another story. The *Sunday Times*, the *News of the World*'s stablemate, was about to run a story that MI6 was investigating the former Governor of Hong Kong and former Tory party chairman, Chris Patten. They were alleging, apparently, that Patten had given secret documents, including intelligence reports, to Jonathan Dimbleby while he was writing *The Last Governor*, the story of Patten's time in Hong Kong.

I asked who was on the story for the *Sunday Times*. Andrew Grice, Sopel said. Grice was the paper's political editor and close to Mandelson. Oh and by the way, Sopel added, he hadn't seen the story yet, either. He'd got the tip-off unattributably from Downing Street.

It whiffed.

Why the unattributable tip? Neither Sopel nor I were going to run a story on that basis, even if it were about to appear in the *Sunday Times*. There was no way I was going to endorse their story without a proper source. And we knew the Foreign Office, the department responsible for MI6, would neither confirm nor deny it. Nor, probably, comment at all.

On the Sunday morning, Sopel and I spoke again but nothing had changed, though in the interim we'd been offered an interview with Mandelson, looking ahead to the 'hundred days'.

Later in the morning, Sopel called again. He'd just spoken to Downing Street, who'd agreed he could source the MI6/Patten story to them. And if we asked Mandelson about it in the *TW2* interview, he'd confirm it.

It still whiffed, but Sopel filed a voice piece for the news bulletins quoting 'Downing Street' and when the moment came in our interview with Mandelson, we asked him about it. His answer was clear, though not a direct confirmation: 'The matter rather than the individual is under investigation ... it would be irresponsible for the government not to take action when there appears to have been a leak of intelligence.'

That was a first. I couldn't remember a government minister commenting on a current intelligence matter before. But with Mandelson's sound bite, the story led the BBC bulletins for the rest of the day and kicked into the following day's papers.

Knocking the Cook sex scandal off the front pages.

Another surprising story found legs that weekend, too. One of the New Labour government's first acts was to announce it was scrapping the royal yacht *Britannia*. The campaign to save it had run out of steam until, on that first weekend in August, the *Independent on Sunday* headlined that the royal yacht had been reprieved. It played in the other papers, too.

Knocking the Cook sex scandal off their front pages.

MI6, Patten and the royal yacht were still around the front pages the following, Monday, morning. The Cook story was on the inside pages with a tired, who-cares feel to it. Not much moral outrage and no call for heads to roll. On the *WATO* newsdesk, we were having fun with the 'who's in charge' saga and starting to look ahead to the 'hundred days'. And we were trying to get to the bottom of the royal yacht and MI6/Patten stories, too.

My phone rang. It was Tim Allan from Downing Street, minding the shop while Campbell was away. He wanted to know if he could help – could he push any interview bids for us? I tended to trust Allan but was still suspicious and replied that he could get us the head of MI6 on the Patten story. Or failing that, the minister responsible, the Foreign Secretary; 'you know, Robin Cook. Oh no … hang on.' I think he saw the funny side.

'I wouldn't bother with that. It's rubbish.' 'Sorry?' I said. It was sourced to you guys in Downing Street, I reminded him. And Mandelson as near as dammit confirmed it, I said.

'Well it's rubbish,' he said again. I wasn't happy. OK, how about getting us Geoffrey Robinson, the Paymaster General, on the royal yacht story?

'I wouldn't bother with that either. That's rubbish too.' I was even less happy. I put the phone down and called a huddle. Martha Kearney, who was presenting *WATO* that week while Nick Clarke was on holiday, came over and a couple of other senior journalists.

We've been used, everyone agreed. Someone said we'd never have run the Cook story anyway. So the fandango over the weekend wasn't about keeping it off *TW2*. It was about getting the BBC to give the Patten story legs to push it up everyone else's news agenda. Sleight of hand was one thing. But I'd never come across anything as deliberate as this seemed. Here was a government that was prepared to plant in the media what it later called 'rubbish' to push their first sex scandal off the front pages. Once the 'rubbish' had done its job, once they'd 'created the truth' and got the government through the immediate crisis, the 'rubbish' went back where it belonged.

There was only one way to respond. Give the *WATO* audience chapter and verse on what had happened. That was the story. And a good one, too. I wrote the script, logging every detail of what had happened. Sopel appeared, giving his account of how Downing Street had explicitly 'confirmed' that MI6 were investigating Chris Patten. And once the Tory chairman, Brian Mawhinney, fully understood what Downing Street had done over that weekend, he was suitably outraged and came onto the programme to tell our audience that.

It was a tetchy start to 'hundred days' week. Mandelson in particular took exception, bollocking Sopel for breaking the lobby code of *omerta*. As far as *WATO* was concerned, he seethed on until the end of the week before detonating during a live interview with us straight after his joint news conference with Prescott. That news conference had gone very badly from his point of view, partly because few journalists there took it at all seriously. He lashed out at one who wondered what he was doing in charge, complaining at the 'stream of vainglorious, self-indulgent questions'. And he took much the same approach to Martha Kearney when she asked why he, a junior minister, had been left 'minding the shop'. We were, he said, 'preoccupied with ourselves'.

If that was tetchy, it got much worse when Kearney asked him about the manipulations over MI6, Chris Patten and the royal yacht. Why had he 'confirmed' a story that Downing Street later dismissed as 'rubbish'? Why had he dropped hints that impugned the integrity of a public figure? Mandelson didn't like it: 'I think the reason why media people like you like talking about news management is because you really rather prefer talking about yourselves and your work and your lives in the media than talking about things that interest the bulk of the population.'

He built up a head of steam: 'This week we've had day in and day out a preoccupation with yourselves. I think it's become very boring and very tedious ... I think you should get back to the subjects that really concern the bulk of the population in this country.' Later that same day, he gave that infamous interview to *The Guardian* in which he declared it was his job to 'create the truth'.

We heard later that, back at New Labour HQ, the staffers had cheered Mandelson's performance on *WATO*. Lack of self-awareness wasn't confined to the Minister Without Portfolio. But that wasn't the end of it. The faux-lads of New Labour were fond of soccer metaphors and what followed was a classic example of playing the man not the ball.

I was due to go on a family holiday to Greece that weekend, the day after Mandelson's outburst on *WATO*. As we were leaving for the airport, I got a call from the BBC press office that an 'unnamed source' had gone for me in *The Observer*. According to that unnamed source, I was 'highly aggressive and highly unapologetic' and was running 'something of a vendetta' against New Labour.

Nothing like this had ever happened before. Rows I'd had with the Tories in government and New Labour in opposition hadn't led to cowardly, anonymous briefings. I had to deal with it. The family went on ahead and I stayed in London for a couple of hours to cobble together some sort of response. Being the BBC, our response was understated: 'Kevin Marsh is a highly regarded BBC news editor. We totally reject any suggestion he is anything other than completely impartial in his political journalism.'

As I travelled to the airport, alone and with time to think, I realised I was anxious. Fearful, even. The adrenalin of chasing the story and the drive to tell the truth about New Labour and its 'truth creation' had blanked out any emotions at the time. But now I realised how serious it was. I'd exposed not just a government deception but how and why they'd put that deception together. And in response, they'd targeted me. Not my work – me personally. Anonymously. That didn't happen in Britain, surely.

It wasn't much of a holiday. I spent most of it on the phone, to the BBC press office and to my bosses at the BBC, all of whom were very supportive though at much greater length than I really needed when the alternative was a few hours in the Mediterranean sun. Some journalists wrote cheering profiles. One or two even saw the row for what it really was.

A fight for the independence of the BBC.

• • •

'Creating the truth' in politics relies on incurious or compliant journalists and on audiences with short memories. The truth is, it works more often than it fails. If it didn't, New Labour wouldn't have done it. Wouldn't have been able to do it.

But when it fails, it's catastrophic. Not just because the truth breaks through. But because the cynicism of the 'truth crea-tion' gets exposed too. The Ecclestone affair was one of those occasions. Its fallout dogged Blair's first term, set the tone for his entire time in power. It was also the next big step in my worsening relationship with No. 10.

Like the Robin Cook sex scandal, the Ecclestone affair cut to the heart of Blair's 'new style of politics'. Both showed that he and New Labour were not 'purer than pure' after all. In fact, as far as questionable deals went, the Ecclestone affair appeared very much worse than anything the Tories managed. New Labour's problems with cash weren't about obscure, greedy backbenchers and junior ministers. Nor about what Blair had called 'people fluttering around the new Government'. They went right to the top.

Bernie Ecclestone, the diminutive boss of the companies that ran Formula 1 racing, had given New Labour a donation of £1 million at the beginning of 1997. Very useful in the coming general election campaign. The donation was undisclosed. Or secret, as most would call it. Meanwhile, in another part of the forest, the party had committed itself to implementing an

EU directive banning tobacco advertising and sponsorship in sport, including Formula 1. It was no casual or vague pledge. Both the new Health Secretary, Frank Dobson, and his junior minister, Tessa Jowell, made public speeches that could hardly be more clear. 'If a car is running at the grand prix here, it won't be carrying tobacco advertising.' The only open question, apparently, was whether it would apply to contracts already in place.

In fact, that wasn't the only open question. In the late summer, an unnamed senior government figure told one newspaper that the government had 'back-pedalled' on the pledge and existing contracts would certainly not be affected. The Formula 1 chiefs, Ecclestone and Max Mosley, lobbied hard. Then, Blair told the German Chancellor and Italian Prime Minister that the EU directive was impractical. Finally, on 4 November, news broke that Jowell had written to the EU Health Council signalling the UK government's U-turn. Formula 1 would be exempted from the ban. That sparked off a colossal media row. Initially about the rights and wrongs of tobacco sponsorship versus the cost to British jobs and expertise if Formula 1 fled the country.

Later that week, details of Ecclestone's and Mosley's lobbying emerged which gave the story new legs. And, by the weekend, there were rumours of financial links between Ecclestone and New Labour. That was puzzling at first. We knew Mosley was a Labour donor but the cuttings seemed to suggest Ecclestone backed the Tories.

The World This Weekend was in a tricky position. Ecclestone's 'donation' was the big political story that weekend. And if some of the claims in the early editions of the Sunday papers were true, it was a massive scandal. But we had no leads and Downing Street was playing for time. They accused the Tories of stirring up the story and insisted they had no record of Ecclestone making any donation up to the end of 1996. That was true, but it was a classic non-denial denial. And when they were pressed on donations immediately before the election, they responded that the records for 1997 would be made public in 1998. Effectively, a confirmation. After all, if he'd given no money, it was simplicity itself to say so.

The new week started with a gift from Gordon Brown, protesting too much on *Today*. In the name of doing 'everything above board', he said, we should wait until the list of donors was published. Again, if there'd been no donation, Brown could have ended speculation there and then. He didn't. And though he'd been New Labour's campaign chairman, spending whatever donation Ecclestone had made, he insisted improbably that he didn't know the size of that gift.

Brown had played them into a lot of trouble – trouble Campbell would have to deal with at the morning's Downing Street lobby. If he offered nothing more, everyone would conclude that the worst allegations in the press were true. If there'd been no donation or it had been a small one, Campbell could say so and kill the story stone dead. More straight bat would look like they didn't know how to explain what had happened. Campbell chose the straight bat and we reported the morning lobby as the series of evasions it seemed to us to be.

Then things did move. On the best possible afternoon to bury bad news. At three o'clock, a fresh judgment was due in the case of Louise Woodward, the British au pair working in the United States who'd been found guilty of murdering the boy she was looking after. We all expected the original murder verdict to be overturned and had piles of background material ready to run. An involuntary manslaughter verdict was duly returned, Woodward freed and the coverage swamped the afternoon and evening news programmes.

Shortly before *PM* went on air, New Labour's press chief David Hill called a snap news conference on Ecclestone for five o'clock. You had to admire the timing.

It was a less revealing news conference than it first appeared. And few news outlets had the space or desire to drill down to the detail of a Westminster village story when they had buckets of human interest in the Woodward story.

Hill admitted that New Labour had accepted a 'substantial donation' from Ecclestone at the beginning of 1997. And that the government had decided to make the U-turn on F1 and tobacco sponsorship in the first week of November. He said the party had asked the chairman of the Committee on Standards in Public Life for advice and that advice had been to send the money back, which they'd done. He added that there'd been no criticism of Labour for taking the money. Giving it back was about the 'appearance' that money might have changed government policy. The appearance that it was 'cash for favours'. But he still didn't reveal the size of the donation, though did say it would be on the list of donors who'd given at least £5,000. No hint that the actual sum was at least two hundred times that.

Hill's timing worked for a while. Woodward swamped the following day's papers. But then, a rumour circulated that Ecclestone's donation had been £1.5 million. Campbell, meanwhile, floated the idea that it might be time to look at party funding 'from top to bottom'. Then, in the middle of the afternoon, Ecclestone confirmed he'd given £1 million. At the time, it was thought he'd been prodded to do it by Downing Street, for the sake of 'clarity'. It certainly achieved that. But once he'd spoken, the affair unravelled rapidly, out of Downing Street's control.

Ecclestone's confirmation made Downing Street's and New Labour's earlier defensiveness look shamefaced, guilty even. That was bad enough. But it turned out that the letter the party had sent to the chairman of the Committee on Standards in Public Life wasn't quite what Hill had implied. The letter hadn't asked for advice on that £1 million donation in January 1997. It had, in fact, asked for advice on a *second* donation. One that Ecclestone hadn't actually offered but which party fundraisers were still hoping to persuade him to give. *After* the U-turn on tobacco advertising and sponsorship.

Once again, it wasn't enough for *WATO* just to tell that story, though we did that. It was another occasion when I felt we had to tell the story of how Downing Street and the party had tried to 'create the truth' by stonewalling and manipulation.

I'd given Nick Jones a pretty free hand to chase down the story for us, though he needed no encouragement. Campbell had shouted him down in the lobby. Hill had berated him for following a Tory lead, for wasting time on 'old news' and tried to scare him off with warnings that Ecclestone would sue. Brown's attack dog, Charlie Whelan, had accused him of 'nitpicking' while Tim Allan had accused him of going off on some Watergate-style fantasy. Campbell ended the week deriding Jones for what he called 'that collective herd instinct you have at the BBC' and *WATO* for spending half its programmes explaining New Labour's diversions and manipulations.

But Campbell couldn't control this story. So he introduced a new strategy, one that was to become familiar. Masochism. He offered Blair up for a live interview on the BBC1 Sunday lunchtime interview show *On The Record* 'to go a few rounds' with John Humphrys and to say 'sorry'.

'I think most people who have dealt with me think I am a pretty straight sort of guy,' Blair told Humphrys. That was to come back to haunt him.

What happened on screen wasn't the sum total of the masochism strategy, though. It also required off-the-record briefings before the live interview to try to fix the headlines and make sure that the lazier journalists got their story 'right'. Blair, he briefed, would 'admit' to failures and would accept they should have been more open. He got some of the headlines he wanted. And even managed to establish the idea that Blair had apologised, though he hadn't. At least, not for what he should have apologised for.

But any welcome headlines sat alongside very much more hostile analysis. Blair was 'truth dodging'. 'Did you lie to us

Tony?' And the *Sunday Telegraph* warned that 'he who lives by image dies by image'.

• • •

Soon after the Ecclestone affair, the editorship of *Today* fell vacant. I wasn't interested and didn't apply. I had more interesting things to do, including developing a new programme, *Broadcasting House*, for the new controller of Radio 4, James Boyle. It left the field clear for two *Today* insiders, Rod Liddle and Chris Rybczynski. Either would do an interesting job, I thought. And whichever got it was welcome to it.

For some reason, the idea of me running *Today* alarmed Campbell. He didn't know and didn't find out that I wasn't interested in the job. But once again, he played the man and not the ball and winged off a letter to my immediate boss, Head of Radio News Steve Mitchell, saying I was 'closed to reason' and guilty of peddling an 'anti-Labour follow-any-old-Tory-guff agenda'. A private letter that somehow got into the papers. Along with the wholly improbable claim that it was nothing to do with the *Today* editorship.

If I had been interested in the job, I might have taken Campbell's intervention a bit more seriously. After all, here was the Prime Minister's right-hand man trying to influence a senior editorial appointment in the national broadcaster because ... well, because of what? Because I insisted on telling the country about the methods New Labour used to 'create the truth'. Once again, I thought it was the sort of thing that didn't happen in Britain. Corrupt dictatorships, perhaps. But not here.

• • •

Within a few weeks, we were into yet another row with Campbell. Again, it was because we insisted on revealing to an audience outside the Westminster bubble the way the truth was being created. Again it led to a personal attack on me. It was an affair known by the single word: Prodi. What academics would call the *'locus classicus'* in any study of Campbell's time in Downing Street.

On Monday 23 March 1998, the Turin-based newspaper *La Stampa* carried a report that Tony Blair had spoken to the Italian Prime Minister Romano Prodi to ask whether his government intended to block Rupert Murdoch's proposed takeover of *Mediaset*, the corporate umbrella under which Silvio Berlusconi ran his media interests. The Italian government had already told Murdoch twice where to go with his takeover bid. He was keen to know, now, whether it was worth increasing his £2 billion offer or whether the Italian government had already made up its mind that it preferred an Italian owner, no matter what the price.

The story was a reminder of Blair's pre-election, unwritten deal with Murdoch, the deal that brought *The Sun* onside. But it made ripples rather than waves at first. Campbell kept the story low-profile by confirming that Blair and Prodi had spoken but refused to confirm, deny or comment at all on what they'd spoken about. The following morning, though, the *Financial Times* political editor, Robert Peston, now the BBC's business editor, ran an account of the two Prime Ministers' conversation under the headline: 'BLAIR INTERVENED ON MURDOCH BID'. The word 'intervened' and its possible meanings became the focus of a lengthy, bitter row.

The BBC political correspondent Nick Jones called me after that morning's lobby and described how Campbell had 'gone off on one'. How he'd turned on Peston. It was 'a complete joke' to say Blair had 'intervened'. It was 'balls'. 'Crap'. 'C-R-A-P'. It was emphatic – but it had the odour of a non-denial denial. Peston kept digging and the following day, he reported that Blair had spoken to Murdoch the week before he spoke to Prodi. It was ponging even more.

Again, Campbell stonewalled, insisting that *if* Murdoch had called Blair, it would have been a private conversation and not something the voice of the government could discuss. It was, he said, a 'non-story'.

On *WATO* we'd been trying to flush out anyone from News International who'd go on the record. At first, there was silence. Then *The Times* media editor Ray Snoddy stepped on stage with what seemed to be Murdoch's version of events. He told how Murdoch had 'used information obtained directly from Tony Blair' to make his judgements over the *Mediaset* bid. Campbell was looking exposed.

'Despite a number of ambiguous statements from Downing Street spokesmen over the past few days it is now clear that last week Murdoch rang the Prime Minister to see if he would find out what the political reaction [in Italy] might be [to a further bid for *Mediaset*].' Snoddy even accused Campbell of coming 'very close to providing misleading information' and insisted that he had dismissed as a 'joke' stories which were 'completely true'. Again, that couldn't have been said without the nod from Murdoch.

According to Snoddy, Murdoch saw his call to Blair as a request for information rather than lobbying. But to those of us on the outside, it looked as if it might be connected with the deal New Labour had struck with Murdoch before the election. Blair, Murdoch and the deal were the story. But so was Campbell.

And by the weekend, it was *all* about Campbell. And not just over Prodi. MPs wanted to grill him about his coup at the Government Information Service. And faxes had been leaked in which he'd 'bollocked' Frank Field and Harriet Harman for talking out of turn on welfare reform. In one of them, he took Harman to task for an interview on *WATO*. It hadn't been 'cleared through his office' and he'd be 'grateful for an explanation'. It was startling stuff. He seemed unable to see the problem with an unaccountable party apparatchik who no one had voted for bullying an elected minister of the crown. Telling her she could only speak to voters with his permission.

The weekend press decided Campbell's days at No. 10 were numbered. He'd breached the first rule of spinning and become the story. And there it might all have ended, with Campbell bloodied and, perhaps, having learnt something. As far as the rough stuff in the lobby went, the journalists there knew they could deal with it. Those who didn't take his dictation weren't going to crumple just because he spelled out the word C-R-A-P at them. But there was another dimension to all of this. Those faxes nagged at me over that weekend, as did Campbell's lack of accountability to the public. Why shouldn't he be held up to scrutiny? Why shouldn't he be made accountable? It seemed to me that Campbell and his team were part of New Labour's fusion of party and state that was alien to Britain.

It was all about accountability. The convention that MPs and ministers shouldn't mislead the House was one of the most powerful in our unwritten constitution. If the Prime Minister himself misled MPs, he'd be hounded. But his mouthpiece and government information supremo was in a position to hide the truth or give out misleading information and there was nothing any MP or voter could do. No one could hold him to account. That was wrong. The Lib Dem peer Lord McNally thought so, too. Enough to call the following week for a statement from the Prime Minister on his press secretary's behaviour.

In the House of Commons, the former Conservative media chief Tim Collins, by now an MP, moved a point of order criticising Campbell for giving out 'a great deal of rapidly changing information', insulting and abusing those journalists who wrote 'proper and accurate stories'. Later that day, the shadow culture secretary Francis Maude joined the attack, demanding the Prime Minister explain how Campbell had briefed journalists over the Prodi affair in a way that was 'at best misleading, at worst deliberately false'.

That might have been effective if he had left it at that. But the following morning, he went on *Today* and, after a bit of fun tagging Campbell an 'over mighty courtier at the court of King Tony', stepped over an important line. 'We want to know', Maude asked, 'if he is doing this off his own bat ... is he specifically authorised to tell lies?' Schoolboy error. The word 'lies'. It got Campbell off the hook.

That morning's lobby, 31 March 1998, has gone down in history, though no two accounts of it agree completely and the recording of it has been mislaid. What's not in doubt is that Campbell, aided and abetted by Maude's use of the 'L' word, laid down a challenge he knew no one could pick up: 'There is not a single person in this room who can say I have lied on this story. If there is, I would like them to say it now because it is not true.'

No one spoke because no one thought he'd lied. Had he asked whether he'd *misled* them, every one of them would have said yes. But, according to the rules of the club, he hadn't lied. He'd stayed within the norms of the lobby, the norms of 'creating the truth'. He'd done it by pirouetting on one fantastically narrow interpretation of the word 'intervened'. Because Prodi had called Blair and not the other way around, he insisted it was 'crap' to say that Blair had 'intervened'.

It was a tactic he became accustomed to use. Find a way of interpreting or reformulating the allegation that was deniable. Or find a small detail that can be challenged in an otherwise accurate account and use it to rubbish the whole thing. It was the tactic he used in the row with the BBC over the September dossier and at Lord Hutton's inquiry.

It was a story *WATO* had to tell. We asked a simple question. Is an unaccountable political appointee who ridicules and abuses journalists who are trying to tell the truth and who stretches credulity to deny the truth, acting in the *public* interest, or in his *party* interest? And if it's the party interest, why are taxpayers paying for it?

It meant putting on air lobby journalists talking about

working at close quarters with Campbell, describing what had become, to them, everyday business. Close-quarter combat they'd become used to. Most of them enjoyed it. Ordinary listeners, though, indeed anyone outside the closed world of the lobby, found their accounts startling. It was the first time those outside the Westminster village heard how Campbell would stand over journalists as they filed their stories, shouting they were a 'load of nonsense'. How he would single out a journalist for derision. How on one occasion he'd mocked a journalist who wasn't sharing his idea of a joke, sneering that he was 'having an orgasm over there in the corner'.

I think it was the only time we'd used the word 'orgasm' on *WATO*.

At the afternoon lobby that day, Campbell launched into a lengthy tirade against the Conservatives, the media, the BBC, *WATO* and me. 'Everyone in this room knows I haven't lied … Political news … [is] very much of zero interest to the great British public … programmes like *WATO* are a joke … in the end that lot at the BBC will have to come to their senses about how they cover politics.'

Two months later, Campbell finally appeared before the committee of MPs who wanted to grill him about how he did his job. The first time he'd come close to parliamentary accountability. Tory MP Andrew Tyrie wanted to go back to 'Prodi' and help Campbell clear up the doubt over whether he'd lied. Campbell dismissed it as a story that was 'obsessing the media'. As if Blair's relations with Murdoch weren't a matter of legitimate public interest. He then turned on me. He accused me of 'getting opposition MPs on to the radio to say that I have misled people, I have lied'.

I've never accused Alastair Campbell of lying. Nor asked anyone to do so. I set out week after week how he and New Labour 'created the truth'. And the effort they put into controlling all that people understood about the government. There's a subtle distinction between 'misleading' and 'lying'. Perhaps that's a condemnation of the way we became used to doing our politics in the New Labour era. Perhaps 'spin', 'mislead' and 'lie' should all mean the same thing. But they don't.

In any event, when Campbell went on to give MPs his account of that, by now, notorious lobby, he told them that the challenge he'd laid down was: 'You know that I have lied to nobody and if there is anybody here who thinks that I have *lied to or misled* them, why don't you just stand up and say so?' He assured MPs that 'no one did'. The addition of that phrase 'or misled' made all the difference.

CHAPTER FOUR

AT *TODAY*

If you want to drop a word in the ear of the nation, then this is the programme in which to do it.

Brian Redhead

'There's a lot of broken glass.'

Mark Damazer, the Deputy Director of News, spoke quickly in a confidential baritone. He was telling me the way he saw *Today* when I took over as editor in December 2002. It was more or less the way Richard Sambrook, the Head of News, saw it. As well as my immediate boss the Head of Radio News, Steve Mitchell and the Radio 4 Controller, Helen Boaden.

'Not what a BBC flagship should be,' Sambrook had told me. 'Wrong agenda and wrong attitudes.'

Today had been without an editor for nearly three months since the previous incumbent, Rod Liddle, had been forced to choose between his *Guardian* column and the BBC – he chose his column. From where I sat, on the other side of the news factory at *The World at One*, it seemed things had been rudderless at *Today* for some time. Broken glass was a good way of describing the result. Once the editorship became vacant, my bosses assumed I was bound to want to clear it up. I wasn't so sure. In the end, though, for few of the right reasons and many of the wrong ones, I decided I'd do it. For eighteen months. Two years max. Clear up the broken glass. And move on.

By the end of 2002, *Today* had been at the centre of British media, political and public life for two decades. Though the weekly audience was sliding, it was a presence in the life of any British adult who took even the slightest interest in news and politics. It set the news agenda. Most news outlets followed its lead and many political news stories had 'speaking on *Today* ...' tagged to their quotes. More than one Speaker of the House of Commons had complained that ministers seemed to prefer to announce new policies on *Today* rather than the floor of the house.

Its presenters were household names: Humphrys, Naughtie, Montague and Stourton. And it wasn't just their journalism that made news. Their mistakes on air and activities off air became stories, too. The press and the public saw them and *Today* as a national possession. But it hadn't always been like that.

In the 1950s, a young BBC producer not long out of university started bombarding his bosses with memos putting forward the idea of a 'morning miscellany' of talk and comment. The producer was Robin Day. And it was a radical idea. At the time, the BBC laboured under self-imposed burdens that made anything like the modern *Today* programme impossible. There was the fourteen-day rule, for example. A rule which forbade any discussion of any matter that would come before Parliament within the next fourteen days.

Deference was the default attitude to authority and live conversation on air was non-contentious, limited to tried and tested formats with tried and tested guests who would stay within the rules. Political controversy, as well as the unscripted voices of working-class folk, was avoided.

Day ground down his bosses. Though when the morning miscellany was finally put on air in 1957, the year of Suez and the first post-war clash between the BBC and the government, it was produced by the tame Talks Department and was little more than two chunks of scripted speech slotted between the 'furniture': news bulletins, religious programmes and so on. It was designed merely as a speech alternative to the music that opened the day on the other BBC radio services.

There was nothing inevitable about *Today* becoming the presence in politics, national and international affairs that it did. In the 1960s, *Today* passed from gentle old 'Talks' to the more edgy Current Affairs empire. It became a regular two-hour programme, still with 'furniture', but with a gradually hardening political and inquiring edge. It wasn't until the early 1980s, under the editorship of Julian Holland, that *Today* began to turn into its modern form.

Holland was a hard news man. He'd come to the BBC from the *Daily Mail* and found the residual deference to authority amongst the BBC top brass wholly alien. Once at the BBC, he teamed up at *The World at One* with a former *Mail* editor, William Hardcastle, the programme's first presenter. With Hardcastle and later with Robin Day, Holland gave *WATO* a sharp and insistent edge that startled and occasionally dismayed his bosses.

Holland was a querulous sceptic. Straightforward, honest and with a good sense of what would outrage middle England or evoke its sympathy or amazement. When he moved to *Today* in 1981, he had no time for the fluff he found there. True, it had begun to toughen up but in Holland's mind it still had a long way to go. He cared about the big stories. Westminster politics. Policy. Big foreign events. He wanted argument. To find out who to blame. And he used to the maximum a power that only the BBC had. The power to drag a minister to the microphone for an uncomfortable five minutes with Brian Redhead. It was accountability in action. Live. In any home that cared to tune in.

It became a very tough place to work. If you were on the *Today* team, it was your life. Long, long night shifts that Holland, briefly, extended to fifteen hours. Chasing down stories in the middle of the night. Calling the people you needed at 5.00 a.m.

Burying yourself in a mound of cuttings to find the key killer fact for that interview. No wonder it became that place apart. You had to believe you were special to put up with it all.

Holland made it even tougher by demanding that they beat the papers to stories. Or take their stories on with angles or interviews they'd missed. The idea was that by the time *Today* listeners opened their morning papers, they were out of date.

Holland more than any previous editor made the *Today* team believe in itself. He knew how important it was to encourage the idea that working on the programme was something close to a vocation. Without some tangible sense that what you were doing was the most important thing in the world, the intense pressure would be impossible to bear. Without that sense, no one could work the hours, sacrificing normal life and, often, relationships.

Today's self-image became its armour against the world. It turned into something close to an independent republic within the BBC. Superior. Sharing little with the rest of BBC News. They kept their plans closely guarded secrets. Hiding their news diaries or writing them in code. Not to protect themselves against external competition, but to confound the real enemy – the rest of the BBC. It was a lynching offence if any member of the team breathed a disloyal word to outsiders.

Nothing showed Holland's disregard for anything that was not *Today* better than the fiasco of the signature tune.

Holland was a jazz fanatic and a good friend of George Melly, Humphrey Lyttelton and clarinettist Wally Fawkes, otherwise known as the cartoonist 'Trog'. Fawkes, as 'Trog', immortalised Holland as a short-sighted Magoo-like character in his long-running cartoon strip *Flook*. It was a characterisation based on cruel fact. As a journalist, Holland had great vision. But nature had progressively taken away his physical vision until, by the time he moved to *Today*, he could barely see at all.

Johnny Dankworth was another close jazz friend and Holland commissioned him to write a short signature tune, called a 'sting', for the programme. Dankworth wrote several, all featuring a breathy clarinet, all with the hint of a red-eyed morning after a late night in a smoky club. The stings divided opinion. Some thought they sounded sleazy. Holland was convinced they were right. So convinced that he omitted to mention them to the Head of Radio News or the Controller of Radio 4.

They both hated them. More importantly, they hated the fact that they hadn't been asked. Failing to consult was always a greater BBC crime than being wrong. Within a few weeks, Holland was ordered to drop the music. His cussedness had been typical. By the time he stood down as editor, *Today*, with the incomparable Brian Redhead at its heart, had established itself exactly where he'd intended. The news programme that set the agenda every day.

Over the decade that followed, three successive editors, Jenny Abramsky, Phil Harding and especially Roger Mosey built on Holland's foundations. But it was Mosey who more than anyone else made *Today* essential listening for the entire media and political establishment. And he did so against genuine competition from TV breakfast shows and 24-hour television news.

'Setting the agenda' came to define rather than simply describe what *Today* was about. Though up until New Labour's election victory in May 1997, it was about beating the press and other broadcasters to every story. Once Alastair Campbell was in Downing Street 'setting the agenda' came to mean something different.

Campbell wanted, felt he needed, a degree of control that was obsessive over both the media and political agenda. To him, to New Labour, the two agendas were the same. It was bound to bring him and *Today* into conflict.

The fight for 'the agenda' had been a struggle within the media until then. Suddenly, it became a political one.

• • •

When the *Today* job came up at the end of 1997, I came under a lot of pressure to apply, especially from the new Radio 4 Controller, James Boyle. He asked me half a dozen times to let my name go forward, even calling me at home the evening before the interviews to tell me it still wasn't too late. But I just didn't want it.

Relations with New Labour were at their most tense. After one on-air clash between John Humphrys and Harriet Harman, the party's entire media team had threatened to withdraw cooperation from *Today*. Press chief, David Hill, complained that 'the John Humphrys problem has assumed new proportions ... we have had a council of war...' that was a meeting of Hill, Mandelson and Campbell as well as the frontline party press officers, and 'none of us feels this can go on.' A Liberal Democrat MP leaked a copy of the letter to the press, which rallied to Humphrys's and *Today*'s defence. Soon afterwards, the *Today* job became vacant after yet another, baffling Birtian reorganisation. Campbell, apparently alarmed at the idea of me working in tandem with Humphrys, wrote to my immediate boss, Head of Radio News Steve Mitchell, and briefed against me in the lobby. He hadn't realised it was a job I didn't want.

Rod Liddle got the call, largely because Mitchell and Boyle thought he could deliver something energetic and original. He'd been at the BBC for about ten years, first as a junior producer on *WATO* when I was the deputy editor there. He'd worked his way up to take charge of *The World This Weekend* under his mentor, Roger Mosey, and then moved to *Today* as an assistant editor.

Liddle had always been attracted to extremes and by his own account had 'no aptitude' for management. A propensity, he said, to 'fuck up spectacularly' when forced into it.[†] That

---

† In July 2001, Liddle told Michael Leapman in an interview for the *New Statesman* that: 'If they moved me to some middle-management job, I would loathe it, have no aptitude for it and sure as likely fuck up spectacularly. If I went anywhere, it would probably be outside. I'd like to do more writing.'

was a problem in John Birt's BBC. He took to fighting his managerial battles in the press, enjoyed feeding the diaries and even took on Campbell in the pages of *The Guardian*. As time went by, he began to enjoy the press profile and when it came to the choice between the BBC and his *Guardian* column, it surprised few that he chose the column.

Around the turn of the century, a new strand of thinking gained traction at the top of the BBC. The idea that we were too cautious. That we didn't break enough stories and weren't taking on the press as aggressively as we should. To some extent, it reflected the transition from Birt to Greg Dyke as Director General.

Journalistically, Birt had an unrivalled reputation for risk aversion. He'd been known to insist on sitting in the edit suite when a controversial programme was being put together. But it was a reputation he didn't entirely deserve. And he was right that a publicly funded broadcaster with a duty to be accurate, impartial and accountable couldn't go the way of a newspaper, serving its chosen section of the market, ignoring the rest and taking risks with the truth in the search for profit.

Dyke was much less buttoned up. He encouraged innovation and creativity and a less constipated approach. The idea that the BBC should be doing more original, 'exclusive' journalism attracted Liddle, amongst others, who argued that in order to deliver it, *Today* needed to import some of the thinking, and some of the people, from what we used to call Fleet Street.

I didn't agree. I was no fan of Birt. But he was right about the responsibilities of public service broadcasting. Nor was it true that we weren't breaking stories. We didn't have much time for the kind of tabloid story that was only ever true-ish and we avoided sensation for its own sake. But *Today*, *The World at One*, *Newsnight* and to some extent Five Live, broke stories and originated news lines on serious subjects as a matter of routine.

We'd all have preferred it if a few more whistleblowers had

turned to the BBC. But the fact is, most broadcast journalism is 'on the record'. Sources speaking for themselves in their own words, something not always attractive to those who'd rather give their testimony anonymously. The last thing we needed, in my view, was to import the values of the press into the BBC. We needed to have more confidence in the things that made us different, not yearn for those that would make us the same. But the idea of a more tabloid agenda, 'breaking more stories', appealed to Liddle.

His argument was that he should produce journalism designed to 'get up people's noses', to force ministers and those in authority to the microphone. That needed more reporters. So he recruited, sometimes in unorthodox ways, the kind of reporters who could turn in the kind of journalism he had in mind. One of those he hired was Andrew Gilligan. He'd left the *Sunday Telegraph* in 1999 after upsetting Con Coughlin, the paper's foreign editor. Amongst other things, Gilligan had deployed himself on assignments without telling his boss. Coughlin thought he was 'an unreliable maverick' and had to go.

The strategy was no more than a partial success. And by the end of 2002, *Today* had other problems too. The regular audience had fallen below the magic six million and in order to pay for the increased number of reporters, editorial and production posts had gone unfilled. There was no full-time deputy editor; more than half the most senior posts were either vacant or filled by more junior staff; while at the next layer down, fifteen out of twenty producer and broadcast assistant jobs – the real backbone of the show – were vacant, filled temporarily or by casuals. It was hurting the programme. Producers were working flat out just to cover the basics. And mistakes were creeping in.

Mostly, they were trivial but as one followed another, enormously damaging. A wrong name or title. Once or twice, though, it was much more serious. The shortage of journalists on the desk combined with pressure to be controversial brought expensive disaster.

•••

Until I decided to move to *Today*, I only knew Andrew Gilligan from a distance. He'd done some decent work on military kit over the years. Radios and rifles that didn't work. Billions wasted on aircraft whose computers didn't work or which couldn't launch smart bombs. His reporting annoyed the MoD and Defence Secretary Geoff Hoon, not in itself a bad thing. But sometimes there seemed to me to be less to some of his scoops than met the eye.

In the autumn of 2002, soon after Liddle had gone, I happened to be walking by the *Today* newsdesk. The day editor called me over. 'What do you think about this?' she asked. It was a Gilligan report alleging that a British arms company had breached sanctions on Mugabe's Zimbabwe by selling baton rounds and tear gas shells to its paramilitary police.

I asked who was the producer working with Gilligan. What do they say? 'We don't do that any more,' she said. So, no one's worked with him at all on this, I wondered. No one ever worked with Gilligan on anything, she told me. Did anyone check Gilligan's scripts? She snorted. I guessed not. Had anyone listened to his interviews or checked out his research. She snorted again. I guessed not again.

Tell me whether I should run it, she said. I ran my eyes over the script. Even on a superficial read, it seemed to me to be full of holes. A campaign group in the UK had a photograph of a spent tear gas shell. It had been spotted on a Harare street after a demonstration. They said. They also said the markings identified the company. Had anyone on the desk seen the photograph? She didn't think so. She hadn't. So, it's all second hand, I asked. Looks like it, she said.

There was another dimension. Gilligan had a history with

this particular arms company. One of his pieces about them had turned into a legal battle. Fine to bust them again if they were up to no good, but I thought he had to do better than this.

'It's a crock of shit,' I told her. A technical term. What should I do, she wanted to know. Bin it, I said. Thankfully, she did.

It made me think that if I was going to show an interest in the *Today* editorship this time round, I needed to find out more about Gilligan. Especially about his dealings with that arms company.

The company was called Chemring, a FTSE 250 company, that started life over a century ago making components for street lighting. Over the next hundred years or so, it diversified and acquired and by the turn of the twenty-first century, it was a leading supplier of pyrotechnics and defence counter measures.

In the spring of 2002, Gilligan picked up a promising lead that a subsidiary of Chemring, PW Defence based in Derbyshire, had offered for sale what amounted to a 'landmine kit' at a London arms fair the previous autumn. The allegation was that the company had set out on its stand E190 fragmentation grenades right next to tripwires. And that the two together comprised a landmine that was illegal under the 1998 Landmines Act and breached the Ottawa Convention.

Gilligan decided the best way to pursue the allegation was by entrapment. To catch a company salesman in the act of selling the grenades and the tripwires together, knowing the buyer intended to use them as landmines. That meant posing as a buyer.

Entrapment, while a standard first resort in the tabloid press, is very definitely a last resort in the BBC. Before using it or any subterfuge, a BBC reporter has to have strong, preferably first-hand, prima facie evidence of wrongdoing. And that normally means lawbreaking. He or she has to have tried all other methods of getting at the facts and has to show to the editor's satisfaction that subterfuge is the only way of getting the clinching evidence they need.

As I looked at the files in the BBC's legal department, I couldn't see any of the kind of prima facie evidence that would have persuaded me to give Gilligan the go-ahead. The alleged crime was serious: selling landmines can land you in jail for fourteen years. But the evidence was thin and ambiguous. One way or another, though, he did wire himself up and posed as a businessman looking to protect the perimeter of an oil production plant in Africa. The sales rep of PW Defence he met appeared from the recording to offer 500 anti-personnel landmines for £25,000.

Gilligan's report won a 2003 Amnesty International award and sparked a Customs and Excise inquiry into PW Defence and the Chemring Group. But then the story unravelled. The investigators could find no evidence of wrongdoing and cleared the company, who claimed Gilligan had confused their salesman.

There was something in the legal files that troubled me. To make the allegation stick, someone had to have seen first-hand the way the grenades, triggers and tripwires were laid out on the PW Defence stands at the arms fair. Certainly the fair's programme had the kit laid out in a way that suggested the land mine 'package'. But the company insisted that on the day, they changed it. I couldn't see from the files how Gilligan could counter their claim. The date of the arms fair was 11 and 12 September 2001. And on those days, as far as I could tell, he was working on a different story. The al Qaeda attack on the Pentagon and the World Trade Centre. In due course, the BBC was forced to concede Gilligan's story wasn't as secure as an award-winning exposé should have been.

• • •

I took over at *Today* at the beginning of December 2002 and had to get stuck in straight away with preparations for covering the Iraq war. We all assumed it was inevitable and would begin in the late winter or early spring and, based on that assumption, Gilligan had got himself an Iraq visa, intending to station himself in Baghdad before the start of any military action. He'd applied off his own bat rather than through the BBC, though as far as the Iraqis were concerned his was a BBC application and that complicated and delayed things when News tried to get the likes of John Simpson into the country. It meant that for several weeks, Gilligan was the only BBC reporter in Baghdad.

That made me nervous. His plans to go to Baghdad at all made me nervous. I'd already made up my mind that the only thing that was going to keep Gilligan away from some journalistic disaster was the shortest possible leash. Out there in Baghdad on his own, the leash was long. And the chances of him making dozens of deadlines a day to serve all BBC outlets without a glitch were minimal. Most of the time, he'd be broadcasting live. It was hard to see how it could end well.

Gilligan was on the agenda, though not at the top of it, when I had a long meeting with my immediate boss, Steve Mitchell, just before Christmas. Top was making sure everyone in the hierarchy really understood that 'clearing up the broken glass' wasn't going to be easy. Nor would it be painless. Too many of my friends, like James Boyle when he was Controller of Radio 4, had made the big changes that those at the top demanded, only to be thrown to the wolves at the first setback. The one thing I wanted to make sure all my bosses were agreed on was that the 'tabloid' *Today* experiment was over. Mitchell agreed. Everyone in the hierarchy agreed. It had seemed a good idea at the time. There'd been occasional brilliant moments but it was hit and miss and the misses had outnumbered the hits.

Gilligan came up twice at that meeting. First I wanted to make it clear I was against him going to Baghdad. 'Tough,' was the answer. If he was the only reporter who ended up with a visa, he'd have to go. Second, I wanted everyone to know how I wasn't entirely thrilled that he was on the books at all.

Mitchell pointed out the obvious problem: all the doubts I had came from stuff that had already been dealt with. And he hadn't been fired or even put on a warning over any of it. Mitchell sighed that I'd have to be patient. We weren't Fleet Street, he said. I couldn't fire him now just because I thought something might go wrong in the future or because I felt he wasn't the kind of reporter I'd have hired. He was right, of course. My only option, we both agreed, was that if things went badly and I still wanted him out, I'd have to 'manage him out'. In the BBC, that took at least two years and a small copse-worth of paperwork.

I had to give him a chance. In the meantime, I had to tighten his leash, hoping somewhere at the back of my mind that he'd find it too tight.

CHAPTER FIVE

HOW ANDREW GILLIGAN'S STORY GOT ON AIR

Intelligence seldom acquires the full story. In fact, it is often, when first acquired, sporadic and patchy, and even after analysis may still be at best inferential.

Lord Butler, *Review of Intelligence on Weapons of Mass Destruction*, 2004

'**D**o you know about Andrew's story?'

It was the *Today* day editor asking the question, the senior journalist who runs the *Today* newsdesk from nine in the morning until handing over to the night editor and the night team at eight in the evening. Miranda Holt was the day editor. It was half past five on 28 May 2003 and she'd just spoken to Andrew Gilligan. He'd called in from his home in Greenwich just after we'd wrapped up the afternoon editorial conference, the 'four-fifteen'. The team, including Holt, were now back at their desks. I was on my way to another meeting somewhere in the subterranean bunker beneath the BBC News Centre where the Radio News senior executives lived. On my way, I'd passed Holt and chucked out a casual 'everything OK?' Rhetorically. She didn't take it rhetorically and told me everything was not OK. She wanted to know if I knew about Gilligan's story.

'He says he's talked to you about it.'

He hadn't. I'd hardly spoken to him at all since he'd come back from Iraq a month earlier. Holt rolled her eyes. I sighed.

'Tell me,' I said. And Holt ran quickly through her brief

conversation with Gilligan a few moments earlier. He'd met a source he trusted who'd told him that the government's September 2002 dossier had been 'sexed up' in the week before it was published. And that it was down to Campbell. That sounded likely.

Who did he see? I asked. I knew nothing about his meeting with Dr Kelly in the Charing Cross Hotel a week earlier. Holt told me what she knew. She didn't know his source's name ... but, according to Gilligan, he'd been involved in producing the dossier. He'd said some of those working in intelligence were unhappy with it. The dossier went further than the raw intelligence. The 'classic' was the 45-minute claim. It was unreliable. It shouldn't have been in the dossier. But if it had to be, his source had said, it shouldn't have been worded as definitely as it had been.

Interesting.

It sounded, on the face of it, like a good, new detail on a fairly well-known running story. There'd been any number of press reports, complete with anonymous quotes, that the September dossier had gone further than the intelligence allowed. That it had overstated Saddam's WMD threat to make the case for war. There'd been reports of full-scale rows between Downing Street and MI6. The press stories had surfaced again in the weeks since the end of the war since no one had found any WMD in Iraq. If Gilligan's source could be trusted, this could be the first concrete example of how Downing Street had manipulated the language of intelligence to create the kind of dossier Blair needed in September 2002.

That's more or less what I said to Holt and I rattled off a series of questions I needed answered before we could even think about running Gilligan's story.

• • •

Just over an hour earlier, I'd called the day team into the glass-walled meeting room for the 'four-fifteen'. All the programme's senior journalists were there. Me, the acting deputy, assistant editors and planning editor as well as the day editor. They sprawled on the purple foam cubes that passed for seating, spilling tea and yawning. It was the most important meeting of the day.

Editorial conferences like this are vital. Programme editors can't possibly know every detail of everything that happens on the newsdesk as journalists chase down their stories and write their briefs and scripts. Nor can you be out on the road with your reporters, stalking their every step. You need fixed points in the day when you can make the big calls. Kill stories that aren't working or change direction with those that might amount to something. You need to decide priorities, spot the ones where you need to take personal charge, the risky stuff, get on top of it. You're responsible for all your team's decisions though you make very few yourself. Essentially, you're working by remote control and much depends on how well you've made and connected up those controls. You set the standards. Hammer home what you expect. Scrutinise decisions your journalists make, endorse them, challenge them. And, sometimes, reverse them. Honestly and bluntly. There's no room for sentiment.

By the time of the four-fifteen, the following day's programme is usually starting to take a kind of shape though most proposed items will still be no more than a collection of options. It's the time to make the big changes of direction and decide what you'd like to hear in the so-called 'leads' at 7.30, 7.50 and 8.10.

Holt, the day editor, was one of the most experienced output editors on *Today*. She'd been down in London for about five years since I'd recruited her to join my team on *The World at One*. Before that, she'd produced *Good Morning Scotland*. She was ambitious. Blunt. Abrasive, even. Questioning and sceptical about everything and everyone. Nothing got on air, nothing even got through the pitching stage unless it passed her hyper-critical inspection.

The list she brought in that afternoon was potentially a brilliant programme. But then, at the 'four-fifteen' they often were. You learnt to live with the later disappointment. That list's highlights were two stories that would accuse two governments of being less than honest. The British and the Israeli. Both stories were sort of coming together. But slowly and with loose ends.

The first would either be the strongest lead story for a while. Or we'd have to kill it and, maybe, come back to it another day. It was fifty-fifty. It was an offer from Iain Watson, a new political reporter I'd persuaded across from *Newsnight*. He was good but untested on *Today*. This was one of his first stories for me. It alleged that the RAF had used cluster bombs in and close to civilian areas in Iraq, in breach of British government undertakings and international protocols.

Watson had heard whispers from a number of New Labour backbench MPs who'd seen evidence from NGOs on the ground that the bombs had been used more indiscriminately than the Ministry of Defence were admitting. Iraqi farmers and children were accidentally detonating unexploded bomblets in areas close to their homes. Houses, schools and clinics had been damaged or destroyed, too.

As with most daily journalism, it was time sensitive. Tomorrow would be the ideal day to run it – Blair was due to visit British troops in Basra. And if we didn't get to the story first, someone else certainly would. But it was stubbornly refusing to come together as tightly as it had to. And it raised one editorial issue after another.

Watson had some strong eyewitness testimony from Iraq, but it was all second hand. We couldn't get independent confirmation on the ground of what the NGOs and campaigners were telling us. While it was legitimate to put their allegations out there, without independent corroboration we couldn't challenge the government's account as head-on as I wanted to. Especially in a lead story.

The law was complex, too. Cluster bombs weren't banned in UK law at the time. They are now. And while the spirit of the international protocols may have been breached, the letter might not have been. It needed more work, careful and precise work, before we could think about pinning allegations of bad faith or dishonesty on the government.

Good four-fifteens were often like this. The promise of a great 8.10 lead. A human story. About right and wrong. And with a political punch, too. About the integrity of the government. It would only fly, though, if the government put up a minister for interview. Otherwise, a decent story but not an 8.10.

I was pretty confident Watson would make it work. I knew he had a knack of getting round roadblocks. He was working down at the BBC offices at Westminster, chasing down interested MPs and looking over their evidence for himself. And the MoD were making encouraging, though not yet definitive, noises about fielding a minister. It was one I was going to have to stay across through the evening and early the following morning.

The second story, which was only slightly lower risk, was about Tom Hurndall, a British peace activist shot and left in a coma by an Israeli army sniper. Hurndall was a student who'd joined an organisation called the International Solidarity Movement in early 2002. It was a group dedicated to protesting against Israeli military activity in and on the borders of the Palestinian territories.

On 11 April, Hurndall and a group of fellow activists had pitched what they called a 'peace tent' near Rafah, a border town in Gaza. Nearby was an Israeli Defence Force (IDF) checkpoint which, the IDF claimed later, came under fire from the Palestinian side. They returned fire; Hurndall and his group ran for cover.

Hurndall saw a group of children caught in the crossfire, unable to move through fear. Wearing a bright orange jacket, he'd run out of cover and into the road to try to protect the children or get them to safety. He'd taken one child to cover and had returned for another when he was shot through the head by a single bullet. A month later, the only inquiry into Hurndall's shooting was an internal one carried out by the IDF. That found he'd been shot accidentally in crossfire while acting as a human shield.

Holt told the four-fifteen that Tom Hurndall was being brought back to the UK the following day. He was still in a coma, severely brain damaged and, frankly, not expected to live. His father, Anthony Hurndall, was travelling with him and bringing a copy of the IDF report. That report, he said, was a lie from beginning to end. The Foreign Secretary, Jack Straw, had asked to meet him. It had the makings of a major row between the British and Israeli governments.

It was a story we had to cover. We had the chance of the first interview with Hurndall senior and that interview would, inevitably, set the agenda on that story for the rest of the day. If the cluster bombs story didn't work, it was a potential 8.10 lead. Especially if Straw would go on the record in a live interview. But there were problems. The Hurndalls were travelling. The journey was complicated and communications had been difficult. We weren't even 100 per cent sure Hurndall senior would make it to London in time to do the interview with us even though he'd agreed in principle. We didn't know exactly the allegations he'd be making, so we couldn't check them out for ourselves. Would he accuse a named individual of deliberately shooting his son? What accusations would he level against the inquiry? How strong was his evidence? Nor had we been able to see the IDF report in any detail. No way of judging whether it was the whitewash a justifiably angry father and campaigners claimed.

Again, my hunch was that this was going to be OK but needed careful shepherding. The night team would have a lot of work to do and we might not be able to make a final decision on what, if anything, we put on air until the morning. It was a fairly typical set of imponderables.

The rest of Holt's list was straightforward by comparison. We wound up the meeting with a lot of work to do. And the possibility of a really good programme in the morning. Or, if neither of the big stories came off, a pretty ordinary one.

• • •

I rattled off to Holt the questions I wanted Gilligan to answer before I was prepared even to think about putting him on air. I'd go to my other meeting and, maybe, she'd have the answers by the time I got back.

The first thing was the source. Even if your reporter has an impeccable track record, it's still an act of faith to put the allegations of a single anonymous source, a whistleblower, on air. You almost never have conclusive 'proof' of their allegations. The best you can usually hope for is that the source will corroborate something you already partially know or strongly suspect. It's often difficult even to try to corroborate their allegations without compromising their identity. So there's a list of questions you need answered about the source before anything else. They boil down to the single question: is this source reportable?

You need to know what's known about them. Not the name, necessarily, but certainly their background. Are they, or were they at the time, in a position to know what it is they're alleging? Do they understand the allegations they're making? Are the allegations theirs or are they second or third hand? Gossip or soundly based? Then you need to know the source's track record? Have we used them before? What's their motive in blowing the whistle? Sources always have a motive and it's rarely altruism. Is it likely their motive is distorting their allegations? Have they got documents we can see? Will they go on the record?

Then, you need to know more about the whistleblower's allegations. What precisely are they? Has your reporter made notes? Did they make them during the conversation or soon afterwards? Are there any agreed quotes?

Then, you think. Have I got enough to put this on air? There are no certainties and you have to make a call based on far less than you would ideally have. If the source is very high quality, a Cabinet minister or a senior public figure with a profile of their own, you might decide the allegations are reportable even though you have no way of knowing whether they're even likely to be true. Or you might ask whether the allegations are consistent with what else you know. Do they add to a partial picture you already have? Do they explain something that's been unexplained to date?

Intriguingly, these are very similar to the questions asked throughout the intelligence community when it's taking in, analysing and assessing secret intelligence. Helpfully, the former Cabinet Secretary, Lord Butler, set them out in his *Review of Intelligence on Weapons of Mass Destruction* published six months after Lord Hutton's report. I didn't have Lord Butler's checklist when I decided to put Dr Kelly's allegations on air. But I had something very similar running through my mind: the BBC Editorial Guidelines, the lengthy and detailed book, built up over many years that sets out the standards of BBC journalism and how they're best realised.

'Governments turn to secret sources', Butler wrote, 'to supplement their knowledge in areas of concern where information is for one reason or another inadequate … information acquired against the wishes and (generally) without the knowledge of its originators or possessors is processed by collation with other material, validation, analysis and assessment and finally disseminated as "intelligence".'

You can say the same about journalism with confidential sources. Although much more information is now freely available than a decade ago, there's still much that is not. And the secret information tends to be the really important, interesting stuff that power wants to hang on to. Journalists turn to 'secret sources' for exactly the same reasons as spies. And just like the spies, they acquire that information against the wishes of those who'd rather keep it secret.

'Before the actual content of an intelligence report can be considered, the validity of the process which has led to its production must be confirmed ... for human intelligence the validation process is vital.' That means answering the kind of questions Lord Butler describes:

> Has the informant been properly quoted, all the way along the chain? Does he have credible access to the facts he claims to know? Does he have the right knowledge to understand what he claims to be reporting? Could he be under opposition control, or be being fed information? Is he fabricating? Can the *bona fides*, activities, movements or locations attributed to those involved in acquiring or transmitting a report be checked? Do we understand the motivations of those involved, their private agenda, and hence the way in which their reports may be influenced by a desire to please or impress? How powerful is a wish for (in particular) financial reward? What, if any, distorting effect might such factors exert? Is there – at any stage – a deliberate intention to deceive?

'The most important limitation on intelligence', Butler wrote, 'is its incompleteness. Much ingenuity and effort is spent on making secret information difficult to acquire and hard to analyse. Although the intelligence process may overcome such barriers, intelligence seldom acquires the full story. In fact, it is often, when first acquired, sporadic and patchy, and even after analysis may still be at best inferential ... analysis assembles individual intelligence reports into meaningful strands ... Intelligence reports take on meaning as they are put into context.'

Finally, in assessing the intelligence it's necessary 'to make choices ... the recipients of intelligence have normally to make decisions on the basis of the balance of probabilities'.

Every word of that applies to journalism and is a very close description of how I planned to assess Gilligan's source and allegations.

• • •

When I got back upstairs to the *Today* newsroom, Holt had the answers I needed.

First, the source. He was a former senior scientist at Porton Down, the government's secret biological weapons research centre. He'd been a lead United Nations Special Commission (UNSCOM) weapons inspector throughout the 1990s, looking for Saddam's WMD; in his case, biological agents and weapons. He was due to go back to Iraq any day now as one of the senior British members of the Iraq Survey Group, the scientists now hunting for any evidence that Saddam had the WMD that had been the cause of war. He was, according to Gilligan, 'the top man in his field' and 'closely involved in preparing the September dossier'.

That put him on the inside. Not a member of the security services, clearly. Not MI6. At least, not formally. But an insider, nonetheless. He didn't have to be the head of one of the agencies or on the Joint Intelligence Committee to know what he was talking about. As an UNSCOM expert, he would have had routine and regular contact with the people looking at the intelligence that, after a bit of polishing for public consumption, went into the dossier. Gilligan told Holt that it went further than that. His source was heavily involved in the dossier, had read it all, critiqued it and contributed to it. He also said he had no anti-war agenda, though he did believe that containment and sanctions had curtailed Saddam's belligerent ambitions. And that he thought there was a one in three chance that Iraq had a WMD programme – but that it was almost certainly small scale, dispersed and probably heavily degraded.

Gilligan said he'd known his source for two years and had met him several times. He'd been the source for a story on *Today* back in 2002, the story that No. 10 was having trouble compiling a dossier on Iraq because there was 'nothing new' to put in it. He'd also been a reliable source of expertise and corroboration of other stories for which he hadn't been a primary contact.

'Did he give you a name?'

'No.' I wasn't surprised. It wasn't something Gilligan was likely to volunteer but, actually, it didn't matter. What mattered much more was his source's authority and credibility. The fewer people who know the name of any confidential source, the better. There's always the risk of a vulnerable source's name leaking out inadvertently, especially in the BBC where scripts, briefs, notes, diaries and so on are all held centrally on a computer database, the Electronic News Production System (ENPS), open to anyone working in News.

Gilligan's answers to Holt had given me far more than I would normally know about any source. More than enough to decide that what he had to say was reportable.

So what about the allegations themselves? And how certain was Gilligan that he could report exactly what his source had said?

Gilligan said he'd taken notes of their conversation and agreed both the quotes he could use and the way he should describe his source. 'Here.' Holt pointed to her computer screen and a transcription of those notes sent via the ENPS.

'WHAT MY MAN SAID' was the title and almost all of it was inside quote marks.

These are verbatim? I asked. That's what he says, Holt told me. We're planning to voice them up, she said. A familiar technique when a source didn't want to go on the record in his own voice but was happy for verbatim quotes to be used.

The notes read:

Q: What about the Blair Dossier [Sept 2002]? When we last met [in spring 2002] you said the dossier wouldn't tell us anything we didn't already know.

A: Until the week before it was just the same as I told you. It was transformed in the week before it was published, to make it sexier.

Q: What do you mean?

A: The classic was the statement that WMD were ready for use within 45 minutes. Most things in the dossier were double source but that was single source. And we believed that the source was wrong. He said it took 45 minutes to construct a missile assembly and that it was misinterpreted [in the dossier] to mean that WMD could be deployed in 45 minutes. What we thought it actually meant was that they could launch a conventional missile in 45 minutes. There was no evidence that they had loaded missiles with WMD, or could do so anything like that quickly.

Q: So how did this transformation happen?

A: Campbell.

Q: What do you mean? They made it up?

A: No, it was real information. But it was included in the dossier against our wishes because it wasn't reliable. It was a single source and it was not reliable.

Then, outside quote marks, the notes continued:

He said Downing Street had asked if there was anything else on seeing the dull original dossier and had been told about this and other things.

Other examples – he mentioned the African uranium, although said he had no personal knowledge of that because he doesn't do nuclear.

And then, back into quote marks again:

What you have to understand is that ten to fifteen years ago there was a lot of information. With the concealment and deception operation [by the Iraqis] there was far less material.

I believe it is 30 per cent likely that there was a CAW programme in the six months before the war, and more likely that there was a BW programme, but it was small because you couldn't conceal a larger programme. The sanctions were actually quite effective. They did limit the programme.

Most people in intelligence weren't happy with it [the dossier] because it didn't reflect the considered view they were putting forward.

CAW, I guessed, was chemical weapons and BW biological. The note ended:

On the aftermath: 'We don't have a great deal more information yet than we had before. We have not get [sic] very much out of the detainees yet.'

It looked sound. It looked a good note of a good source. Enough to go with. But I wanted to think more. Were the allegations 'true'? Part of the bigger truth of the dossier. Give me a couple of minutes, I told Holt and went into my office to dig out some notes and think.

• • •

One of Hutton's most serious mistakes – encouraged, it has to be said, by some of the evidence he heard – was to think that it was Gilligan who made the decision to put his story on air. That wasn't the case. It could never have been the case. Hutton thought he understood, but didn't, how *Today* worked, how any news programme or newspaper works. And because he

decided he didn't need to hear how I'd considered the allegations of Gilligan's source, he assumed I hadn't thought about
them at all.

The BBC didn't help itself either. It didn't ensure that
Hutton understood what the 'editorial system' actually was
at *Today*, that no BBC reporter can make the decision to put
themselves on air. That allowed Hutton and his counsel, James
Dingemans QC, to question Gilligan about his research, checks
and corroboration without realising they were only to decide
whether or not to offer the story to the *Today* newsdesk. They
were not the checks that went into deciding to put his source's
allegations on air. Only I or one of my output editors could
make that decision. And in this case, it was me.

Reporters always make the kind of checks Gilligan described
to decide whether or not they have a story. Most prefer to
chew it over with a senior producer or assistant editor, testing out what they think they have, talking through possible
pitfalls or what else they need to corroborate what they have.
They might even write up a half-pager setting everything out
in detail and bring it to one of the editorial conferences where
the senior team will try to thrash it to death.

Gilligan didn't like doing it that way. He preferred playing
things much closer to his chest. Protecting his sources and
contacts. He would routinely present his stories at the last
possible moment and only occasionally at one of the routine
editorial conferences. I always assumed he was hoping
to smuggle them past an inattentive or indifferent editor.
That might have worked in the past; it wasn't going to
work now.

It's difficult to understand why it never occurred to Hutton to
ask, once he'd heard Gilligan describe his preliminary checks,
'and what did your editor say when you offered your story?',
a question he would surely have asked had he understood the
'editorial system'.

Gilligan's preliminary checks occupied the week between his

meeting with Dr Kelly and offering his story. He'd begun by speaking to other political and security contacts. They weren't especially helpful, though they did suggest he 'keep digging'. That it looked like he was on the right lines.

Then he called some defence experts, including one at the International Institute for Strategic Studies. They weren't much more help, though one did point him to well-reported stories suggesting friction between the White House and the US intelligence agencies. Helpful, but no real corroboration.

He looked over the text of the September dossier again. Was there anything in the content or language consistent with what his source had told him? He noticed that one part of the dossier, for example, read that Iraq wasn't actually producing chemical agents but could do so within months. Another part read that there was a 'continuing research and development programme'. While a third part read that Iraq had 'continued to produce chemical agents'. At best, it was confused and confusing. At worst, it showed that the way the intelligence had been worded was inconsistent, perhaps pointing to more than one hand with more than one interest. It seemed overwritten in some places but not in others. And the more alarming judgements were in the more political parts of the dossier. The Prime Minister's foreword and the executive summary. Neither seemed to Gilligan an accurate reflection of the rest of the dossier.

Then there was the language itself. It didn't read like the collection of Joint Intelligence Committee assessments Blair had given the impression it was. Those assessments tended to be more circumscribed, their judgements qualified. Again, it was consistent with the kind of thing Dr Kelly had told him, but it was a long way from corroboration.

Then he looked at the 45-minute claim. Was there anything to suggest that it wasn't the unqualified certainty it appeared to be in the dossier? Well, certainly it had slipped out of government speeches since the turn of the year. And that would be odd if it were as solid and robust as the dossier made it appear. Again, helpful but no corroboration.

So what about the circumstantial evidence? Well, pre-eminent was the 'dodgy dossier'. The February 2003 dossier, cobbled together for Campbell by the Coalition Information Centre (CIC), a propaganda outfit based in the Foreign Office but answerable to him and to the White House, using old information culled from public sources and copied from a PhD thesis on the internet. That dossier had been as cynical as it was careless. The language of it tweaked, with Campbell's approval, to make Saddam seem more of a danger than any real intelligence suggested he actually was. Much the same as Dr Kelly was alleging with the earlier September dossier.

Gilligan also knew, as we all did, that at least one of the claims in the September dossier was a fraud. The claim that Saddam had tried to buy uranium from Niger. The International Atomic Energy Authority had said in March 2003, two months before Gilligan met Dr Kelly, that the claim was based on forged documents. If one piece of questionable intelligence had been included in the dossier, it was at least possible that there was more.

Gilligan looked over the press cuttings, too. In one, *The Times*'s defence editor, Mike Evans, had quoted 'a senior Whitehall official' saying that at the end of August, the dossier was not revelatory. In another, *The Guardian*'s security correspondent, Richard Norton-Taylor, described a conversation with a Whitehall official at the beginning of September, at about the time the Prime Minister gave the green light to the dossier, saying it wouldn't have much of a role to play in the debate over the threat from Saddam because there was nothing to put in it.

There were other articles in the cuttings, too, that had appeared in the spring. One claimed Campbell had had rows with the agencies over the dossier. In another, the Liberal Democrat foreign affairs spokesman Sir Menzies Campbell reported a conversation with members of the agencies saying they were unhappy at the way in which the government was using intelligence selectively and removing context. These, Gilligan thought, seemed consistent with what Dr Kelly was telling him.

There'd been the speeches in Parliament, particularly one by the former Foreign Secretary Robin Cook. He said he'd seen no intelligence while in Cabinet that suggested Saddam was the urgent threat the dossier claimed.

And, finally, there was the simple fact that the most alarming claims in the September dossier had turned out to be wrong. Saddam had no WMD. Either the intelligence was unreliable. Or the judgements and language of the dossier were overstated. Perhaps both.

Gilligan knew none of this was conclusive. None of it was even strong circumstantial corroboration. But given Dr Kelly's credibility, Gilligan decided to offer the story. Before he did so, he wrote up exactly what the allegations were and how he intended to report them. And at half past five on 28 May 2003, he phoned the *Today* editor to make his offer.

• • •

I spent no more than four or five minutes thinking about Gilligan's story. Set out here, though, in complete sentences, it seems to have taken much longer. It seems more ordered and rational too. In fact, on occasions like this you make a lightning raid on bits of memory helped by the odd note you've kept, just in case. Snippets of stories you've covered, some remembered in great detail, others mere headlines. Lines from interviews. Phrases from conversations. Unanswered questions at the end of an interview or a programme. In a year of covering a story, such as the road to war in Iraq, you store up thousands of impressions, thousands of half-answered questions that you keep coming back to. There are trigger words and thoughts.

The sudden realisation that a new thing connects with an old one. And remember, at the time, Iraq and WMD was a story we were all living with every day.

Right at the front of my mind, though, was a conversation I'd had with a former Cabinet minister that lunchtime. As well as an earlier conversation with the head of MI6, Sir Richard Dearlove. Both conversations had confirmed what I'd thought about the dossier on the day it was published. Now, they made the allegations of Gilligan's source ring true. Very true.

I'd never thought that the dossier was anything other than a political, rhetorical document. Propaganda, if you like. A fairly typical piece of 'truth creation' out of Downing Street. Designed to make the case for war. I'd never seen anything wrong in the government making the strongest case they could, incidentally. That's politics. Prime Ministers have every right to argue their case as strongly as they can; oppositions have every right, too, to argue theirs. What neither has the right to do is present a partisan, rhetorical, political document as something it is not. In this case, a dossier of hitherto secret intelligence, written for the politicians by the spooks.

It had never occurred to me when I first read the September dossier that it was anything other than a routine Downing Street political publication. I certainly didn't think it was the dispassionate work of British intelligence and don't know anyone who did. Nor did it claim that it was. It described itself as 'based, in large part' on intelligence and 'the assessment of the British government'. It was, self-evidently, a statement of Blair's beliefs accompanied by a selective interpretation of intelligence to justify those beliefs. The judgements and the language were, we all thought, Downing Street's.

I'd always had the habit of keeping files on running stories. At first on paper, then on my PC. I had several on the Iraq war. One was called 'Intelligence' and I used to drop into it newspaper articles that caught my attention, most of them about the reported rows between the government and the intelligence agencies during the run-up to war. There were articles in there like the one from February 2003 – *The Independent*'s Chief Political Correspondent Marie Woolf's 'Monday Interview' with Menzies Campbell, the Liberal Democrats' Foreign Affairs spokesman: 'There's no doubt that the intelligence services have been very, very concerned about what they see as the misuse of information, in the sense that they believe the Government is inclined to use what supports the Government's political case without taking full account of the qualifications attached to such information, which is a necessary part of intelligence assessment.'

Gilligan had seen that one too, though I didn't know it at the time. Then one from March: *The Observer*'s foreign affairs specialist Peter Beaumont and its political editor Gaby Hinsliff had written a kind of background piece about intelligence which reported 'a close observer' of the security services saying that 'they have come into conflict with the politicians over Iraq. They feel that their long history is in danger of being undermined by the uses made of the intelligence product by No. 10, and that the way information has been spun has corroded the public's belief in what they do.'

There was tension 'visible beneath the surface … as intelligence officials have briefed against the more outrageous claims made by the Government', they wrote. While the team working on the September dossier 'led by Alastair Campbell … began by deciding what messages derived from intelligence material should be put across, and then attempting to find publicly available information backing them up'.

'The September dossier went through two or three final drafts, with Campbell writing it off each time, and had already resulted in fairly serious rows … the essence of the disagreement is said to have been that intelligence material should be presented "straight", rather than spiced up to make a political argument.'

Oh, and then this on 27 April by the foreign editor of the *Independent on Sunday*, Raymond Whitaker. Titled,

'REVEALED: HOW THE ROAD TO WAR WAS PAVED WITH LIES'
it delivered more or less what it promised. That intelligence
agents on both sides of the Atlantic had accused President
Bush and Tony Blair of 'distorting and fabricating evidence
in [the] rush to war' by the 'selective use of intelligence,
exaggeration, use of sources known to be discredited and
outright fabrication'.

The agencies were 'furious' and one source had told him the
two governments 'ignored intelligence assessments which said
Iraq was not a threat'. Whittaker's sources had 'demolished'
the argument that Saddam Hussein was a real and present
danger. A declassified CIA report had said the chances of
Saddam actually using WMD were 'very low'. But that report
had been cherry-picked, while still secret, to portray him as an
imminent threat.

It went on:

> We were not lying, but it was just a matter of emphasis … you
> cannot just cherry-pick evidence that suits your case and ignore
> the rest. It is a cardinal rule of intelligence, yet that is what the
> PM is doing … what we have is a few strands of highly circum-
> stantial evidence, and to justify an attack on Iraq it is being
> presented as a cast-iron case. That really is not good enough.

There was more. Articles I'd saved from the weeks immediately
before the dossier was published. A briefing from 'officials' that
the agencies weren't coming up with the goods. Sources saying
the dossier was in trouble because the material they had was too
dull. Predictions that there would be nothing to put in it that
would show Saddam had to be dealt with and dealt with quickly.

I mouse-clicked through them. Did any mean Gilligan's
source was right? No. Though they were consistent with what
he'd said about the last-minute transformation at the behest
of Downing Street. They suggested, too, that some in the intelligence community were unhappy at the way Downing Street

had used 'intelligence' to make the dossier 'sexier' to persuade us all that Saddam was an imminent threat.

None of it corroborated the detail of the 45-minute claim. Nor that anyone in intelligence was unhappy with that specifically. But it did tilt the balance of probability. And in any event, the 45-minute claim was never more than an example of the broader transformation, the 'classic' illustration.

There was the February 2003 'dodgy' dossier, too. If Campbell had overcooked one dossier, it could be no surprise that he'd overcooked an earlier one in September 2002. And there was no doubt in my mind that that both dossiers were nothing more than political tools, designed to get Blair over the next bump in the road and to secure the next day's headlines. After all, once the September dossier had done its job, it had disappeared completely from the political debate.

Back in September 2002, Blair had been under enormous pressure. From Cabinet colleagues, from former ministers, from Labour backbenchers, from the trade unions, from the press, from the public. Many of his critics believed he'd made a secret agreement with Bush to support the US in whatever military intervention the President chose to oust Saddam. Many in his own party believed he had slipped too easily into Bush-speak, talking about 'good' and 'evil'. And that, like the White House, he disdained the policy of weapons inspection and containment as well as the UN, the EU and international law.

He'd talked about 'regime change' while in Texas, straight after the Crawford summit. And since then, he'd repeated again and again that of all the 'rogue states', Saddam's Iraq was a special case. An imminent threat and one that had to be dealt with urgently. Echoing the belligerence of the transatlantic neo-cons, Cheney, Rumsfeld, Rice and the President himself.

The problem was, whenever we'd looked at the evidence on *The World at One* and *The World This Weekend,* it had seemed to point in the opposite direction. Over the decade since UNSCOM, the United Nations Special Commission, had begun its weapons inspections in Iraq in April 1991, we'd carried dozens of reports on their work inspecting Saddam's post-war WMD stockpiles, attempting to ensure compliance with UN resolutions. It was this body that Gilligan's source had worked for as a senior scientist and inspector. The compliance/non-compliance picture was familiar to all of us and UNSCOM directors Rolf Ekéus and Richard Butler, as well as its chief inspector, Scott Ritter, were frequent 'big interviews'.

By the time UNSCOM left Iraq in 1998, the clear impression I'd formed was that if Saddam still had chemical and biological weapons, they weren't in good shape. I was no expert, but I listened carefully to those who were. And their message seemed to be that, probably, he had nothing immediately usable. Nothing of any significance to make him an imminent danger to the UK. And few people who knew what they were talking about seemed to think that he'd re-armed significantly in the intervening four years.

The same was true with his nuclear programme. Hans Blix, the director general of the International Atomic Energy Agency (IAEA), was a regular guest on our programmes too. And he was clear that Saddam's efforts to develop his own nuclear weapons hadn't been successful. They'd come close, but containment meant they'd been unable to make or buy weapons-grade nuclear material.

The message from the inspections had always seemed to me that Saddam was nasty, secretive and had ambitions to get his hands on some pretty evil military kit. But he was weaker than he had been in 1991, the time of the first Gulf War, and no clear and present danger to anyone except his own population.

Blair, though, believed he was that imminent threat and became increasingly keen to prove it. Over the summer of 2002, Washington finalised the military timetable for a full-scale invasion of Iraq and Blair was committed to standing shoulder to shoulder with Bush. Though he still pursued the diplomatic route, looking for support from the EU and a resolution at the UN that would specifically authorise military action, he knew that war was all but inevitable. And that he had next to no time to persuade a sceptical party and people that his beliefs were justified. The idea of producing a dossier containing elements of intelligence had been around, though semi-frozen, for much of 2002. In the autumn, Blair thawed it out.

I remembered his extraordinary news conference on 3 September 2002. Extraordinary for several reasons. He'd called it in his Sedgefield constituency, giving it a personal touch. As if he were saying 'trust me ... this is me ... speaking as a constituency MP ... not as your Prime Minister'. It was bad tempered, too. Most of the journalists seemed shocked at the gap between Blair's judgements and language and what was known about Saddam's WMD.

'What is the threat?' he'd snapped back at the journalist who'd asked that question. 'The threat is an Iraq that carries on building up chemical, biological, nuclear weapons capability...' He'd made the humanitarian case with the zeal of an evangelist: 'We're dealing with a regime that routinely tortures and executes its political opponents, that probably was responsible for up to 100,000 Kurdish people dying in a brutal campaign in order to enforce Iraqi rule.'

But the journalists in the room had kept coming back to the question, why now? Blair listed the 'why nows'. Twenty-three breaches of UN demands over their WMD. Vast amounts of chemical and biological weapons unaccounted for. Vast amounts? That wasn't quite what the inspectors had been saying. And there was Saddam's mindset to think about, too. When he hadn't been contained, he'd gone out and attacked people. And his was the only regime that had actually used chemical and biological weapons to kill thousands of innocent people.

'Either the regime starts to function in an entirely different way – and there hasn't been much sign of that – or the regime has to change. Now that is the choice, very simply.'

Blair's conviction seemed a long way from the judgements of those who were following developments in Iraq more dispassionately. And if he was in any doubt about the scale of the task involved in bringing his party round, let alone the country at large, he only had to listen to his own constituency agent, John Burton. He wanted more proof. So did union leaders preparing for the TUC. They wanted a dossier and they wanted Parliament recalled. Blair needed a dossier, too. Something that would appear to endorse his beliefs. Something that, on the face of it, was authoritative and impartial. But which also 'proved' what he believed to be true.

I remembered, too, that a couple of weeks before the government's September dossier was published, another dossier landed in our in trays. The International Institute for Strategic Studies (IISS) paper called 'Iraq's Weapons of Mass Destruction: A Net Assessment'. It was inevitable that we paid the IISS paper even more attention than we might have done otherwise. Knowing that we'd be comparing the two later that month.

The IISS is positioned at the hawkish end of things. It's well connected and is routinely able to draw on the expertise of those who've just stepped down from government or from senior command in the military or intelligence services. When I picked up their dossier, I expected to read the strongest possible case against Saddam. I assumed it would echo much of what Blair had said at Sedgefield. But it didn't. Saddam's WMD were a threat, true. But a threat now? And directly to the UK? Not quite.

On nuclear weapons, its headline was startling enough. Saddam could assemble nuclear weapons 'within months'. But only if he could get his hands on fissile material from abroad. If he wanted to make his own, that would take several years and a lot of foreign help.

On biological weapons, Saddam had 'perhaps' kept

thousands of litres of anthrax from his stocks prior to the first Gulf War – stocks that were now a dozen years old. He could 'resume production ... in weeks'. But, the IISS conceded, no one knew for certain. Ditto chemical weapons. He'd probably kept a few hundred tonnes of chemical weapons and precursors – the material needed to make the agents themselves. And he could jack up production again 'within months'. But as with biological weapons, there was nothing even close to certainty.

As for ballistic missiles, the IISS's best estimate was that Saddam had kept about a dozen missiles with a range of 400 miles that could strike Israel, Saudi Arabia, Turkey, Iran and Kuwait. He might also have kept hold of missiles with a 125-mile range. But again, no one could be sure.

Two overriding impressions had stayed with me from the day we reported the IISS dossier. First, even the IISS, with all its connections to government, the military, intelligence and so on had next to nothing that was new. Nor was anything certain. Second, Saddam's WMD arsenal was much depleted and while he still had programmes in place and could crank them up in time, he was in no shape to threaten anyone right now.

The IISS concluded with the dilemma: 'Wait and the threat will grow ... strike and the threat may be used.' When the government's dossier came out, its certainties were a sharp contrast.

The morning it was published, Nick Clarke and I sat with a copy each in the *WATO* green room, looking for the Campbellisms. The clever tricks of language that appeared to say more than they actually did. They started with the title: 'Iraq's Weapons of Mass Destruction'. No messing about with doubt and uncertainty normal in intelligence, then. The foreword was a masterpiece of suggestion: 'The Assessment of the British Government ... based in large part on the work of the Joint Intelligence Committee ... at the heart of the British intelligence machinery ... made up of the heads of the UK's three Intelligence and Security agencies ... its work ... is largely secret'. Most people would miss the meaning of 'the assessment

of the British government based in large part on...' and assume
the dossier was 'intelligence'. Funny, we thought, that Blair's
credibility had reached such a low point that he had to rely on
a group of people whose tools of trade were perfidy, mendacity, treachery and betrayal.

It was a Campbell classic, we both concluded. Strident and
fear-inducing to the point of irresponsibility. Even the hawkish
IISS had conceded what it didn't know and hedged around
what it thought it did with qualifications and concessions.
Campbell's handiwork, by contrast, was bold, assertive and
unqualified. It even claimed to be able to see inside Saddam's
head, thanks to 'secret intelligence sources'.

Where the IISS had Saddam only able 'to resume' chemical
and biological weapons (CBW) production in weeks or months,
the government dossier had him still producing them and
with military plans and the intent to use them. Where the IISS
had him holding on to a dozen 400-mile-range missiles, the
government had him keeping twenty and testing missiles that
could hit 'Sovereign Base Areas in Cyprus'. And so on. No
qualifications. No room for ambiguity or doubt. It was the
case for a war against a dangerous threat. 'I am in no doubt
that the threat is serious and current, that he has made progress
on WMD, and that he has to be stopped,' Campbell wrote in
Blair's name.

Like most people, though, I still thought that such intelligence
as there was in the dossier was accurate and, probably, accurately represented. The edition of *WATO* I edited that day went
heavily on what seemed to be the most alarming revelation:
that Saddam had tried to buy uranium from Africa to expe-
dite his nuclear weapons programme. When the International
Atomic Energy Agency raised doubts in March 2003 about the
documents on which the claim was believed to be based, saying
they were 'in fact, not authentic', I felt personally duped.

• • •

All of this was perfectly good context and I had no doubt that the general thrust of Gilligan's source was spot on. But it wasn't the general thrust that mattered; there was little in that that was new. It was the specifics that made it a story.

Those specifics were that a dull, intelligence-based dossier had been 'transformed' at Campbell's behest to make it 'sexier'. And that it had happened in the week before it was published. The 'classic' example – and it was no more than an example – was the statement that Saddam's WMD could be ready for use within 45 minutes. That came from a single source, a source some in intelligence believed had got it wrong. And it had been included against their wishes because it wasn't reliable.

There was little chance of ever getting the evidence to prove beyond doubt that any of that was true. But those two conversations I'd had with my own sources persuaded me that there was a very strong chance that it was.

Those conversations, with Clare Short and Sir Richard Dearlove, were the kind every editor has daily. Conversations where you pick up bits of gossip, background, confidences. Someone's perspective. And for one reason or another, they never amount to a story that you can use straight away. Instead, they hang around in your memory until something else comes along and you make a connection.

It was the conversation over lunch with Sir Richard Dearlove, his deputy Nigel Inkster and another spy chief, Nigel Backhouse, that was most significant. That persuaded me that even at the top of MI6, they didn't believe Saddam was the urgent, imminent threat Blair and the dossier said he was.

From late 2002, we'd been trying to arrange a meeting with MI6, in part because they'd dropped us strong hints that they wanted a more open relationship with some parts of the media. For some reason – and I find it difficult to persuade myself it was coincidence – Dearlove finally put out his invitation to John Humphrys and me during the later stages of the coalition advance on Baghdad. By the time we actually met, the advance was over, Saddam had fallen and the unhindered search for WMD was on. There were conditions. We had to agree not to report the lunch or anything said there. And though I kept to our side of the bargain, somehow journalists learnt about the lunch and even what we'd talked about.

It wasn't until Humphrys and I were getting out of the car near MI6 HQ at Vauxhall Cross on the south bank of the Thames that we realised we didn't know where the front door was. And to make it harder, there was a wooden builders' screen all the way around the building. They were having their fence repaired and painted. Not only couldn't we see where a front door might be, we couldn't see any way through the screen. We walked around, feeling foolish, assuming someone, somewhere inside was watching two middle-aged men stalking the spooks' home.

Suddenly, a group of office workers emerged from a gap in the screen. Clue. Head towards them. If they were coming out, we could go in. Through a narrow gap we could see a temporary cabin and uniformed security people. Success. Inside the cabin, there were forms and photographs. We had to empty our pockets. Abandon our mobile phones. And wait for an escort.

We went into the building proper through tall, individual, cylindrical Perspex pods. I was sure I felt the floor dip slightly as if I was being weighed. Was someone somewhere already doing the calculation? Entry bodyweight plus lunch weight minus lavatory visits (estimated). Inside, there were no identifying marks on the walls, doors or lifts. Nothing to say which floor you were on. Nothing to tell you any office numbers or directions. Just doors and panels in light-coloured wood.

We were escorted into a lift and up who-knows-how-many floors to a suite of rooms somewhere high in the building with views over the river and London. Dearlove and Inkster greeted us. Dearlove, a smiling, gentle-faced man, hair mostly absent.

At first impression, he seemed rotund but was too tall for that. Inkster, wiry, slender, sharp faced. Unsmiling. You could imagine him telling you your cover was blown and that this was, I'm afraid, farewell.

We chatted for a while in a functional but expensively panelled ante-room with green tinted windows half-overlooking the building itself, half-overlooking the river and Vauxhall Bridge. We sipped mineral water. Humphrys struck up a conversation about John Le Carré and spy fiction generally and we all agreed that Le Carré was very credible. At least, his early stuff. We all agreed, too, that he'd been left stranded by the end of the Cold War and was yet to find a new voice. But his portrayal of the infighting and inter-agency politics was still pretty compelling. 'I imagine it used to be pretty much true,' Dearlove smiled. I didn't confess I'd never read any Le Carré.

Over the first course of prawns – not quite prawn cocktail – Humphrys pitched in with a head-on interview bid: 'I'd very much like to speak to you on the programme.' It worked sometimes. But not this time. Dearlove charmingly, smilingly explained how it wasn't something he could ever see himself doing. Though perhaps we should feel more able to speak to them from time to time. For background.

Over the chicken main course, we talked about the war. Not the September dossier, which was by then ancient history. Nor the February 'dodgy' dossier, which had slid into infamy. But we did talk about how it was that Saddam's Iraq had become the rogue state at the top of Blair's list. And whether it really had needed the urgent military attention that others hadn't.

Dearlove was Delphic. Smilingly Delphic. 'On any Cartesian analysis, Iraq was not the main threat.'

It was a striking phrase. Maybe 'Cartesian' was an adjective Dearlove routinely used. Maybe it was a phrase he'd carefully planned. Either way, it made Humphrys growl. Really? Who's the main threat, he wanted to know. I was still stunned by what I'd heard, though. Had he *really* just told us that Saddam wasn't the urgent, imminent threat Blair had claimed he was over and over again to make the case for war? And that when Blair insisted that it was the intelligence that had persuaded him, the man responsible for that intelligence didn't seem to see it quite that way?

Dearlove answered Humphrys's question: 'Iran and Islamic fundamentalism … in roughly that order.' Casually. As if everyone knew that. Crikey, I thought.

Inkster changed the subject: 'What do you think the reaction would be in the media if we never found any WMD? But did find paper trails, evidence of WMD *programmes*?'

'I think we'd laugh,' I said.

'We thought you'd say that.' Inkster smiled. More crikey. Saddam's regime had just fallen. British and American weapons inspectors could now scour Iraq, unhindered and with leads from the information that Saddam's experts were giving up, voluntarily or otherwise. If the weapons were there, as Blair and the dossier claimed, if Saddam had stepped up produc-tion, if they were held at 45 minutes' notice, now was the chance to prove it. Yet here was one of the top men in British intelligence telling me they would only find a paper trail. That they wouldn't find stockpiles held at 45 minutes' notice nor evidence of 'continued' production.

In the car back to the office, Humphrys and I tried to fathom what it had all been about. These guys do nothing by accident, we thought. Surely the lunch had been engineered to drop those gems into our laps? But why? We'd agreed we couldn't report anything we'd talked about. Mystery.

As soon as I got back to the office, I made a note of Dearlove's 'Cartesian' comment and Inkster's 'programmes not weapons'. I showed it to Humphrys, who agreed it was his recollection, too. Then I filed it away. I didn't know when it might come in handy.

The second conversation was at lunchtime on the day Gilligan offered his story. Clare Short was by then out of the

Cabinet after finally and, in the eyes of some, belatedly resigning over the war. But she'd been in the Cabinet when the September dossier had been written and published. Our lunch that day, though, was nothing to do with Iraq or the war or the dossier. One of my planning editors, Peter Hanington, had been negotiating with Short to return to Rwanda to make a series of features for us about how the country had got back onto its feet after the genocide that had left a million people dead.

Over lunch, we talked about the features she planned to make. I stressed we'd be treating her as a partial broadcaster. That there was no point pretending she was impartial – and anyway, that wasn't why we'd asked her. I said we'd be commissioning contrary views as we saw fit. Fine, she said.

We'd finished. And were about to leave. As a parting shot, I wondered whether she regretted now not resigning sooner. At the same time as Robin Cook. If they'd gone together, might it have put pressure on Blair and forced him to rethink?

'It was unstoppable,' she told me. War was inevitable. She told me she genuinely believed she'd got an assurance out of Blair that the UN route would be exhausted before war began. That if there was a war, it would be legal. And that reconstruction after the end of the conflict would be well ordered and well planned.

So did that mean she agreed with Blair? That Saddam had to be dealt with? That regime change by force was the only answer? No, Short said. Over the whole of 2002 and the beginning of 2003, she'd seen nothing from her Cabinet seat to show Iraq was an imminent threat. Plenty that he was evil, cruel, an affront to any civilised country. But an imminent threat to us, no.

Once Blair had decided that he was going to support Bush and join in the invasion planned for the spring of 2003, that decision had shaped the way Blair interpreted the facts and the intelligence.

'Alastair was absolutely central to the policy and

decision-making and was totally controlling the presentation,'
she said. Presentation that was overstated. It was just another
exercise in spin, she said. When the September dossier was
published, it looked like the policy was driving the way the
intelligence was interpreted. And Campbell was 'in control'.

Short had many reasons to be resentful. She'd called Blair
'reckless' and been bollocked for it. She'd hung on in Cabinet,
then resigned because she felt Blair had betrayed her. She was
temperamentally and intellectually opposed to the war and
had been hammered by her natural allies for not resigning
sooner. I took all of that into account as I thought about what
she'd said on the way back to the office.

Like hundreds of other conversations, it lodged somewhere
in the back of my mind. I never knew when it might come
in useful. I had no way of knowing it would be in a couple
of hours.

• • •

It was decision time.

Gilligan's source was credible, there was no question of that.
Had he been prepared to go on the record, to do an interview
in his name and his own voice, no one would have hesitated to
put him on air. There was no possibility of him doing that, but
he passed every 'reportability' test.

Gilligan had presented us with what he said were agreed,
verbatim quotes. The broad thrust was familiar. Upset spies,
rows between the intelligence community and Downing Street.
A political document dressed up to look like intelligence.

The specific allegations about the 45-minute claim were new,
though. That it was single sourced and that some in intelligence
believed that source was wrong; that it didn't refer to WMD
and was actually about conventional, battlefield missiles.
That Campbell was behind the 'transformation', though he
hadn't made anything up; it was real intelligence, but had

been included without qualifications and against the wishes of people like Gilligan's source because it wasn't reliable.

I went through the checklist again: source credible; allegations consistent with what we know, or at least think we know; Campbell's form; Dearlove torpedoing the dossier's central message; my conclusions at the time over the September dossier; Clare Short's account of what she saw, or didn't see, from her Cabinet seat and her conclusion that it was Campbell who was 'in control' of the spin.

I went back out into the office, over to Holt's seat on the end of the *Today* desk. 'OK,' I said, 'let's go with it' but with conditions. I wanted to check with Gilligan one last time whether his source would go on air himself. I wanted the allegations put to the government. And Gilligan had to script what he was going to say. In good time for me to check it. Later that night, if possible.

'Looks like we're going to get an MoD minister on the cluster bombs story,' Holt told me. 'Fine,' I said, 'make sure they know about this – let's extend the bid to cover it.' I wasn't interested in ambushing anyone. That wasn't my way.

And I went into another meeting. Thinking about cluster bombs. And Tom Hurndall.

CHAPTER SIX

THE ROW WITH CAMPBELL – THE BEGINNING

There are two types of crazy people: those who are just crazy, and who are therefore dangerous; and those whose craziness lends them creativity, strength, ingenuity and verve. Alastair was of the latter sort.

Tony Blair, *A Journey*

It's tempting to think now, with the benefit of hindsight, that there was something inevitable about the course of the dossier row with Downing Street. That's not so. Until Alastair Campbell made the conscious decision at the end of June 2003 to re-ignite it and move it to a different level, it had died away like every previous fight he'd picked with us.

By then, Campbell was by his own account angry and frustrated. We were refusing to acknowledge his re-interpretation of Dr Kelly's allegations and Andrew Gilligan's reporting. We were refusing to apologise for allegations we didn't believe we'd ever made or reported. But that was what he was demanding: that we apologise for saying he'd 'inserted false intelligence' into the dossier, knowing it was false and against the wishes of the intelligence agencies. That was his reformulation that was very similar to the actual allegations and readily deniable. And even though Gilligan had made mistakes with his language, we couldn't apologise for something he'd never said.

Campbell couldn't get us to acknowledge his insistence that all the judgements in the dossier were those of the Joint Intelligence Committee (JIC) either. It wasn't true – at least, not in the sense of complete, qualified judgements such as those you'd find in a JIC assessment. Downing Street's first non-denial denial that 'not one word of the dossier was not the work of the JIC' was patently false. The published dossier didn't make that claim. Nor could he force us to accept that we shouldn't have reported allegations from a single, anonymous source unless that source was on the JIC or one of a handful of very senior people in the agencies. That was absurd. Gilligan's source was sound and his allegations reportable.

It wasn't just the BBC that was making Campbell angry and frustrated. As he records in his diaries, just before the row broke out, relations with the hawks in Washington hit a new low. Defense Secretary Donald Rumsfeld had helpfully said WMD might never be found in Iraq – indeed, Saddam might never have had them. And there were reports that another leading hawk had called WMD a 'bureaucratic convenience' to get the UK into the war. In a style which reflects his aggression at the time, Campbell recorded that his first instinct was to retaliate in kind.[†]

Just before he chose to re-ignite the row with us, it had become clear that he was going to have to account for himself to the MPs of the Foreign Affairs Select Committee. And that they were certain to give him a hard time – not over the September 2002 dossier but over the later February 2003 'dodgy' dossier. That February 'dodgy' dossier was a permanent stain on his and the government's reputation. It was dishonest and had tainted everything the Prime Minister had said about Iraq, Saddam and WMD before the war. Campbell

---

† Campbell writes in his diary for 28 May 2003: 'Rumsfeld had not helped set up the visit to Iraq with a statement that we may never find WMD, or that he may never have had them...' The following day he records that the press was dominated by Rumsfeld's comments: 'When I thought of what we could do to fuck them up in the same way. We then heard, though we couldn't get it substantiated, that Paul Wolfowitz had said that WMD had been a bureaucratic convenience to get us into the war.'

had taken one beating over it, in the media at the time. Now, he was going to have to take another and both he and the Prime Minister risked coming out of it looking like serial offenders when it came to 'intelligence' dossiers. Unless he could divert attention elsewhere. To the row with the BBC over the September dossier.

There appeared to be another motivation, too. A personal one. A determination to conclude what looked to us like a vendetta against Gilligan, what he saw as the BBC's weak flank. Years later, in his memoirs, Blair described how at this time Campbell had 'probably gone over the edge'.[†] Certainly, that was how it looked from the outside. While calculated, his behaviour had the appearance of a man out of control. An obsessive.

• • •

THURSDAY 29 MAY 2003: ANDREW GILLIGAN'S 6.07 TWO-WAY

'Just read the fucking script. What's wrong with you?'

It was another exasperating live performance from an exasperating reporter. I listened to Andrew Gilligan's live two-way, his first shot at reporting Dr Kelly's allegations about the September dossier, while I was on my way into the office. Sitting in the back of a minicab as it threaded its way through St John's Wood.

Gilligan's live performances were always clumsy, his delivery halting. Peppered with 'ums' and pauses as he searched for words. This morning was not one of his best. He sounded barely awake, struggling to make sense. He seemed unable to get his story out. And not much of it sounded like the script I'd read before leaving for the office barely an hour earlier. The script he was supposed to have in front of him as he did this live two-way with John Humphrys.

---

† Tony Blair, *A Journey* (London: Arrow Books, 2011), p.7.

Gilligan's wasn't the only script I'd looked over just before dawn that day. It wasn't the most important either. That was Iain Watson's report on cluster bombs. I'd looked over a couple of interview briefs, too, using the laptop I had at home linked to the BBC's computer system.

The cluster bomb script looked sound. Watson had good quotes, graphic detail and a hard case for the minister to answer. That was going to be defence minister Adam Ingram. The brief for the interview looked fine as well. Overnight, the MoD had agreed that Ingram would take questions on Gilligan's story about the dossier, too. That he'd give the government's response, live on the programme.

Gilligan's script was fine, too. He'd use it verbatim at 7.32 and it would be his 'core' script for his live two-way at 6.07 a.m. That was the usual format for *Today*. Reporters and correspondents on the main stories would always give a taster in the form of a live two-way between 6.00 a.m. and 7.00 a.m.

Gilligan's two-way was not on track, though. As well as his stumbling, sleepy delivery, he seemed to me to be off script. His source, he said, was 'one of the senior officials *in charge of* drawing up the dossier'. That wasn't the phrase in the script, I was pretty sure. The description there was 'a British official who was *involved* in the preparation of the dossier'.

It got worse. As he fumbled towards his source's central allegations, his control over his words got looser and looser. I muttered the obscenity under my breath. I don't think the driver heard me.

Most reporters, if they lost their thread in a live two-way as Gilligan clearly had, would take a deep breath and just read from their script. OK, so it would lack spontaneity but at least it would be right. And they'd sound less of a fool. Plus, this was one of those stories where getting it right and not sounding like a fool were more important than usual. Allegations from single, anonymous sources have to be reported word perfectly. You have to be precise about the exact words and about the difference between what it was the source said and what you inferred from them.

Gilligan had lost control of that precision. 'What we've been told is that the ... the government probably ... erm ... knew that that 45-minute figure was wrong, even before it decided to put it in.' I didn't remember 'wrong' being in the script. The word I remember was 'questionable'. And the phrase 'put it in' hadn't been in the script.

This wasn't going at all like a live two-way should. It sounded as if Gilligan had got up late and was doing it off the top of his head. Bad call. He needed a bollocking for that.

When I got into the office it was obvious something was up. The 'interferer' – the senior journalist who came in early each morning to keep an eye on the team – was on the phone, looking irritated. It was Gavin Allen, an assistant editor, one of the two or three most senior people on the programme, very sharp and with well-developed political antennae. He'd joined my *WATO* team years earlier as a young junior producer with a history first from Cambridge. He went on to become my deputy at *Today* and then the executive editor in charge of *Question Time* and *The Politics Show*. Allen was tough when he needed to be, especially when politicians tried to put the squeeze on. But he was no hip-shooter either and he wasn't interested in defending what couldn't be defended just to look tough. Exactly the sort of guy you wanted on deck on a difficult morning.

As I walked in through the door, I saw him standing by the *Today* newsdesk with a phone clamped to his ear. He pointed to the handset and mouthed the words 'Downing Street'. It was about 6.35. It was a long call and once he'd put the phone down, he told me they'd said 'the Gilligan story is 100 per cent untrue'.

I knew that it wasn't. So, what are they saying wasn't true? I wanted to know. They hadn't said. But they wanted to know why we hadn't put the allegations to them last night. Weird. I'd checked, three or four times the previous evening that we'd told the MoD about the story and that they'd agreed Ingram would give the government's response. Live on the programme. And there he was, in the running order at 8.10.

'They want us to broadcast a denial in the news bulletin at seven,' Allen said. I said they'd have to talk to the newsroom. We didn't write the news bulletins. They came from the newsroom, up on the first floor. But they wouldn't include a 'denial' of a *Today* story without my say-so.

This kind of early morning call from Downing Street or from a government department was fairly normal. Usually, by the time the programme was over we'd have had two or three. A line in a script was 'wrong', they'd argue. We'd misquoted some statistic or taken it out of context. We'd given the opposition the last word rather than them or taken an unwelcome tack in an interview. We'd get similar calls from opposition parties or organisations who'd appeared on the programme. Or who hadn't and wanted to know why not. It was part of my daily routine to spend the first hour after the programme came off air sweeping up after this kind of complaint. It was wearying but necessary. Often, they'd misheard something. Or wanted us to 'correct' something a guest had said in the middle of a discussion. Occasionally, they'd have a point. We'd oversimplified. Or got the wrong end of the stick. Or just been unfair. When we had got it wrong, I always apologised straight away. Apart from anything else, it usually stopped the complaint right there. A sincere apology was all that most people ever wanted.

But it had to be different with Campbell, Downing Street and the New Labour media machine. They'd carried instant rebuttal as their weapon of first resort from opposition to government. And it was no more about simply 'correcting' errors and mistakes than it had been in opposition. It was about fixing the headlines and punishing those, like me, who refused to take their dictation. Flinging handfuls of grit into the machine, just like they had in opposition.

It was easy to overload the *Today* morning team and they knew it. We never had more than four or five journalists on deck when the programme went on air at 6.00 a.m. And those who weren't in the studio keeping the programme on air were scuttling around recording and editing interviews; checking facts and chasing down new stories, monitoring breakfast TV; finding the guest who'd wandered off; defusing the row in the green room; finding the radio car or guest's cab that had gone missing.

Even if this one did turn out to be a nuisance call – and all the signs were that that's exactly what it was – I still had to take it seriously. Did they give you any clues, I asked? Allen said no; they'd just said Gilligan's story was completely untrue. And they wanted us to say so.

That was never going to happen. The story wasn't 'completely untrue'. Gilligan's performance had been less than 100 per cent. He certainly hadn't followed his script. But I wasn't going to put a misleading non-denial denial on air. The government would have the chance to rebut the allegations at ten past eight. That's the way we always handled contentious reports.

Shortly after seven, Downing Street called again. Allen took the call and soon became exasperated. Again and again he asked 'what exactly are you saying is wrong?' They kept saying 'everything'. In the meantime, Humphrys had wandered out of the studio and into the office while the bulletin was on air. It was one of the few chances I ever got to speak directly to the presenters during the programme and usually we'd talk quickly about the items in the next hour of the programme. This time, though, all we could do was stand by Allen as he explained to Downing Street we weren't going to put on air a 'denial' that we knew was untrue and misleading. He kept asking what it was about Gilligan's story they were saying wasn't true. Were they saying the dossier hadn't been transformed by No. 10 in the week before it was published, for example? They said they 'wouldn't discuss processology'.

I tried to talk John through the next few items but his attention was on the Downing Street call. He was amused. He had more of a taste for these early morning scraps than

I did but by the time he had to go back into the studio, we still hadn't resolved anything. Allen was still on the phone trying to get sense out of Downing Street. The world and the programme moved on and round about 7.15, in the middle of the interview with Tom Hurndall's father, Downing Street called again to dictate to us one of the most tortured pieces of prose I've ever come across. I've no idea who actually wrote it. I imagined Campbell dictating it over a whistling voice link from southern Iraq, furious that no one in Downing Street had told him about Gilligan's story the night before.

'These allegations are untrue,' the statement began. 'Not one word of the dossier was not entirely the work of the intelligence agencies. The suggestion that any pressure was put on the intelligence services by No. 10 or anyone else to change the document are [*sic*] entirely false.' Problem. I knew that statement wasn't true and that it was 'denying' something that a sleepy Gilligan, fumbling for words and meaning, hadn't said, meant or implied.

I knew that Campbell had written the foreword, for example. No one had ever claimed that was the work of the intelligence agencies or even the Joint Intelligence Committee. And the most anyone had ever claimed about the rest of the dossier was that it was 'the assessment of the British government' and '*based, in large part*, on the work of the Joint Intelligence Committee'. Nor had Gilligan ever alleged or reported an allegation that 'pressure was put on the intelligence services by No. 10 ... to change the document'. It was almost comic.

It was a dilemma. I was no fan of putting untruths on air. But however untrue I knew Downing Street's statement to be, they had said it and we had to reflect that in some way. And time was running out.

Allen and I went through to the studio with his shorthand note. I'd decided the only way we could use the statement was to read it, then qualify it immediately to make it clear it was 'denying' something no one had said. And hope that somewhere in the forest of double negatives the audience would find something comprehensible.

The control cubicle of a live news programme is not a great place to do anything complicated. And this was complicated. At the heart of the glass-walled room is the studio manager controlling the desk. Opening and closing the presenters' and guests' microphones and those in remote locations and radio cars. Listening to levels and sound quality. He or she is the most important person there. They need to hear everything that's going out on air as well as all the instructions being shouted around them.

The output editor sits at the back at a kind of *Star Trek* console. A desk with a computer screen and keyboard with wires, headphones, flashing lights, keys to press to speak to the presenters through their headphones. To the right of the studio manager is the studio producer. They call the shots. Which item is next. When it's time for a presenter to wrap. Which guest has gone missing. All fortissimo. The editor responds. Fortissimo. Changes the running order or an intro. Also fortissimo. Barks at the presenters. Also fortissimo. Producers come and go with gobbets of information. Also fortissimo. It's rushed, hectic, all against the clock. You can't stop the programme to sort out a problem. Nor is there a golden thread attached to the words uttered on air. You can't pull them back once they're out there. And when it's a live programme, not everything that gets out there is exactly what you want.

Allen started to speak to Humphrys through his headphones. I was shouting at the studio producer to get Gilligan's line up so I could speak to him. Humphrys, meanwhile, was gesticulating. He couldn't say anything because the sport report was going out and was in the middle of a live item. He ripped his headphones off and came through to the cubicle. 'I can't read this rubbish …' 'You have to…' He winced. I tried to cut through it. Read the statement then he and Gilligan would improvise a live Q & A making it clear that Downing Street was denying something neither Gilligan nor his source had said. Then Gilligan could go into his prepared script. Sticking to it this time.

We were into the 7.30 news bulletin. The studio producer told Gilligan what he had to do. It had to happen. The only alternative was dead air. Live news broadcasting is often like this.

Humphrys was back in the studio. The green light went on telling him his mic was live. In a fraction of a second, he had to fashion in his head a new introduction to Gilligan from the script he had in front of him, now outdated, and from the tortured English of the Downing Street statement. And he had to turn it all into a question to which Gilligan could answer 'that's not the allegation'. He overcooked it, describing the dossier as 'cobbled together at the last minute with some unconfirmed material that had not been approved by the Security Services'. That wasn't right at all. Though the whole point was for Gilligan to say it wasn't right at all: 'Are you suggesting,' Humphrys went on, 'let's be very clear about this, that it was not the work of the intelligence agencies?'

Gilligan replied: 'No, the information which I'm told was dubious did come from the agencies, but they were unhappy about it, because they didn't think it should have been in there. They thought it was, it was not corroborated sufficiently, and they actually thought it was wrong, they thought the informant concerned, erm, had got it wrong, they thought he'd misunderstood what was happening.'

It was far from ideal. And Gilligan implied it was the agencies, MI6 in this case, rather than others in the broader intelligence community who 'didn't think it should have been in there'. But the moment had passed. It was live. The words were out there. I couldn't pull them back.

Then we were into the script and it all became calmer. We were finally getting the story out there in the form I'd approved and, in half an hour's time, we'd hear the government's response.

• • •

That response came a little after 8.10 in the live interview with defence minister, Adam Ingram.

Ingram was a querulous, combative Scot whom no one pushed around. You didn't carve your way up through the Scottish trade union movement and Labour Party without busting a few noses, figuratively speaking. Prior to becoming a defence minister, he'd been Neil Kinnock's parliamentary private secretary and a Northern Ireland minister, an appointment not entirely without controversy given his membership of the Orange Order as a young man.

He was one of those New Labour ministers who enjoyed fighting with Humphrys though his chances were few. He wasn't senior enough. But if needed, he could slug it out while keeping to his brief and making sense. He didn't take nonsense either. If he thought we were ambushing him or a question was off-topic, he'd say so. On air and off it.

The clock ticked over to 8.10. The news bulletin finished and Watson's report on cluster bombs was on air. It was hard-hitting. British forces had used cluster bombs close to and in civilian areas. They'd caused horrific casualties. Destroyed family homes. Left a lethal legacy. Then the interview. Humphrys was as tough as Watson's report. 'And you have no idea how many children will be blown to bits by the cluster bombs that did not explode and now are abandoned and left around the built up areas?...' 'Well that's a ridiculous allegation...' 'Oh you can tell me can you?...' 'That's a ridiculous allegation...' 'Ah you've found them all then have you?'

Ingram wasn't intimidated. He played a poor hand well. Humphrys moved on: 'Let me put to you another point if I may, and that is this whole question of weapons of mass destruction that Saddam Hussein was supposed to have. It is active, detailed and growing, said Tony Blair. It is up and running now, it could be activated within forty-five minutes.

We are now forty-five or more days since the war ended, none has been found.'

If this was an ambush, as Downing Street later claimed, I have no doubt Ingram would have cried foul. He didn't. He'd been briefed on the detail of the dossier. So well briefed, he shocked us all by confirming one of Dr Kelly's most important allegations without being asked; that the 45-minute claim was single sourced. Humphrys's question had been an open one: 'Why was Tony Blair in a position back last year, last September, to say that these weapons could be activated within forty-five minutes?' Ingram's answer was startlingly specific: 'Well, that was said on the basis of a security source information. Single sourced – it wasn't corroborated.' Humphrys was taken aback. He wanted to be sure: '...single sourced. So you concede that?'

It was an important moment. Without any prompting, a government minister had confirmed one of the allegations of Gilligan's source. One of the allegations I couldn't be certain about and that I'd had to make a judgement on: was it likely to be true? It was. In my mind, that increased the likelihood that the other allegations were true, too. If nothing else, it affirmed the authority of Gilligan's source.

Ingram swerved: 'I think [that] has already been conceded ...' It hadn't. And it's not clear exactly what he meant by it. The MoD certainly hadn't conceded it. Nor had Downing Street. Then, the diversion. Gilligan's report was based on a single source who 'said that this report [i.e. the dossier] had been concocted under pressure from No. 10. There was no pressure from No. 10...' Nowhere had Gilligan used the phrase 'concocted under pressure from No. 10...'. Humphrys tried to correct him: 'No, no, can I tell you what the allegation was because I think you may have been a little misled on that. The allegation was not that it was concocted by No. 10. The allegation was that report was produced; it went to No. 10; it was then sent back to be "sexed up" a little...' An oversimplification, but not a million miles off.

Ingram hit back with a denial and an intriguing description of the dossier. 'When we present a dossier on behalf of the security services it has their authoritative and best assessment ...' That was how Downing Street wanted us to see the dossier – the work of the security services. But it wasn't. It was exactly what it said on the cover. The work of Downing Street, the government's assessment of intelligence. A political document. But Ingram persisted: the dossier was 'not concocted by No. 10 or pressure from No. 10 to produce it in a particular way'. It was the agencies' 'best knowledge and their best assessment to what they could play out into the public domain...'

There's always a moment of relief when you've gone out on a limb with a story and you get the confirmation you need. Any story based on a single source, however reliable, is always like that. Ingram's confirmation that the 45-minute claim was single sourced was that moment. It didn't give us cast-iron confirmation that the rest of what Gilligan's source had told us was true. But Ingram hadn't denied the detail of those allegations, even though he had the chance. Instead, he'd put out there an inaccurate but deniable version of them. That felt like a classic non-denial denial. A confirmation in the New Labour universe.

By half past eight that morning, it looked like Gilligan, in spite of shambling sleepily around in one of some twenty broadcasts that day, had stumbled on the truth.

THE FIRST PHASE: 29 MAY TO 4 JUNE
DOWNING STREET AND THE 'ROGUE ELEMENTS'

I forget exactly when my immediate boss, Steve Mitchell, showed me the fax from Downing Street. It had rattled down to him from the 'Fifth Floor' – where BBC News top brass had their offices. Slightly odd it had come in that way, I thought. Complaints usually came straight to me, usually as we came off air. This time, though, it must have been mid-afternoon by the time I got to see it.

I was half expecting something from Downing Street, but

it wasn't exactly top of my list of things to think about. That included giving Gilligan a bollocking for his shambolic 6.07 two-way. If I could find him. He'd done all his broadcasting for *Today* from home. That was something I wanted to stop. By mid-morning, though, he was in Television Centre, touring the News studios with his story, complete now with a new top line: 'Defence minister Adam Ingram confirms one of the key claims in the September dossier was single sourced.'

I ran into him, literally, in the corridor when I was between meetings and he was between broadcasts. It was a snatched conversation. I said it was a good story and well done. But that his early two-way had been 'fucking awful'. And that we needed to talk. He blinked owlishly. He said he had to be in a studio in a couple of minutes. He said, too, he had another story for the next morning and that he thought he should write an essay on the dossier story for Saturday's *Today*. A kind of round-up, think piece.

Oh. And a piece for the *Mail on Sunday*.

The idea of a Saturday piece was a good one. The idea of a piece for the *Mail on Sunday* wasn't. He'd written for them, and *The Spectator*, while he'd been in Iraq. And it had been a nightmare. There was a rule that a senior editor, in Gilligan's case me, had to vet anything that BBC reporters wrote for other outlets. It made sense to have a second pair of eyes looking out for damage to the reporter's credibility or impartiality. And to the BBC who paid their wages.

All the other reporters who did this kind of thing made a point of getting their copy to me early. In good time to make changes. Gilligan didn't. He'd often sent me his *Mail on Sunday* copy from Baghdad after the paper's deadline had passed. If he intended to evade vetting, he never succeeded. Twice, I'd had tense discussions with a stressed *Mail* feature desk late on a Saturday evening. I got the changes I wanted but I could have done without it.

I told him the idea didn't thrill me. He said the *Mail on*

Sunday piece would 'add nothing' to what he'd already said on the BBC. I doubted the *Mail* would be hugely interested in that. Plus, I was going to be away that weekend and that meant someone else would have to vet it. I reminded him it was his responsibility to get it done. He shambled off to do his next live broadcast. In the event, he wrote the piece but failed to find anyone to vet it.

Mitchell shoved the Downing Street fax in front of me. It was from Anne Shevas, the chief press officer there but someone I didn't know. I read it quickly. It was garbled and wrong. Its main complaint was that we hadn't contacted them about the dossier story. That was strictly true – we hadn't called Downing Street – but then, we never did unless we wanted an interview with the Prime Minister. It was standard practice to call the departmental press office of the minister most likely to give a government response to a story like this. If they thought it was nothing to do with them, they'd send us elsewhere. Only if everyone thought it was nothing to do with them would we call Downing Street. Or, more usually, they'd call us.

This time, we'd approached the Ministry of Defence, partly because we were already speaking to them about the cluster bombs story, partly because the MoD was one of two departments responsible for questions of arms proliferation. They took both bids, so there was no need to go direct to Downing Street. And since Campbell had centralised the government information machine and put it under his direct control, departmental press offices were required to tell Downing Street about every ministerial bid. Was it credible that they knew nothing about Gilligan's dossier story the night before? I didn't think so.

Before I replied, I checked with the producer who'd twice contacted the MoD about the dossier story. And with the night editor who'd made two further calls chasing up the interview bid and who'd taken the call confirming that the 8.10 ministerial interview would cover both cluster bombs and the dossier. I learnt later that Gilligan had also spoken to the MoD, though no one had asked him to.

There was a second strand to the complaint. That we had made 'serious and untrue allegations about this office over the presentation of a dossier relating to Iraq'. I puzzled over the phrases 'about this office' and 'the presentation of a dossier'. Did they mean Downing Street? Or the Downing Street press office? And Gilligan's source had made allegations about the content of the dossier as well as the way that content had been worded. I'd been satisfied that Gilligan's source was credible and reportable before the event. Now that we had Adam Ingram's confirmation of a key detail, I was even more satisfied, if that were possible.

It was rubbish. The kind of thing Campbell and his team in Downing Street had sent us as a matter of routine for years. I wrote a reply and forgot about it. That, I was sure, was that.

Gilligan, meanwhile, seemed to me to be putting substantial effort into avoiding me and the bollocking he must have realised was inevitable. My calls were going straight to voicemail. I emailed him: 'It's really good to have you back here in the UK...'; that stuck in my craw. 'Great week; great stories, well handled and well told...'; and so did that. Insincerity always did. 'We still have to have that conversation ... but since you're entirely nocturnal while I'm a normal human being, we don't seem to meet too often. Maybe you could creak the coffin lid open next week during daylight hours???'

Any other reporter would have taken the hint. Gilligan took a holiday. To Orkney.

Meanwhile, the dossier story wouldn't go away. Pretty well every BBC and Fleet Street journalist with any security contacts had followed up Gilligan's story with their own sources, finding similar allegations. Over the weekend, two other BBC journalists spoke to Dr Kelly without knowing he was Gilligan's source. That was less of a coincidence than it seems. He was many journalists' 'go to' man for questions about WMD, the Iraq inspections, UNSCOM and the UN Monitoring, Verification and Inspection Commission (UNMOVIC). Dozens of journalists knew him as an open, reliable expert who would always try to be helpful with briefings and background. He was used to speaking to journalists but was no serial gossip or loose talker. He was always careful and measured and, apparently, had no interest in undermining government policy.

For one of those BBC journalists, the *Newsnight* science reporter Susan Watts, it was the second time she'd spoken to him about the dossier. The first time, he'd said much the same to her as he'd later said to Gilligan, but she took his allegations as 'chatter'. The second time, realising she'd probably 'missed a trick', she took the precaution of recording the conversation. He was diffident about the fuss Gilligan's story had caused. He feigned ignorance or perhaps genuinely thought at that time that he wasn't the source. Nevertheless, everything he said to her was consistent with Gilligan's story, at times reflecting Gilligan's actual words on air.

Tony Blair's denials, made on the road in Iraq, Poland, Russia and France did nothing to lower the temperature. Nor did those same denials when they were repeated at the Downing Street lobby briefings. There was a simple reason for that. Any journalist following the story could see they were denying allegations no one had made. And anyone with good security contacts was hearing that Gilligan's source was on to something.

• • •

Campbell first learnt about Gilligan's story when he and Blair were in Basra, visiting British troops there. According to his diary, he wasn't impressed. It was 'ghastly', he thought. Nor did he think it of any significance: 'clearly a repeat of the stories at the time' that 'the spooks were not happy with the dossier'.

But once he and the Downing Street entourage had moved on to Warsaw, he found Gilligan's story had started a media firestorm – and that's what really mattered. The press was grim.

Blair saw it as yet another attack on his integrity and asked Campbell to go through with him how the dossier had been written.[†] It is here that we see the account eventually given to Hutton taking shape. It was 'the work of the agencies', Campbell told him. And the idea that anything in it was 'made up' was 'absurd'. Campbell then called the JIC chairman, John Scarlett, who said he was happy to deny verbally that Downing Street had pressured him over the dossier – but he baulked at the idea of putting that in writing.[‡]

That weekend, the media firestorm intensified. Gilligan's *Mail on Sunday* article was only a small part of it. Campbell came back to London briefly on his way to a private funeral in New York. He called Scarlett again, this time to check whether there'd been any unhappiness in the intelligence community over the dossier as Dr Kelly had alleged and Gilligan reported. Scarlett told him that some people 'lower down' may have been unhappy but those at the top were content.

Campbell's absence abroad in that first week of June may have been a factor in one of the most bizarre episodes of the whole row. The mystery of the 'rogue elements'. A diversion that pointlessly raised the temperature.

---

† Alastair Campbell, reflecting the moral indignation of his master, quoted the Prime Minister in his diary for Friday 30 May 2003, 'It's another attack to go to the heart of my integrity' and went on to write: 'He was a bit jumpy about the spooks [September dossier] stuff and said we had to get him all the facts on it. I said the facts were that it was the work of the agencies and the idea that we could make these things up was absurd.'

‡ On the same day, Campbell ruefully noted: 'John S said he was emphatic in saying to people that it was not true that we pressured them, and they were saying that. But he stopped short of agreeing to do a letter about it. He was very much up to helping us but only so far.'

One of the journalists who picked up Gilligan's story at the beginning of that first week of June was a political correspondent on *The Times*, Tom Baldwin. He was often spoken of as one of Campbell's trusted allies. A firm New Labour supporter, he became Ed Miliband's press secretary in 2011.

Baldwin had been away when Gilligan's story went out. When he came back, he tried to catch up. Not by doing what other journalists had done, putting in calls to his sources to test the truth of Gilligan's story, but by trying to find out who the source had been. Why, I wondered, had he made that decision. Did he know something we didn't?

Baldwin's first shot was to speak to two Blair ultra-loyalists, Chief Whip Hilary Armstrong and Leader of the House John Reid. The result was an extraordinarily hyped lead story in *The Times* of 4 June: 'Rogue elements within the intelligence services are using the row over weapons of mass destruction to undermine the Government'. Baldwin reported that unnamed 'senior Cabinet ministers' believed the government was the victim of 'skulduggery'. That 'figures within the intelligence establishment were motivated by their political opposition to a Labour Government' and 'unhappy about publishing this dossier'. They were, he reported, out to 'settle scores' with the Prime Minister and Alastair Campbell.

When I saw the story, my first thought was that Campbell was behind it. And that he'd prompted Labour's attack-dog-in-chief John Reid to go on the record with his extraordinary claim that 'There have been uncorroborated briefings by a potentially rogue element – or indeed rogue elements – in the intelligence services.'

The more I thought about it, the more unlikely it seemed. If the intelligence services really were at loggerheads with No. 10, putting it out into the open wasn't going to help. It revived memories of Harold Wilson's paranoia about the security services. More importantly, Reid's accusation that there were 'rogue elements' in the intelligence services who were 'colluding' with journalists to share their discontent effectively confirmed a story that was even more remarkable than Gilligan's.

Baldwin denied Campbell had anything to do with his story. But we couldn't ignore it and had to invite Dr Reid onto the programme. Unsurprisingly, he accepted. Somehow, Gilligan, who was lying low in Orkney, got wind of what was happening and called me, pleading to be allowed onto the programme. It wasn't ideal. He was six hundred miles from the office with limited access to the BBC's Electronic News Production System. But he argued that Reid would inevitably make specific allegations about him and his source. At the very least, he had the right to respond to them. He was right about that. We had a short conversation about what the hell he was doing in Orkney and that it would be a good idea if he were to get his arse back to London. But I couldn't deny him the opportunity to respond to the *Times*'s story and Dr Reid.

That turned out to be far from the best call I made in the whole business.

The following morning, Humphrys was again on duty and looking forward to an 8.10 brawl with Dr Reid. But before that, he was to put Baldwin's 'rogue elements' story to Gilligan. 'These are the rogue elements who presumably spoke to you, Andy?' he kicked off. The only accurate answer to that was: 'No.' Gilligan knew his source wasn't in the security services and would never describe himself as a 'rogue element'. Gilligan had made that clear in his original reporting.

For some reason, Gilligan said: 'Yes ... it is the kind of thing you find in an airport paperback...' I wasn't happy. But it got worse. As he went on, he both contradicted himself and multiplied his sources: 'The people who spoke to me were not rogue elements.' People? Then, when he tried to remind listeners what the original allegation was, he made another mess with another slip of the tongue. 'Uncorroborated evidence of the 45-minute threat was given undue prominence in the dossier at the behest of the Prime Minister or his staff ... to the disquiet of the intelligence committee.' He intended to say 'community'. But that wasn't what came out. He seemed now to have upped the allegation, saying it was the Joint Intelligence Committee that was unhappy with the way the claim appeared in the dossier.

Humphrys realised that was wrong and tried to give Gilligan a way out: the chairman of the JIC, John Scarlett, had said he was in 'complete agreement' with the dossier. It was too delicate a hint for Gilligan: 'I think in a way he's almost bound to say that ... now the fact that he may have kind of bureau-cratically signed off on this report does not mean that he and all his colleagues were entirely happy with it because they were not.' Gilligan hadn't a scrap of evidence for that. Nor for what he said next. That his source 'does represent real feeling within the intelligence services'.

Immediately before the 8.10 interview with Dr Reid, we heard claims from another source, this time on the record, that some of Britain's intelligence assessments before the Iraq war had been 'skewed by some political pressure'. That source was Andrew Wilkie. He'd been a senior analyst in Australia's most senior intelligence agency and had resigned just before the Iraq invasion. He told us that he'd seen no intelligence, neither raw nor assessed, from either the United States nor Britain, that justified the coalition's claims about the level and urgency of threat that Saddam's WMD posed.

There'd been, he said, 'some overrating of the threat posed by Iraq' and that 'governments ... latched on to those parts of the assessments [that] best suited their political purposes and tended to exaggerate them to justify going to war ... the intelligence agencies were being put under great pressure politically to come up with a smoking gun'. It was the same picture Gilligan's source had drawn.

And then we were into the Dr Reid interview. I never looked

forward to Humphrys's tussles with the New Labour bruisers. They created headlines, maybe the odd mis-speak or gaffe, but rarely any genuine enlightenment. When I was at my grumpiest, I saw them as a bout between a couple of ageing, bare-knuckle prize-fighters, groggily shuffling round an imaginary ring, jabbing and weaving, looking for the killer punch that both knew would never come.

This one began in an aimless flurry over how many sources Gilligan actually had. Then drifted off in an exchange over the February 2003 dossier, Campbell's 'dodgy dossier' – nothing to do with the allegations of Gilligan's source. It was utterly confusing. Then, Dr Reid got around to what he called 'the final untruth'. Gilligan's story was not, he said, one about the language of the dossier or overemphasis: 'At seven minutes past six last week ... Andrew Gilligan said this: "the government probably knew that the 45-minute figure was wrong, even before it decided to put it in".'

It was the first time anyone had highlighted that phrase, one that Gilligan had used only once, in the 6.07 two-way, and by mistake. He'd intended to say 'questionable', just as it was in his script. Dr Reid went on: 'If any of your listeners can interpret that [as] anything other than an allegation of dishonesty, of putting in information we knew to be wrong, then it would confound me if they can decide that.' It was, he said, an accusation that the government had deliberately misled the people of this country.

Humphrys jabbed back: 'We have had absolutely not a single shred of evidence to prove that that 45-minute claim was right.' Reid weaved and counter-jabbed: 'We were not accused of something which may be right or may be wrong, we were accused of dishonesty John, we were accused of forcing the security services to produce information in a public document in an attempt to dupe the people by putting in false information.'

Humphrys saw the chance of a straight right: 'Forced you?

Forced the security forces to provide information to dupe the people of this country? I don't remember me saying that, I don't remember Andrew Gilligan saying that.' Nor had he. But that didn't stop it becoming a formulation Campbell would repeatedly use throughout the row.

I'm not sure what the audience made of the interview. I knew all of the background and in minute detail, yet even I found it baffling. Dr Reid had again denied allegations that had never been made. But there'd been one moment of clarity: that the government's real beef was with that allegation that they 'probably' knew the 45-minute claim was 'wrong' before they decided it should be included in the dossier. But even that had been wrapped around with allegations of forcing the security services to dupe the public.

There was an intriguing postscript.

During the interview, Humphrys had said he'd 'spoken to one or two senior people in the intelligence services who have said things that suggest that the government has exaggerated, did exaggerate the threat from Saddam Hussein and his weapons of mass destruction, this is not something that's been got up by a few disaffected spooks.'

He was referring to that meeting he and I'd had with the MI6 chiefs back in April. After the programme, one of those we'd met called him. Was that a reference to that meeting, he wanted to know. Humphrys said, disingenuously, that it wasn't meant to be. He seized the moment, too, to ask whether there'd been 'cherry-picking' with the intelligence in the dossier.

It wasn't quite the right question to ask. But it got the response: 'inevitably'.

Campbell, meanwhile, had arrived back in London on an overnight flight from New York and one of the first things he did was to check that the paper trail – emails and so on – showed he was 'in the clear' over the dossier. And he checked with Scarlett once again that he was fine with the public line that no one had overridden him.

THE SECOND PHASE: 6 TO 12 JUNE
CAMPBELL TAKES IT UP AND A DOWNING STREET LUNCH

Campbell became directly involved just over a week after Gilligan's original report.

It wasn't immediately clear whether he was picking up the row over the dossier specifically or simply mounting a new attack on Gilligan, whom he was clearly still determined to undermine. The first fax he fired off was characteristically angry but uncharacteristically broad and ill-focused.

It was his response to a 'think piece' Gilligan had broadcast the day after the 'rogue elements' interview with Dr Reid. It wasn't his best piece ever as he tried clumsily to explain how British intelligence worked. Campbell took exception to it in a lengthy fax to the Head of News, Richard Sambrook. Gilligan, he wrote, 'continues to display an extraordinary ignorance about the workings of intelligence', and he denied that there'd been a 'rather major row' at the JIC, as Gilligan had claimed. Insisted, too, that 'all the intelligence in the September dossier was there with the complete authority of the JIC ... Do you accept that what Gilligan said this morning about the composition and role of the JIC is inaccurate? What, if anything, do you intend to do about it?'

Campbell's complaints about the dossier allegations took second place and were focused on the reliability of Gilligan's source. That, he complained, hadn't been discussed anywhere on the BBC. Did we have a 'process to filter out potential misinformation, gossip, unreliable or uncorroborated information?' he wanted to know.

There was one classic Campbell passage. Gilligan, he wrote, 'cites Adam Ingram as having corroborated his story that the 45-minute claim was based on intelligence from only one source *and that it was added into the dossier by me*'. No one had ever said that the 45-minute claim was 'added into the dossier' by Campbell nor that Ingram had confirmed it. But he went on to say that both the Prime Minister and the JIC chairman,

John Scarlett, had made it clear that 'this piece of information was not inserted into the dossier by No. 10'. These 'denials' of allegations no one had ever made were destined to become the focus of the row.

Sambrook had been away when we broke the dossier story. Once Campbell's fax had arrived, I spent the best part of an afternoon with him and his deputy, Mark Damazer, going through a detailed account of why I'd decided to put Gilligan on air. Why I thought the source was credible and reportable. Why my own sources led me to judge that the allegations of Gilligan's source were likely to be true. And why I thought those allegations offered us 'a couple of good, new, details on a running story'. I explained how we'd put the allegations to the government via the MoD, what it was that defence minister Adam Ingram had confirmed. I explained, too, how Gilligan had done a lousy two-way at 6.07, departing from both his script and the 'notes' he'd shown me the day before. But that we'd got him back on script after that.

Greg Dyke had been out of the country, too, when Gilligan's story had originally gone out and he first became aware of it when he heard Humphrys's interview with Dr Reid. By coincidence, he had a routine meeting later that day with his Controller of Editorial Policy, Stephen Whittle, the executive in charge of the BBC's editorial standards. He mentioned Gilligan's story to Whittle: 'Good stuff. How did they get it?' he said.

It was an aside. But Whittle interpreted it literally and went off to find out. He did it, however, without speaking to me and wrote a note for Dyke based on a conversation with my immediate boss, Steve Mitchell – who knew nothing about the details of the story and couldn't have been expected to – and on his own slightly outdated understanding of how *Today* worked. That note turned into one of the most lethal pieces of evidence at the Hutton Inquiry. Its description and omissions together gave a misleading impression of what Hutton came to call the 'editorial system' at *Today*. Had it remained the private note it was intended to be, it wouldn't have mattered. Hutton, though, took it to be an accurate account of how the story had got to air and wasn't sufficiently curious to check his assumptions, neither with Whittle nor with me.

Whittle's note called it 'a strong and well-sourced story'. That was true. What wasn't true was that it came from 'two separate but related information sources'. It came from a single source that was consistent with other sources. The note also gave a generic description of the kind of conversation that might go on between an editor and senior journalists about 'the strength of the source (not the name) and about whether the Gilligan story was consistent with the separate Intelligence sources we were aware of who had expressed concern about the handling of intelligence before the Iraq war'.

The paragraph that did the damage, however, was Whittle's description of the editorial process before Gilligan went on air: 'The live two-way at 0610...' – that was the 6.07 two-way in which Gilligan had broken his story – '...was discussed in general terms by the programme with Gilligan while John Humphrys had a brief, written overnight, to work from.' That just wasn't right. There were stages of approval missing and it didn't note that Gilligan had scripted his story. The idea that Gilligan had no script, an idea that was to kill us at the Hutton Inquiry, was already there in Whittle's note. But it was wrong.[†]

I didn't see this note until it was disclosed to the inquiry. At the same time Whittle was writing it, I was dealing with Campbell's rambling fax. That looked like it would need at least two days' work. Going back over scripts and recordings when I had far better things to do. I knew that was the idea. But it made me angry and I let the anger show: 'It's all drivel ... the man is flapping in the wind,' I wrote to Mitchell.

---

† See Appendix for the transcript of Andrew Gilligan's 6.07 two-way and the script he prepared prior to broadcast.

It was all drivel. 'We stand by the original story and the processes that got it to air ... apart from the one key fact, the 45-minute claim,' I wrote. 'The rest of what the source told us on this occasion (about unease in the security services) was consistent with what we were hearing from a number of sources.'

I wrote, too, how I'd followed the BBC's Editorial Guidelines on single, anonymous sources to the letter and had made a balanced editorial judgement, looking hard at the allegations and running them against what was already in the public domain and 'what I knew from my own sources'. It irked me, too, that Campbell had already nudged the allegations away from the words Gilligan had used and reformulated them in a way he could deny. He could easily deny 'inventing' or 'making up' intelligence or 'forcing the security services to act against their will' or even 'inserting' anything into a dossier. But they weren't the allegations. So in my draft reply, I tried to pull it back on track: 'We have never claimed that anything was inserted into the dossier that was not the work of the security services – simply that uncorroborated intelligence was given prominence.'

I spent far too much of the next few days riding up and down in the glass lift between the *Today* offices on the ground floor and the 'Fifth Floor'. There, in a side-office about the size of a large cupboard, Damazer was crafting our response, typing furiously, his planet-sized brain paragraphs ahead of his fingers. Sometimes, he would have a sudden thought that he'd send to himself in an email. He had over 7,000 of these emails in his inbox. Most unopened.

I'd slouch in a corner surrounded by his memorabilia from American Presidential elections past. Damazer would type and talk without verbs. He'd try out a paragraph on me, we'd argue about it, he'd have a completely different idea, email it to himself, save the draft he was working on as 'untitled246. doc', or whatever number he was up to. From time to time, I'd slide away back downstairs to my day job. Twenty minutes later, Damazer would call: 'Can you come up to look at this?' And so it went on for the first part of the following week. Once we'd done, I really hoped that was the end of it.

We didn't know it then, but we were going to have to work much faster than this.

• • •

It was still impossible to get too far away from the September dossier in that second week of June. The papers were carrying more and more revelations about the way intelligence had been used – some would say abused – here and in the US in the run-up to war.

After we'd finished that response to Campbell, I had a visit from Frank Gardner, the BBC's Security Correspondent. Gardner's contacts in the intelligence agencies were excellent. Those of a more paranoid turn of mind thought a little too excellent. His clipped accent and suave manner would have suited him perfectly for a life in espionage, though perhaps in the 1950s rather than the 2000s. He'd been at the BBC for eight years. And though he'd been a correspondent in Cairo, it wasn't until 9/11 that the BBC started to value his expertise properly. He was an Arabist through and through, inspired while a schoolboy by meeting the explorer Sir Wilfred Thesiger, and one of the most authoritative sources in the country on al Qaeda and Islamist terror.

Most reporters and correspondents who wanted to see me just bowled up in the *Today* office. And though that meant interrupting whatever else I was doing, it was the way I preferred it. Gardner, with the impeccable politeness of a lost age, phoned ahead. We had coffee and he wanted to talk about Gilligan's source. I was wary. He asked if I was clear about the difference between the agencies and those on the fringes of intelligence. I was wary. I didn't want to share what I knew about Gilligan's source too widely, though I did assure him that he wasn't MI6.

Gardner told me he'd been talking to some people who thought he was probably on the Defence Intelligence Staff (DIS), the intelligence analysis arm of the Ministry of Defence. I said nothing. 'The thing is,' he said, 'the agencies look down on the DIS. They call them "dweebs".' I wondered whether Gardner was telling me this to be helpful. He finished by saying 'the people I've been talking to' hoped Gilligan was sure about his source.

It's only now, a decade or so on, that I realise how important this conversation was. 'The people I've been talking to' were his contacts in intelligence, in MI6. And they were telling him that there were reservations in the DIS, part of the intelligence community, about the dossier. They hadn't rubbished those reservations, though they didn't necessarily share them.

I told Gardner that a conversation I'd had with 'people in the agencies' led me to think Gilligan's source was reflecting genuine concerns over the dossier. We finished the coffee and Frank politely excused himself.

Gardner had a similar conversation with Damazer too, who took from it that MI6 were pretty keen to make it known that Gilligan's source wasn't one of theirs. Not a 'rogue element'. Interestingly, though, Gardner had explicitly told Damazer that his sources hadn't claimed Gilligan and his source had got it wrong. Damazer concluded that the broader 'intelligence community' was 'not united' over the dossier. 'Some think fine – some think not. That's reportable and fine.'

Whether Gardner intended it or not, these were very important conversations in shaping my and Damazer's attitudes. Especially over the simple question: should we have reported the allegations of Gilligan's source, irrespective of whether we had independent corroboration? Damazer insisted that 'proper questions' had been posed by a source that was 'completely understandably and defensibly anonymous'. He was clear: the allegations were 'proper, serious and require answers'.

I didn't disagree with him. But I went further on two points. First, I preferred to argue that the source's allegations were both 'reportable' and that they rang true. Second, whatever else Gilligan had done, he'd made a complete mess of his 6.07 two-way. And I thought we might end up having to apologise for that.

By a bizarre coincidence, a small group of us, including Richard Sambrook and Mark Damazer, was due to have lunch with Blair and Campbell in Downing Street in this second week of June. It had been arranged months before but now it would, we assumed, be either the opportunity for some kind of reconciliation or a nasty brawl over the meat and two veg.

Campbell hadn't especially liked our reply to his first complaint. We'd tried to drag things back to the actual allegations and away from his reformulations: 'We have not suggested that the 45-minute point was invented by anyone in Downing Street against the wishes of anyone in the intelligence community…' We'd also dismissed his complaints about the source: 'If we had thought the single source incredible we would not have reported the allegation at all … It is fanciful to imply that Andrew – or anyone else for that matter – can simply put stories on air without discussion with his editorial management.' Campbell had countered immediately, but once again it was aimed directly at Gilligan. He claimed, too, to 'know that the source of this specific piece of information is not a member of the JIC, nor was directly involved in the publication of the dossier' – a reference to a conversation he'd had in Downing Street with Sir David Omand, the Prime Minister's intelligence and security advisor, who believed the source was someone in the DIS. He'd bundled a few new complaints in, too. About the Editorial Guidelines, about the way we'd covered the annual report of the Intelligence and Security Committee of MPs and about how news outlets had repeated a *Sunday Telegraph* story alleging he'd 'written a letter of apology' to the head of the MI6 saying sorry for 'abusing intelligence'. He insisted the story was untrue – but it was a Campbellesque interpretation of an untrue. He'd apologised all right. Verbally, for the shambles that was his February 2003 'dodgy' dossier. There was no letter.

It was hard to work out what Campbell was really complaining about. There was so much to choose from. Sambrook sent a cooling reply on the morning of the Downing Street lunch, pointing Campbell towards the Programme Complaints Unit 'which functions completely separately from production arms of the BBC such as BBC News and reports to the Director General with a right of appeal to the governors. If you feel it would help, you could make a formal complaint...' Campbell never made a formal complaint.

As we travelled across town towards Downing Street, Damazer and I sat in the back of a half-empty people carrier with copies of faxes and scripts spread out on our knees. We went through them all word by word, stopping at anything that we might need to defend. Our views weren't exactly as one, but they more or less amounted to the same thing. I said again I thought Gilligan had made a complete mess of the 6.07 two-way; what had come out of his mouth wasn't what I'd passed for broadcast. 'Probably knew it was wrong' ... 'an official in charge of drawing up the dossier' and so on. The inferences he'd made, too. Were they reasonable? Or did they misrepresent his source's allegations? We both agreed they were reasonable.

We trooped into Downing Street, apprehensive. Wary. Wondering exactly how fax-wars would play out over the lunch table. Would Blair or Jonathan Powell have to step in as peacemaker? We smiled at the idea of being thrown out for brawling.

We needn't have worried. Over lunch, Gilligan, the dossier, Campbell's faxes, Iraq, WMD were never mentioned. We picked at lasagne and salad and sipped mineral water, talking about the EU. The special relationship. And public sector reform.

• • •

Life went on. We took the Downing Street lunch as a kind of reassurance that the dossier row was over. It had been a piece of political theatre. The kind of thing that had happened many times before ending, as seemed to be the case this time, without any real resolution.

As well as running *Today*, I had a heavy schedule leading yet another project to squeeze another few million pounds out of the BBC's News budgets. Gilligan seemed still to be avoiding me. I did manage to arrange a clear-the-air session – but then the MPs on the Foreign Affairs Select Committee came temporarily to his rescue.

The committee had announced on 3 June that it would hold an inquiry into 'the decision to go to war with Iraq', investigating whether the government had presented 'accurate and complete information to Parliament in the period leading up to military action in Iraq'. Removing WMD had been the government's prime objective in going to war so the intelligence about them was what the MPs planned to look at. Amongst other things, it meant picking over the various government dossiers, including the September 2002 document, and what Gilligan's source had said about it. Inevitably, they invited Gilligan to appear. He couldn't refuse. They invited Campbell, too. But at first he said no.

For several days in that third week of June, Gilligan was locked away with Damazer, preparing for his appearance. They set up a temporary camp in the BBC's Millbank Office just along the embankment from the Palace of Westminster and, as the date for Gilligan's appearance drew nearer, a steadily growing and more senior band of BBC executives attached themselves.

When Gilligan finally appeared before the committee, he got a nasty first ball from the committee chairman, Labour veteran Donald Anderson, who quoted from a recent article in the *Sunday Telegraph* which said of Gilligan that he was 'poached by the *Today* programme's then editor, Rod Liddle, with a brief to cause trouble'.

'Is that your understanding of your brief?' Anderson asked.

'Not entirely,' Gilligan mumbled. A straight 'No' would have been better. I despaired. He really hadn't realised the world had changed. Damazer, sitting alongside Gilligan to ensure he didn't stray too far off-piste or make up BBC policy on the hoof, visibly stiffened. But that was the worst moment. The MPs didn't seem to know where they wanted to go. Some ill-focused to-ing and fro-ing about the intelligence services, journalists and sources and how many Gilligan had for his story.

Then a spat with Tory Sir John Stanley over the integrity of the JIC. Sir John seemed unaware of the irony in one of his questions. Was Gilligan saying that 'the JIC system, including the chairman, was effectively a party to including unreliable intelligence assessments material in a document going round under the JIC's imprimatur?' That, of course, was exactly what had happened.

But Gilligan got through it without any major injury. And we assumed there'd be another lull, at least until the MPs produced their report.

June in the BBC means appraisals. This was my first appraisal round at *Today* and was part of the dreary business of detaching some of the reporters. The end had to begin with a bad annual appraisal. It was a wretched, drawn-out affair but the only way it could be done. Sometimes, though, they'd take the bad appraisal as the hint it was and suddenly discover they'd be happier elsewhere.

For all of them, those I wanted to go and those I wanted to stay, I sketched out the way I wanted them to work. The kind of thing I expected them to take responsibility for without me chasing them. Talking their stories through with me face to face. Volunteering to talk their sources through, too, rather than me having to squeeze it out of them. Always working with producers on contentious stories. Filing their scripts in good time so I could make changes.

There were a dozen and a half of these draft appraisals and they were pretty dull except to the reporter concerned. One, though, excited the BBC and government lawyers at the Hutton Inquiry as well as Lord Hutton himself. It was the draft of Gilligan's, the only one caught up in the document trawl because I'd sent it in draft to my immediate boss, Steve Mitchell, as an email.

That email began with how I planned to start my conversation with him. The dossier story captured what I saw as his problems perfectly. It was 'good investigative journalism marred by flawed reporting'. That's to say, he got stories but had a tendency to screw up the way he broadcast them. His 'loose use of language and lack of judgement in some of his phraseology' were problems that he seemed unable to control. 'The biggest millstone around our necks' was how I described it. And not just on the dossier story.

I ground through them all, and planned to email Gilligan's appraisal to Mitchell the following day. But that was the day Campbell chose to re-ignite the row. It put everything else on hold and the email didn't get sent until the end of what felt like three days of madness.

The three days that brought Greg Dyke centre stage.

CHAPTER SEVEN

THE ROW WITH CAMPBELL – THE END

In the later stages ... Alastair had probably gone over the edge.
Like all creative people, he can snap...

Tony Blair, *A Journey*

From the moment Dyke took control, his mindset was critical. He'd become increasingly involved in responding to Campbell during the first two weeks of June. I'd gone through with him why I'd put Gilligan and his source's allegations on air. I'd told him, too, I'd wished Gilligan had put in a better performance and kept to his script. But I also told him I thought the allegations were true, otherwise I wouldn't have put them on air.

Dyke himself had grilled Gilligan over exactly what his source had said. He'd asked him outright whether he'd used the words 'the government probably knew the 45-minute claim was wrong before it included it in the dossier'. Gilligan assured him more than once that he had.

The idea that Dyke 'bet the farm on Gilligan', as one critic at the time put it, based on nothing more than a casual assurance is simply wrong. Like the rest of us, he knew he could never be certain that the allegations were the truth, the whole truth and nothing but the truth. But like the rest of us, too, he was certain that they'd been made by a credible source and should have been reported. And the more Campbell threw out increasingly prolix non-denial denials, the more vehement he became, the more

Dyke knew it was his job, as editor in chief, to defend the BBC's independence. He knew Gilligan was the BBC's weak flank and that defending his reporting was more hazardous than anyone would have wished. But Dyke's choice – between defending the BBC and capitulating – wasn't a real one. Capitulation wasn't an option. That was the mindset that mattered.

Much was made at the time and has been since of the weight on Dyke from his closeness to New Labour. He'd been an open supporter before becoming the BBC's DG. He was still part of that world, socially if not politically, and it was inevitable that the press would look for any sign he was still a 'Labour luvvy'. Such as caving in over the dossier allegations. But that never seemed to me to be the motive that drove him to take personal control of the row with Campbell. It was very much simpler. We were right and Campbell was wrong.

He was also mindful of the message of a seminar he and a handful of very senior BBC journalists, executives and academics had held shortly before the Iraq invasion. That seminar had concluded that, at times of conflict, it was only when the BBC took a backward step that things went badly for the corporation.

Dyke had shown his reluctance to take a backward step a few days before the war had begun. Blair had written to him complaining that there'd been 'a breakdown' in the BBC of the separation between news and comment. That news programmes had got the balance wrong between support for the war and opposition. Dyke's response had been brusque, to say the least: 'Your communications advisors are not best placed to advise whether or not the BBC has got the balance right between support and dissent … for you to question the whole of the BBC's output … because you are concerned about particular stories which don't favour your view is unfair.' And his sign-off was as nuanced as a finger jabbed into the eye: 'that our conclusions didn't always please Alastair is unfortunate but not our primary concern.'

Some 'wise voices' also argued during the row and after-wards that Dyke was too ready to take Campbell on. That once Campbell had re-ignited the row, Dyke should have paused. Tried to take the heat out of it. Maybe set up some kind of independent inquiry under one of broadcasting's great and good.

It would have made no difference.

The mistake those 'wise voices' made was to think that by defending our reporting we ensured the first two phases escalated inevitably to the third and from there to the terrible climax of Dr Kelly's death. That's not how it was. There was a clear hiatus at the end of the second phase. The temperature lowered in mid-June and the row was all but over.

Campbell made a conscious and deliberate decision to re-ignite the row for his own very specific reasons. And those reasons meant he had no interest in letting things cool again. He'd already ignored one offer from Sambrook and discreet approaches to find some sort of mediation had failed, too.

Campbell's determination to 'fuck Gilligan' also meant that once Dr Kelly had come forward to his MoD bosses as the possible source, Campbell was keen for the name to get out.[†] And it was that, not the row with the BBC per se, that created the pressure on Dr Kelly and the 'shame' that ended in his death.

• • •

THE THIRD PHASE: 25 TO 27 JUNE

It was inevitable that the Foreign Affairs Select Committee would want to hear from Campbell. It was inevitable, too,

---

† His diary makes grim reading: 'The BBC story was going away because they were refusing to take on the source idea [an offer to give the BBC Dr Kelly's name as Gilligan's possible source, effectively asking the BBC to confirm or deny it]. There was a big conspiracy at work really. The biggest thing needed was the source out.'

that if he appeared, it would be bloody. And not just for him. The MPs would want to look in minute detail at his and the Prime Minister's increasingly discredited communications strategy over the Iraq war. And that would include not just the September 2002 dossier but also the February 2003 'dodgy' dossier, the one plagiarised from the internet. Nor was there any guarantee that the New Labour majority on the committee would offer him any protection.

At first, he refused to appear. As late as 18 June, a fortnight into the inquiry and the day before Gilligan gave his evidence, Blair told MPs that 'it had never been the case that officials have given evidence to select committees'. That wasn't quite true. And Campbell wasn't any old official, either. The Tories tried to crank up the pressure but overstated their case, calling for an independent inquiry to look at how intelligence was 'twisted and fiddled and spun by people like Alastair Campbell'.

Dissident former Cabinet ministers exerted genuine pressure. They'd been around the Cabinet table in the lead-up to the war. Clare Short went into print in the *New Statesman* with an account very similar to what she'd told me in private on the day I'd passed Gilligan's report for broadcast. Campbell, she said, was at the centre of exaggerating the threat Saddam's WMD posed. Later, both she and the former Foreign Secretary Robin Cook told the MPs' inquiry that neither of them had seen any intelligence showing Saddam was the kind of threat described in the September dossier.

The pressure on Campbell built and finally he decided the best thing to do was to appear, 'to get my retaliation in first'. His 'anger' and 'frustration' at the way the BBC was winning the row was one cause. Gilligan's performance before the committee had been more sure-footed than he'd hoped. Most importantly, though, he was getting a hammering over that February 2003 'dodgy dossier'. The risk was obvious. If he didn't appear in person to defend himself and divert attention from the 'dodgy dossier', the MPs and the public would conclude that its cynicism was representative of the government's entire pre-war 'communications' strategy.

The February 'dodgy dossier' was the most cynical act of propaganda in British political history. It went far beyond anything that was legitimate in political argument, enraged the intelligence agencies, endangered lives and caused the Prime Minister to tell a clear untruth to the House of Commons. Yet because it grew out of almost a decade of New Labour 'truth creation', even when it was exposed we did little more than shrug, saying 'what do you expect?'

The only thing most people remember now about the 'dodgy dossier' is that part of it was plagiarised from a previously published PhD thesis. Cut and pasted from the internet, complete with spelling and punctuation mistakes. There was no new intelligence in it and publicly available material was twisted to make it look more alarming. Its purpose, though, tends to be forgotten.

It was cobbled together to undermine the UN weapons inspectors who'd returned to Iraq and after three months of inspections were reporting that Saddam appeared to have next to no WMD. Nor was there any evidence they could find of current production, let alone WMD held at 45-minute readiness, two of the most alarming claims in the September dossier.

The inspectors of UNMOVIC had returned to Iraq at the end of November 2002 under UN Security Council Resolution 1441. There was some initial friction with Saddam's officials, but by January 2003 they'd carried out hundreds of inspections, many of them in locations identified by British and American intelligence, and were starting to form the view that if they were allowed to continue their work Saddam might be disarmed completely.

It was still early days and no one was making a cast-iron case. But the inspectors' was an authoritative voice of doubt that London and Washington didn't need to hear. For

Bush and Blair, only the military timetable mattered. The British and American troop build-up was beyond the point of no return.

We wheeled the armchair generals onto *Today* to talk us through that military timetable. To tell us how it would be too hot to fight after the end of March. And how the coalition of the willing would be distinctly unwilling to keep a force of that size in theatre into the autumn. Everyone's best guess was that war would come in the last week of February, which meant a stampede to cancel or re-arrange skiing holidays. Over in Whitehall, though, Defence Secretary Geoff Hoon held onto his chalet booking in Chamonix. Just in case.

The UNMOVIC chiefs, Hans Blix and Mohamed ElBaradei, were cautious but gave the clear impression their inspectors were making headway. Blix told the UN Security Council on 9 January that they hadn't found a 'smoking gun' while conceding that it wasn't impossible that Saddam was concealing prohibited weapons and activities. But as the inspectors visited more sites, the picture became less equivocal. And as international pressure increased on Saddam so did his, apparent, willingness to co-operate.

By the middle of January, the inspectors were able to go more or less where they wanted, when they wanted. Surveillance aircraft had open airspace and the Iraqis were starting to offer up stocks for destruction or provide evidence that they'd destroyed them themselves. UNMOVIC's 200 or so staff, including over eighty inspectors, were gaining in confidence. They were well equipped, better equipped than UNSCOM had been, and Iraqi officials were making a great show of helping them get established on the ground. There were even whispers about the possibility of effective disarmament by the summer. It was what Paris, Berlin and Moscow wanted to hear. Since it was looking like Saddam was no immediate threat and UNMOVIC seemed to be working, why not give the inspectors three or six months to complete the job?

Meanwhile, in the UK, popular opposition to the war was growing. The Stop The War Coalition was drawing support from a broad spectrum and was promising an anti-war demonstration of unprecedented size in mid-February. In Downing Street, Blair felt that, once again, he was losing control of the debate. The feeling he'd had back in the summer of 2002 that resulted in the September dossier.

The first week of February was going to be crucial. The US Secretary of State, Colin Powell, asked for and got a special UN Security Council Session on 5 February. Over the weekend of 1 and 2 February, Blair was to fly to Washington for the summit we all assumed would settle the invasion plan. And there would be another debate in an increasingly sceptical Parliament after Blair's Washington trip and before the UN Security Council special session.

It was essential to counter UNMOVIC's optimism. It needed another dossier. But instead of turning to the intelligence agencies, the JIC, the Foreign Office, Downing Street's foreign and security gurus or even his own press team in No. 10, Campbell tasked a group called the Coalition Information Centre (CIC).

The CIC, which also played an important role in fashioning the early drafts of the September 2002 dossier, had begun life in Washington in October 2001, as a 'quick response war room at the White House to counter the Taliban's anti-American propaganda'. Effectively a multi-national rapid rebuttal and propaganda unit. After the start of the war in Afghanistan, it set up offices in London and Islamabad.

Though it was staffed by FCO officials on secondment, it was answerable directly to Campbell and, bizarrely for a unit so close to the heart of the British government, to an American. A Bush loyalist called Tucker Eskew, the President's representative to No. 10 for communications strategy. It was accountable to no minister.

The CIC had a very poor reputation amongst journalists. War reporters in Afghanistan openly called it a 'disinformation centre'. They saw it as a propaganda machine with a very relaxed grasp on 'truth'. Little more than a joke. For its masters, though, the CIC brought with it the advantage that it would do exactly as it was told. During the latter part of January, it produced a document that Campbell handed out to journalists on 3 February called 'Iraq: Its Infrastructure of Concealment, Deception and Intimidation'.

It began: 'This report draws upon a number of sources, including intelligence material, and shows how the Iraqi regime is constructed to have, and to keep, WMD, and is now engaged in a campaign of obstruction of the United Nations Weapons Inspectors.'

Its three sections claimed to brief journalists on Saddam's efforts to conceal his WMD; to give 'up to date' details of Iraq's intelligence and security organisations whose job it is 'to keep Saddam and his regime in power, and to prevent the international community from disarming Iraq'; and to show the effects of Saddam's security apparatus on ordinary people.

It was the middle section, the 'up to date' picture of Saddam's intelligence and security machine, that was plagiarised from a ten-year-old academic article called 'Iraq's Security & Intelligence Network: A Guide & Analysis' by a PhD Student, Ibrahim al-Marashi. It had been cut and pasted from the web, complete with typos but with one or two tweaks to sex it up a little.

So, where the original article had Saddam's security apparatus 'monitoring foreign embassies in Iraq' the 'dodgy dossier' had 'spying on foreign embassies in Iraq'. While 'aiding opposition groups in hostile regimes' was sharpened to 'supporting terrorist organisations in hostile regimes'. For the most part, though, the February 2003 'dodgy dossier' was about UNMOVIC. It stressed the inspectors' limitations: they are 'not a detective agency ... they can only work effectively if the Iraqi regime co-operates pro-actively ... but Iraq has singularly failed to do this'.

That wasn't wholly true. By the beginning of February, UNMOVIC inspectors were visiting five or six sites a day all over Iraq. They reckoned they'd visited 350 sites in the first three months, including 44 new ones, making 550 inspections. 'All inspections were performed without notice,' they reported, 'and access was in virtually all cases provided promptly. In no case have the inspectors seen convincing evidence that the Iraqi side knew in advance of their impending arrival.'

There was more, again calculated to undermine the inspectors: 'There are presently around 108 UN Weapons Inspectors in Iraq – a country the size of France … vastly outnumbered by over 20,000 Iraqi Intelligence officers.' By the time the dossier was handed out, the number of inspectors was many more than that, but it was irrelevant. So was the size of the country. The inspectors weren't just wandering aimlessly through the desert. They were visiting specific sites, some already known to them. They were inspecting sites, too, that British and American intelligence had pointed them towards. A pattern was starting to emerge. When the inspectors went where the spies said there were WMD, they were finding nothing.

Then there were the claims that the inspectors were victims of psy-ops. 'Before UNMOVIC personnel arrive in Iraq, their names are sought by at least one and probably several of the Iraqi intelligence and security services. They will find out as much as possible. Do they have family, do they have any weaknesses that can be exploited? Are they young, nervous, vulnerable in some way?'

The inspectors were, of course, almost to a man and woman the world's leading experts in their fields. Many were seasoned veterans who, like Dr Kelly, had been round this track when Saddam really was putting the squeeze on. The picture of nervous young men and women, sweating in panic in hotel rooms, surrounded by Saddam's thugs, was a compelling one for the CIC. But it was fantasy.

The message was simple. Inspections and containment

couldn't work; Saddam's concealment and fearsome 'systems of control and intimidation' meant such talk was misleading. The US Secretary of State, Colin Powell, planned a similar message for the Security Council. He was preparing to show more intelligence, more evidence of Saddam's WMD capability, including persuasive pictures of mobile labs and recordings of telephone intercepts. He'd also selected quotations from Blix and ElBaradei that stressed caution rather than optimism: 'Iraq appears not to have come to a genuine acceptance, not even today, of the disarmament which was demanded of it,' from Hans Blix. And ElBaradei's dismissal of Iraq's copious weapons declaration that 'did not provide any new information relevant to certain questions that have been outstanding since 1998'.

The February 2003 'dodgy' dossier was a prop in this piece of political theatre. And like many theatrical props, it was a sham. How much Blair actually knew about its true status remains an open question. But as Campbell was handing it out to journalists, Blair was telling MPs 'the evidence of co-operation withheld is unmistakable ... As the report we published at the weekend makes clear ... there is a huge infrastructure of deception and concealment designed to prevent the inspectors from doing their job.' That 'report' comprised 'intelligence ... about the infrastructure of concealment'. And just in case MPs hadn't understood that the February dossier was real intelligence, he added that 'it is obviously difficult when we publish intelligence reports, but I hope that people have some sense of the integrity of our security services. They are not publishing this, or giving us this information, and making it up. It is the intelligence that they are receiving, and we are passing it on to people.' No doubt hoping that, once again, the unquestioning respect that many had for those whose trade was treachery would rub off on him.

There was, indeed, some intelligence material in the 'dodgy dossier'. However, the agencies hadn't approved its use and it had been hyped and overstated. Within the week, everyone knew the truth of it and there was no way Campbell could spin what he'd done. A Cambridge academic recognised the plagiarised source and the sham unravelled. Downing Street squeezed out a truculent apology, not for the cynical, though incompetent, effort to mislead but for failing to credit all its sources properly. No. 10 even criticised the media for its 'obsession with spin', insisting that the 'underlying truth' was 'accurate'. The working assumption, as with other examples of New Labour's 'truth creation', was that once it had done its job it would be forgotten.

It wasn't forgotten, though. And in the first two weeks of June, it figured in session after session of the Foreign Affairs Select Committee.

The 'dodgy dossier' undermined the earlier September dossier. It cast doubt over every argument for war. And Campbell winced at that thought, that all his efforts to justify Blair's pre-war beliefs would be 'judged upon the basis of a single error by a single individual'.

If Campbell needed any hint of how serious the Foreign Affairs Select Committee's criticisms might be, he only needed to look at the findings of the MPs on another committee, the Intelligence and Security Committee. They'd spanked him soundly for putting intelligence out there in the 'dodgy dossier' without asking the agencies: 'although the document did contain some intelligence-derived material it was not ... checked with the agency providing the intelligence or cleared by the JIC prior to publication.' That kind of thing normally ended in a long prison sentence under the Official Secrets Act. All the same, they were persuaded that the earlier September dossier had, by contrast, been produced with the full knowledge and co-operation of the agencies.

Campbell and Scarlett had to maintain that position. They had to continue to argue that the September dossier had been put together with a 'meticulousness' and 'seriousness' absent from the 'dodgy dossier'. If Campbell did that with enough vehemence, he might be able to suppress some of the flak and prevent it hitting the September dossier, too.

That flak was coming from all sides. The former JIC chairman, Dame Pauline Neville-Jones, had told the Foreign Affairs Select Committee that the 'dodgy dossier' had been a 'serious mistake'. The PhD student whose thesis had been plagiarised told them it had endangered his family's lives. Then the Foreign Secretary Jack Straw appeared before the committee and poured derision on it. The 'dodgy dossier' was 'an embarrassment ... a complete Horlicks'.

Campbell decided he had to appear. He had to prove – or at least argue loudly and vehemently – that the September and February dossiers weren't the same. And that meant re-igniting the row with us over the September dossier – a strategy he'd agreed with Blair shortly before he appeared.[†]

The strategy, as Campbell records it in his diary, was to stay calm and treat the committee with respect; apologise to the plagiarised PhD student; and go for the BBC over the September 2002 dossier, demand an apology and 'get up the big picture message about the cynicism of people who say that the Prime Minister would go to war on the basis of this'.

His performance delivered.

And performance was exactly what it was. Carefully scripted and directed, it made compelling TV. One clip, complete with jabbing finger, looped round on the TV news shows: 'I find it incredible and I mean incredible that people can report based on one single anonymous uncorroborated source ... that the Prime Minister, the Cabinet, the intelligence agencies, people like myself connived to persuade Parliament to send British forces into action on a lie. That is the allegation.'

It wasn't. But to bolster his case, he'd even brought a prop. A correspondence file: 'I tell you, until the BBC acknowledge

---

† See Alastair Campbell's diary entry for Wednesday 25 June 2003 (p.617).

that is a lie, I will keep banging on, that correspondence file will get thicker and they had better issue an apology pretty quickly.'

It was a breathtaking gamble. If it came off, everyone would finally forget the February 'dodgy dossier', he'd have defended the September dossier and finally landed a blow that mattered on the BBC, something he'd never previously been able to do.

Campbell was now repeating – and perhaps even believed himself – a misleading reformulation of the allegations that 'we or I inserted false intelligence into the dossier against the wishes of the agencies whilst probably knowing [it] to be untrue'. No one had ever said the intelligence was 'false' nor that he'd 'inserted' it into some otherwise neutral or apolitical intelligence document that had arrived in his in tray, written by the spooks.

Lobby journalists heard something similar on the morning of Campbell's appearance, 25 June: 'no one in Downing Street had inserted or exaggerated [the 45-minute claim]'. Again, the 'insertion' word. And we all heard much the same when Campbell appeared in person. He told the MPs that 'they are basically saying that the Prime Minister took the country into military conflict ... on the basis of a lie...' No one had accused the Prime Minister of lying. The accusation was that he and the Prime Minister had presented a piece of political rhetoric as intelligence and then told the country that 'intelligence' justified war. 'What is completely and totally untrue is that I in any way overrode [the JIC's] judgement...' Dr Kelly hadn't alleged and Gilligan hadn't reported that he'd overridden the JIC's judgement. 'The serious allegation against me is that I abused intelligence ... that I abused British Intelligence ... against the wishes of the intelligence agencies...' That wasn't the allegation.

Meanwhile, the other part of the strategy was to hammer away at presenting the dossier as a 'neutral', independent piece of work wholly owned by the agencies. 'The entire [September dossier] was the product of the pen of the Joint Intelligence Committee chairman...' That simply wasn't the case. 'That document [i.e. the dossier] was the document which was presented to us...' Again, not the case. 'The changes we made in relation to it had nothing to do with the overriding intelligence assessments...' Some in intelligence, especially the analysts in the Defence Intelligence Staff, would beg to differ.

Campbell's anger at the committee was familiar, too, to anyone who'd watched him over the previous few years. 'The story that I "sexed up" the dossier is untrue: the story that I "put pressure on the intelligence agencies" is untrue: the story that we somehow made more of the 45-minute command and control point than the intelligence agencies thought was suitable is untrue.'

Once he'd done, we needed to put something out quickly. And to try to drag coverage back to the original allegations, away from Campbell's reformulations. More charging up and down in lifts, more snatched huddles. We put out a short statement saying we had nothing to apologise for and regretted Campbell's accusation of lying: 'Our senior and credible source told us that he and others in the intelligence community were unhappy that real intelligence based on a single source was given undue prominence in the dossier of September 2002. That the dossier was transformed ... it remains unclear why the assertion that Iraqi weapons of mass destruction could be ready within forty-five minutes, based on a single source, was given such prominence.' Sambrook decided, too, that he'd come on *Today* the following morning, 26 June, to repeat and underline the allegations we'd actually reported and argue that 'the BBC was not making allegations but reporting them'.

I'd never been totally comfortable with that argument. I'd decided to put the allegations on air not just because they were 'reportable' and from a credible source but because I judged they were more likely than not to be true, based on all else I knew at the time. Campbell seized on the line of argument immediately.

'It means you don't know if the story you broadcast was true.' It was obvious how this one was going to play out.

But the appearance before the MPs wasn't the end of it. Campbell also sent two faxes. One was relatively calm and addressed to Greg Dyke. The other angry and addressed to Sambrook. He was clearly in no mood to calm things down, demanding answers to a long list of questions 'by the end of the day'. And just to make sure the temperature stayed as high as possible, he also released his letter to the press.

The questions asked whether we 'still stood by' the allegations, though once again his interpretation comprised allegations no one had made. That 'No. 10 added in the 45-minute claim to the dossier … and that we did so against the wishes of the intelligence agencies'. Or that 'both we and the intelligence agencies knew the 45-minute claim to be wrong and inserted it despite knowing that'. Or that 'we ordered the September dossier to be "sexed up" in the period leading up to its publication'. We were getting used to this tactic now.

Again, though, much of it was aimed straight at Gilligan – and not just over the dossier. Did we stand by his assertion that 'the JIC is not part of the intelligence community, but a No. 10 committee which exists to arbitrate between government and the intelligence agencies' and that its chairman only 'kind of bureaucratically signed off his report'. Questions about his source: how many there'd been, whether he was on the JIC, a 'senior official involved in drawing up the dossier' or a source 'in the intelligence services' and whether it was now 'normal BBC practice not to seek to corroborate single source stories'. Plus, a couple of jibes aimed at Gilligan's writing for the papers.

And he attacked what he saw as a new weak point. Our insistence that we were not making the allegations, we were reporting them.

Dyke and Sambrook were out of London with the rest of the BBC top brass when the fax came in. Campbell's decision to release it to the press meant they had to act quickly and that meant heading back to Television Centre.

We gathered on the Fifth Floor. Gilligan seemed nervous. Dyke took off his jacket and rolled up his sleeves. He asked Gilligan again whether he stood by every word of every one of his reports. Was he certain his source had used the phrase 'sexed up'. And that he'd said the government 'probably knew' the 45-minute claim 'was wrong before it decided to put it in the dossier'. Gilligan answered once again, 'Yes.'

'You'd better be fucking right,' Greg told him. Then, turning to the rest of us, 'He'd better be fucking right.' He sat down at the nearest computer and began a frenzied assault on an innocent keyboard. This was now his scrap and he was determined to fight it in his way.

His response to Campbell tried once again to counter the way he was now routinely 'misrepresenting our journalism'.

> You have said we accused the Prime Minister, the Foreign Secretary and other ministers of lying. We have not. You have said the BBC deliberately accused the Prime Minister of misleading the House of Commons and of leading the country into war on a false basis. We have not. You have accused the BBC of damaging the integrity of the political process. We believe we have done the opposite.
>
> The nub of what the BBC reported was: unease among some of the intelligence community about the use of intelligence in government dossiers; the assertion of one senior and credible source – who has proved reliable in the past – that the '45-minute claim' was wrong and was inserted late into the dossier.

None of us thought this was about the truth of the September dossier any more. 'We have to believe', the reply concluded, 'that you are conducting a personal vendetta against a particular journalist whose reports on a number of occasions have caused you discomfort.'

And then: 'If the information provided by our source is proved to be incorrect we would make the fact very clearly known to our audiences and we would express regret. As we stand today, that is simply not the case.'

Campbell's response was double-barrelled. First in a scathing press statement, then an unscheduled appearance on *Channel Four News*.

His statement began as I feared: 'The BBC broadcast a story that was hugely damaging to the integrity of the Government and the Prime Minister without knowing that story to be true and without any effort to check whether the story was true or not ... It confirms our central charge that they do not have a shred of evidence to justify their lie, broadcast many times on many BBC outlets, that we deliberately exaggerated and abused British intelligence and so misled Parliament and public.'

He made the most of what he saw as a gift: 'If the BBC are now saying that their journalism is based upon the principle that they can report what any source says, then BBC standards are now debased beyond belief. It means the BBC can broadcast anything and take responsibility for nothing' ... the story 'is not true and ... [the] journalist made no effort to check its veracity'.

We might have had the law on our side – and we did – but I wondered how many ordinary members of the BBC audience would agree with Campbell that our defence, that we were reporting allegations not making them, amounted to 'weasel words, sophistry and a defence of unethical journalism'.

We were still digesting his statement, watching *Channel Four News* and wondering where the hell this could go next when, suddenly, he was there.

Again, his target was the 'weasel words ... [that say] we didn't make the allegation. We reported a source making the allegation. What does that say about journalism?' he asked. 'They now say you can say anything you want on the television because somebody said it to you. It doesn't matter if it's true. It doesn't matter if you check it. It doesn't matter if it's corroborated. You can say it.'

Then, more classic Campbell. 'The charge that I distorted British intelligence, that I inserted a claim that was not true, that I knew it not to be true. They are serious allegations ... there were no errors of fact in the WMD dossier in September 2002.' I mouthed the words, 'no one ever said any of that'. But so what.

It was a Friday evening in late June. The height of summer and I'd never felt more wretched.

It was out of control.

THE FOURTH PHASE: 30 JUNE TO 6 JULY
THE BEGINNING OF THE END

We were in unknown territory.

It felt like the moment just before a pub fight breaks out. Everyone nervy, knowing mad things were happening but not how to stop them. Gilligan had started to behave in a way that was genuinely worrying. Damazer and I wondered whether he'd become a danger to himself. We couldn't put him on suicide watch. But Damazer kept talking about our duty of care without really saying what he meant.

As far as I could see, Gilligan was indeed in a dangerous place, but not because he was vulnerable. Because he was set on hitting back at Campbell in his own way. He'd got some of that retaliation in first with a *Today* piece on the day that Campbell appeared at the select committee. 'The questions Campbell must answer'. That had unforeseen consequences. One of the Foreign Affairs Select Committee members, the Conservative MP for Croydon South Richard Ottaway, heard the piece and called the *Today* office looking for Gilligan. He wanted a briefing so that he could grill Campbell better, he said. That first contact became a conduit to MPs on the select committee that Gilligan would ill-advisedly exploit.

In the meantime, there were sideshows. The Deputy Leader

of the House of Commons, Phil Woolas, accused Gilligan of misleading Parliament. 'You and the BBC are in full retreat from the original allegations because you know them to be untrue,' he said. It was bunk. It felt part of something co-ordinated. As did Ben Bradshaw's interview on *Today* on the Saturday after Campbell's *Channel 4 News* gatecrash.

I'd known and worked with Bradshaw for many years and considered him a friend. He'd taken me by surprise in September 1996 when he told me he'd been selected to fight Exeter for New Labour. I didn't even know he was a party member. He certainly never showed leanings that way when we worked together. But once he'd been elected, he became visibly and enthusiastically Blairite and rose rapidly. After the 2001 election, he'd become a junior Foreign Office minister, moving in 2002 to become Deputy Leader of the House and then to the Department of Environment, Food and Rural Affairs. With his BBC background, he was a regular media performer. Fluent, serious and loyal. On Saturday 28 June he clashed with Humphrys, more in sorrow, he said, than in anger. But it was one of the angriest confrontations of the whole affair.

Humphrys was uncompromising. Bradshaw was alarmed, he said, at the way the BBC was damaging its own integrity. 'When you have an anonymous un-attributable source you must, as the BBC ... go out of your way to try to corroborate that anonymous source. You did not.' Bradshaw also voiced the charge that we hadn't put the allegations to the government. 'Certainly before you broadcast such a serious allegation you give the opportunity to the Government to deny it.' We had told the government about the story and they'd taken the opportunity to field a minister, live, to respond. But the belief seemed to have taken hold in the MoD and Downing Street that none of that had happened.

Humphrys challenged Bradshaw, but he hit back, repeating the charges: 'There was no attempt to corroborate and there was no attempt to give a right of reply to the Government before you broadcast the most serious accusation that I can ever remember being levelled against a government in my lifetime.' Listening was extraordinarily frustrating. If only he'd known what had actually happened, he couldn't possibly have said that.

The press that weekend was hyperactive. One of the New Labour loyalists on the committee, Eric Illsley, briefed journalists that they were going to exonerate Campbell and criticise both Gilligan and the BBC. That made Gilligan even more anxious to retaliate. I was keen for him to calm down. But he wanted to marshal his own defence in his own way and in his own words.

Working through the night, he assembled a minutely detailed, five-page analysis of Campbell's evidence to the MPs. He began with his track record over the 'dodgy dossier' and ended with an account of how he thought the allegations had got on air. It wasn't a helpful account: it wasn't quite right, largely because he hadn't been in the *Today* newsroom when my day editor and I were making our decisions about his story, nor had he spoken to either of us about it.

He decided, too, to brief some of the MPs on the committee with his analysis and his running commentary on their inquiry so far. He spoke again to Richard Ottaway and to another Tory, John Maples. They reassured him that those press reports that Campbell would be exonerated were untrue. Gilligan then called Sambrook to share the 'good news'. But whatever relief Sambrook felt at that was far outweighed by his alarm that Gilligan now appeared to be in regular contact with committee members.

On the Saturday evening, Gilligan called me at home to tell me that *The Observer* was planning to run a story the following day. 'I thought you should know Kamal Ahmed has got the story about your lunch with Dearlove...' Ahmed was the political editor of *The Observer* and I'd known him for years. He was close to No. 10, but this time I didn't suspect Campbell was his source. I was pretty sure I knew who was.

It was half past eight. I knew very little about the print times of the Sunday papers but I assumed the early edition of *The*

Observer would be close to going to press if it hadn't already. Gilligan's 'tip' left me next to no time to do anything about it. After I'd spat all the obscenities I could think of, I called Ahmed. Yes, he said, it was the front-page splash, already set and about to go. Why didn't you call me, I asked? I got it from a very senior BBC source, Ahmed said. They're very keen to get it out there, he added. What's the gist, then? I asked, and he read me his opening paragraphs.

There was a small flaw in his piece. A very small flaw but it gave me an opening. That's wrong, I said. I'm not confirming or denying anything but if you print that, you'll have MI6 down on you and they'll be able to prove you've got it wrong. I'll have to say I told you it was wrong. You'll be in the shit.

Ahmed butted a few 'buts'. Said again that it was from someone very senior in the BBC. 'It's one of your bosses that wants this out there, Kevin...'

'All I can say, Kamal, is that if you print that it will be wrong.' 'Shit,' he said. 'I'd better go.' I don't know what happened next. I guess it wasn't pretty. He had to stop the presses that had already started to roll. The story didn't appear. Not that weekend, at least.

The following day, Monday, Gilligan sent us all that analysis of Campbell's evidence he'd been working on. I glanced at it. It seemed obsessed. He'd lost perspective. I was a long-term fan of close textual analysis but there were limits and this was way beyond them.

First he says the changes he made were only presentational changes (Q974). Then he is asked (Q1018): Q: Can you try to visualise for us how different the September dossier would have been if it had not been for your discussions on presentational issues? A: Other than literally drafting points I cannot recall any substantial changes being made to the executive summary. This seems to imply that he did make substantial drafting changes to the executive summary.

There was more. Much, much, much more. Too much more. I understood why Gilligan felt he had to do it but I just couldn't take it. I never read the fine detail. Gilligan wanted to distribute it to his friendly MPs on the select committee. He called Sambrook to ask permission. Sambrook said no – but promised to include parts of it in the BBC's submission to the select committee.

Gilligan argued. He didn't want it subsumed into a corporate submission. Could he send it in addition, he wondered. Again, Sambrook said no. Gilligan persisted. Could he 'communicate the contents [to] one or two members'. Sambrook was worn down. He couldn't offer it, but if any MPs on the committee asked for it, he could brief them. Sambrook meant sending nothing on paper. Gilligan assumed something different.

Meanwhile, Damazer had dragged from the back of his impressive brain a half memory that the BBC *Newsnight* science specialist Susan Watts had broadcast two reports about the dossier; one on 2 June and the other on 4 June. Both were, Damazer's memory told him, similar to Gilligan's. Bizarrely, at no point in the very public and increasingly acrimonious three-week row with Campbell had Watts or her editor, George Entwistle, who in July 2012 became the BBC's Director General, put up their hand to say 'what about this...?'

Damazer looked at the tapes and realised they were even more similar than he remembered. Either Gilligan and Watts had the same source or they had different sources and a second voice from within the intelligence community had given testimony very similar to that of Gilligan's source. Whichever, Watts's reports tended to validate Gilligan's.

Watts had quoted her source as saying that the 45-minute claim was 'seized on ... that's why there is the argument between the intelligence services and No. 10'. Downing Street, her source told her, was 'obsessed' with finding intelligence that proved an imminent threat. The judgement that Saddam was an immediate threat was 'a Downing Street interpretation of an intelligence conclusion'.

Neither Campbell nor anyone else in No. 10 had complained to or about Watts. Yet *Newsnight* was one of the BBC programmes that Downing Street routinely monitored. And while her phrasing was more careful and her language more measured than Gilligan's, her thrust was the same. The September dossier was 'sexed up' at the behest of Downing Street; the 45-minute claim was contentious at best; and, as it was expressed in the dossier, it was the cause of unhappiness in the intelligence community.

Sambrook went down to the *Newsnight* office to ask Watts and Entwistle about the reports and was immediately exasperated. They were cagey. Neither was a fan of Gilligan and both were reluctant to corroborate his story. That may be why Watts failed to mention at that meeting that she'd recorded her second conversation with her source, who was, of course, Dr David Kelly.

Sambrook suspected that her source and Gilligan's were the same. More importantly, he realised it was urgent that the Foreign Affairs Select Committee should see Watts's reports. Whether she and Entwistle were comfortable about it or not, those short films did tend to corroborate the allegations in Gilligan's story. Campbell's failure ever to complain about them tended to confirm the suspicion we all had that amongst his motivations was settling scores with Gilligan and *Today*.

Sambrook sent the tapes to the Foreign Affairs Select Committee chairman, Donald Anderson, along with a briefing note, setting out the similarities between Gilligan's and Watts's reports. Gilligan, though, was losing patience.

He was now in regular contact with three or four MPs on the committee, feeding them his thoughts more or less as they occurred to him. He would appear unexpectedly outside the glass walls of my office or by my seat on the newsdesk ready to offload his latest unhappiness. And he would share with me, or anyone who'd listen, the fine detail of yet more analysis he'd done of Campbell's committee evidence or a new contradiction he'd discovered in the text of the dossier.

On one occasion, he suddenly materialised beside me and, without speaking, gesticulated that I should come outside. I followed him out into the corridor. He put his finger to his lips, making a 'shhh' sound and walked towards the door that led to the 'doughnut' – the circular open space at the heart of Television Centre.

'We can't talk inside…' he finally told me. 'Let's walk around.' He asked me if there'd been any workmen in my office over the past few days. I said no. Had we had trouble with the phones? I said no. Well we can't take the risk, he whispered, glancing around. They'll have bugged your office somehow. I started to ask who … but there didn't seem much point.

We walked. He talked. I despaired.

THE FIFTH PHASE: 30 JUNE TO 10 JULY
NAMING GILLIGAN'S SOURCE

It was on 30 June, five days after Campbell had decided he needed to re-ignite the row with us, that Dr Kelly wrote to his MoD boss to say he'd met Gilligan. In the interim, he'd been abroad and, he said, not following the row especially closely.

At the end of that same week, on 4 July, the MoD head of personnel warned Dr Kelly he'd broken the rules by meeting Gilligan. That was in spite of Dr Kelly's insistence that he hadn't met Gilligan to talk about the dossier and that he'd spoken to journalists dozens of times before without sanction and saw it as an important part of his job. It seems, on the face of it, an excessively oppressive response. One that was not entirely motivated by personnel considerations.

It's impossible to know the effect such an interview had on a man of such integrity as Dr Kelly. With hindsight, it does appear to be the first turn of a screw that built unsustainable pressure on him.

That same day, 4 July, Richard Sambrook had lunch with a group of *Times* journalists where, inevitably, the dossier and the row with Campbell was more or less all that anyone wanted to talk about. One asked whether he or Gilligan had spoken to the source again. Sambrook said no. 'Is that because he's out of the country?' Sambrook was alive to the danger and tried to evade: 'Something like that,' he said.

Tom Baldwin, the *Times* journalist behind the 'rogue elements' diversion, and who was very close to Campbell, pricked up his ears. He'd spent most of June trying to track down Gilligan's source, without much success in spite of Downing Street briefings.

The day after the lunch, Baldwin ran a story describing Gilligan's source as 'a military expert who is now based in Iraq'. That was wrong. Dr Kelly was not in Iraq. BBC journalists, Baldwin wrote, 'have been told that Mr Gilligan's anonymous source is among the 100 British intelligence and weapons specialists currently in Iraq as part of the American-led survey group searching for Saddam's missing weapons of mass destruction'. That was wrong, too. Very few BBC journalists or insiders knew anything at all about Gilligan's source. No one had been told anything. In any event, once the story ran, one analyst in the Defence Intelligence Staff said 'they've all but named Kelly'. That could not have suited Campbell better. At that stage, though, while the MoD and Downing Street knew Dr Kelly had met Gilligan, they couldn't be sure he was Gilligan's single, anonymous source. But over that weekend, they all but persuaded themselves that he was. Blair asked for the confusion to be cleared up. The Joint Intelligence Committee chairman, John Scarlett, thought that could only be done with 'a proper security style interview in which all these inconsistencies are thrashed out'. Given Scarlett's early career in Cold War Moscow, one can only imagine what he meant by 'a proper security style interview'.

On the Monday, 7 July, the Foreign Affairs Select Committee

finally published its report. It was a messy score draw, as far as the September dossier was concerned. The MPs concluded, though not unanimously, that 'Alastair Campbell did not exert or seek to exert improper influence on the drafting of the September dossier'. Nor had they seen any evidence that 'a senior intelligence official dissented from the contents of the dossier'. But, 'the language used in the September dossier was in places more assertive than that traditionally used in intelligence documents'.

For much of that morning in No. 10, there was a 'rolling meeting', un-minuted, discussing what to do about Dr Kelly and how to respond to the committee's report. Some of those involved were anxious that if Dr Kelly's name was revealed now, or if he was even thought to be Gilligan's source, the committee would want to question him. One official warned that it would mean his 'uncomfortable views about specific items on which he had views' would be revealed. In other words, there was the risk that he would repeat in public the concerns about the 45-minute claim he'd shared in private with Gilligan and Watts.

Campbell, though, had persuaded himself that if it could be shown that Gilligan's source was not on the JIC or at the very top of the agencies, he would win a clear victory. Dr Kelly was neither. Ergo, if his identity were revealed, the BBC's defence of Gilligan would collapse. He was wrong about that – often the best sources are nowhere near the top of organisations. Nevertheless, he pushed to get a press statement out as soon as possible that said Gilligan's source wasn't a 'senior official in charge of drawing up the dossier'. He wanted that statement to understate as far as possible Dr Kelly's status. A statement in those terms was duly drafted, though no one was entirely sure how they were going to use it. Dr Kelly was shown the draft later that day and told that it would only be used 'if necessary', whatever that meant. But that in the meantime, he should be prepared for his name to be revealed. He continued to insist that, while he'd spoken to Gilligan, he wasn't his source for the dossier story. Again, we can only imagine the pressure this placed on him.

It was all too slow and lacking 'clarity' for Campbell. He called the Defence Secretary, Geoff Hoon, and tried to insist that the MoD release Dr Kelly's name, even though no one was 100 per cent certain that he was the source and Dr Kelly was still denying it. Hoon as well as Campbell's own trusties in Downing Street, Godric Smith and Tom Kelly, weren't so sure.

Over at *The Times*, meanwhile, Baldwin was somehow picking up hints that the identity of Gilligan's source would soon be revealed. He was preparing for Tuesday's edition a story that 'some [BBC] executives have hinted that he may be in Iraq searching for WMD'. 'Loose talk at the BBC,' he wrote, had persuaded the government that Gilligan's source wasn't a spook, didn't work on drafting the dossier 'but more likely is a WMD specialist at the Foreign Office'. I doubted very much that it was the 'hints' of 'senior BBC executives' or 'loose talk' that were his source.

At the MoD, the press office got a briefing to use if they were contacted by journalists looking for more information. If they were asked: 'What is his name and current post?' the press officer was instructed to respond: 'We wouldn't normally volunteer a name. (If the correct name is given, we can confirm it and say that he is senior advisor to the Proliferation and Arms Control Secretariat.)'

There were still those in the MoD who were urging caution. Some still doubted that Dr Kelly was the source but they were in a minority and by the evening of Tuesday 8 July, the general view was that he was the source and that Gilligan had embellished whatever he'd said. Downing Street and the MoD decided to make it public that someone had 'come forward'. That guaranteed Dr Kelly would eventually be named.

A little before six in the evening of 8 July, the MoD put out a statement that 'an individual working in the MoD has come forward'. It went on to say that the individual met Gilligan on 22 May and that during their conversation 'Mr Gilligan raised the Iraqi WMD programme, including the 45-minute issue. The official says that Mr Gilligan also raised the issue of Alastair Campbell.' The statement described the 'individual' as 'an expert on WMD who has advised ministers on WMD and whose contribution to the Dossier of September 2002 was to contribute towards drafts of historical accounts of UN inspections'. He is not 'one of the senior officials in charge of drawing up the dossier' nor a member of the intelligence services. The MoD statement said he hadn't seen the 45-minute intelligence report and when Gilligan asked him about the role of Alastair Campbell with regard to the 45-minute issue, he made no comment and explained that he was not involved in the process of drawing up the intelligence parts of the dossier. When Gilligan asked him why the 45-minute point was in the dossier, he says he commented that it was 'probably for impact'.

The MoD admitted that it didn't know whether 'this official is the single source'. But, it went on: 'The BBC has recently said that it was reporting the allegations of the source, rather than making the allegations themselves. That is why the question of the source is important.'

We had a problem.

I was with Dyke in Birmingham for the Radio Festival. We were both on stage at various times during the day and communicating with each other, with Sambrook and Damazer and with the BBC press office by mobile phones, struggling with dodgy signals and keen not to be overheard by the thousands of radio journalists milling around.

I was anxious that we give absolutely nothing away. The risk of jigsaw identification, a gobbet of information here combining with another there, was high. And by now, it wasn't just journalists close to Campbell like Tom Baldwin who were chasing down Gilligan's source. The MoD and Downing Street had made the identity of the source an issue. *The* issue.

There was much in the MoD/Downing Street statement that was wrong, but we couldn't take any of it on. We had an absolute duty to do all we could to protect Dr Kelly's identity. After seemingly endless agitated conversations, we came up with a statement that said: 'The description of the individual contained in the statement does not match Mr Gilligan's source in some important ways. Mr Gilligan's source does not work in the Ministry of Defence and he has known the source for a number of years, not months.'

We added: 'For the single conversation which led to the *Today* story, Mr Gilligan took comprehensive notes during the meeting with his source which do not correspond with the account given in the MoD statement. These notes have already been deposited with the BBC legal department...' We didn't realise at the time what a hostage to fortune that was. The statement concluded: 'We note that the MoD statement says that "we do not know whether this official is Mr Gilligan's source".'

It wasn't great, but it was the best we could do. We were now on the defensive and sounded like it. Not because we had any doubts about Dr Kelly, his credibility and standing but because we couldn't really take issue with any of it without the risk of identifying him.

The following morning, Wednesday 9 July, there was clear enough evidence we were right to be cautious. The *Daily Telegraph* reported that we'd admitted Andrew Gilligan met his contact at a central London hotel on 22 May, apparently corroborating the Downing Street/MoD statement. I couldn't remember us doing that but was nowhere near a secure computer to check. Plus, I was due on the Radio Festival stage that morning, alongside Clare Short, talking about spin, deception and honest government. I didn't expect it to be a particularly rough ride: I didn't expect the opening question from Eddie Mair, who was chairing the session, either. 'Which one of you hates Alastair Campbell the most?'

My mouth was paralysed. I knew that anything I said
would go straight into the papers. Short rescued me: 'It's not
about hating...'

Mair's questions didn't get any less tough. But it was pretty
clear that the audience was on our side. It would have been
odd if they hadn't been. Someone asked about the pressure of
it all. I said it was great to have Dyke by your side: 'I hardly
dare think what it would have been like under Birt,' I added.
After the session was over, my old mentor Jenny Abramsky,
who was by then Managing Director of Radio, tapped me on
the shoulder. It was a rebuke. Birt, she assured me, would have
carried out a proper inquiry much earlier. I smiled and tried
not to look as pained as she did.

That same afternoon, Tom Kelly chaired the Downing Street
briefing and added new detail to the statement. It looked to
me like a nudge, designed to ensure Dr Kelly's identity would
come out that day. The 'individual' was a technical expert who
was currently working for the MoD, he said, though their
salary was paid by another department. There weren't many
people that description matched.

Then, *The Guardian*'s Richard Norton-Taylor picked up
from somewhere the line that Gilligan's source had been an
UNSCOM inspector. Only a dozen or so of them had been
British. He mentioned it to colleagues, who suggested some
possible names. He did an internet search, quickly finding
a lecture Dr Kelly had given, complete with a short CV. He
seemed to fit the description the MoD/Downing Street had
put out. At the same time, other journalists on other papers
were going through similar hoops trying to narrow down
the name.

The scene that afternoon in the MoD press office would
have been ludicrous if it hadn't also been part of a lethal game.
Around half past five, the *Financial Times*'s Chris Adams called
the press office and put Dr Kelly's name to them. The press
officer followed the brief: 'If the correct name is given, we can

confirm it and say that he is senior advisor to the Proliferation and Arms Control Secretariat.' The name was confirmed.

Richard Norton-Taylor called soon afterwards with three names, including Dr Kelly's which the press officer again confirmed. *The Times*, in spite of Baldwin's six-week obsession, was less fortunate. Its journalists had to try twenty names before they got to Dr Kelly. One journalist was even said to have offered to read the entire government phone book if that's what it took to find the name.

THE SIXTH PHASE: 10 TO 18 JULY
THE END

I had an endless number of phone calls that Wednesday afternoon. From the BBC press office, from the *Today* office and from Sambrook. I was still in Birmingham at the Radio Festival and from mid-afternoon it was just a question of waiting.

By the time I was travelling back to London, I knew that at least three papers were going to name Dr Kelly as the 'individual' who'd come forward and almost certainly name him as Gilligan's source. That would mean that both the Foreign Affairs Committee and the Intelligence and Security Committee would want to call Dr Kelly. There could be no certainty about how that would turn out.

I spoke to Sambrook from the train. We were still clear that we owed Dr Kelly a duty of confidentiality. There was no question of us confirming anything or denying anything that might narrow the search. Paradoxically, Dr Kelly was clearly bound to be the number one topic on every BBC news programme and discussion show that evening and the following day.

Back in London, the MoD/Downing Street statement had needled Gilligan by describing his source as a mere 'technical expert' and 'middle ranking official'. But the statement changed nothing. Dr Kelly was a credible, reportable source. By this time, Dyke knew that Dr Kelly was Gilligan's source though the chairman, Gavyn Davies, didn't. Now that his name and

CV were all over the serious papers, they asked for more information on Dr Kelly, a briefing note that Gilligan 'compiled from open sources about the man the MoD claims to be my source'.

He also contacted the MPs he'd been speaking to on the Foreign Affairs Committee, John Maples and Richard Ottaway, ostensibly to inquire about their plans for questioning Dr Kelly. He learnt that MoD were trying to set conditions for any appearance: they wanted the MPs to agree only to ask him about his contacts with Gilligan, not more generally about the dossier, WMD and his experience. It was a condition the Tories, Lib Dems and most New Labour members could never allow.

The likelihood that Dr Kelly, who we'd still not confirmed was Gilligan's source, would appear prompted the committee chairman, Donald Anderson, to write to Gilligan asking for more information about his source. That wasn't something we could offer. He asked, too, whether Gilligan was 'satisfied' that all the evidence he'd given to the committee in his appearance on 18 June was 'in every particular truthful and accurate'. He gave Gilligan a deadline of 4 p.m. the following day to reply. It seemed unnecessarily aggressive.

The following morning, Gilligan went into conclave with Sambrook, a lawyer and two other BBC executives to draft a response. We were still determined to give nothing away. Gilligan, though, was becoming increasingly frustrated. At one point, he pulled Sambrook out of the conclave to demand that he be allowed to take on Donald Anderson, the committee, Campbell, the world in his own terms. Sambrook told him to calm down – he'd be thankful for everyone's 'expertise and experience' in time. In the end, the BBC's reply was a vision in vanilla. It went out in Gilligan's name and insisted that he was going to protect his source and that his evidence was indeed 'truthful and accurate'.

Recollections differ over what happened next. Sambrook is

adamant that once they'd finished drafting that response, he and Gilligan went their different ways and neither of them spoke any more about further contacts with members of the Foreign Affairs Committee. Gilligan, however, recalls that Sambrook told him it was 'important' that the quotes Susan Watts had used in her *Newsnight* pieces were put to Dr Kelly when he appeared. And that he, Gilligan, should dig out the quotes and send them to his contacts. Sambrook explicitly denies this.

The following Monday, 14 July, Gilligan emailed John Maples, Richard Ottaway and, via a Liberal Democrat press officer, David Chidgey. He included some of the 'open source' material on Dr Kelly that he'd circulated the previous week within the BBC. Even with his disclaimer, 'we are not ruling anyone in or out as the source', Gilligan was all but admitting to the three MPs that this was his source. His 'Questions for Kelly' were clearly designed to point them towards areas that would endorse his account of their meeting.

But once again, he was caught out by his loose use of language. Clumsily and almost certainly without realising what he was doing, he named Dr Kelly as Susan Watts's source. Ironically, he didn't actually know at the time that Dr Kelly *was* her source. But the wording of his memo left anyone reading it with no other conclusion to draw. He begins one paragraph with 'Kelly told *The Independent* (etc)...' And then begins the following paragraph: 'He also told my colleague Susan Watts ... who described him as "a senior official intimately involved with the process of putting together the dossier"...'

Whatever he was thinking, he'd committed the cardinal sin of revealing Dr Kelly as Susan Watts's source.

• • •

Dr David Kelly appeared before the Foreign Affairs Select Committee the following day, 15 July.

It's almost impossible to disentangle thoughts then from

thoughts now. No one could have had any idea that within seventy-two hours Dr Kelly would be dead. No one could have known then about the pressure building on him and how that pressure would affect a man of such high principles and integrity. Nor did we know then about the contents of the tape recording Susan Watts had made of her conversation with him. When we did finally hear that tape, it suggested that he wasn't as completely frank with the MPs as he might have been. And that the need to dissemble probably stretched every moral sinew in him.

Yet I'm sure that anyone watching closely and with any insight felt as uncomfortable as I did.

I felt an instant empathy with him. He had the calm, patient demeanour of a favourite teacher. He spoke quietly, too quietly at times. And deliberately. Often he would seem to be searching for the consequences of using any word before speaking.

He was clearly a very brave man. He'd faced down the thugs of one of the most brutal regimes on the planet. He'd forced a path through Saddam Hussein's deceptions to the truth. He'd tracked down deadly toxins. But this was an alien world. The contrast between the quietness of this careful man with the silver beard and the bickering, grandstanding pomposity of the MPs couldn't have been more stark.

As I watched him being challenged about the dossier ... about what he'd said to Gilligan ... about the possibility he was the source and what he'd thought about the dossier and the way it had been produced ... something didn't quite feel right. There were contradictions. Or impressions given in one answer that turned out, in a later one, not to be quite as they'd first seemed.

He was 'familiar' with the dossier; he was 'really not involved'. He'd only met Susan Watts once; he'd spoken to her several times on the phone. He was 'on leave or working abroad' in late August and early September; he was 'in the country but didn't participate in meetings' in early and mid-September. The 45-minute claim only 'became apparent on publication'; or maybe he was aware of it 'forty-eight hours beforehand'.

On the specifics of the allegations that Gilligan reported, he seemed to me to have a great difficulty of some kind. Where there might have been a 'yes' or a 'no' there were circumlocutions. 'I do not recognise those comments,' he said. But when he was asked 'Is there anything in Mr Gilligan's accounts that you dispute?' Dr Kelly replied: 'I think you would have to ask me the specific question.'

Did the 'Campbell word' come up? Someone wanted to know. It 'came up in the conversation'. How? 'What I had a conversation about was the probability of a requirement to use such weapons. The question was then asked why, if weapons could be deployed at forty-five minutes' notice, were they not used, and I offered my reasons why they may not have been used.' Yet he believed he was 'not the main source'.

The care he took to say nothing, not to speak an untruth even by omission, became tortured.

Tory John Stanley asked: 'Can you tell me absolutely whether you named or otherwise identified Alastair Campbell or did you say anything which Mr Gilligan might reasonably have interpreted as identifying Mr Alastair Campbell as wanting to change the dossier or "sex it up" in any way or make undue reference to the 45-minute claim?'

Dr Kelly replied: 'I cannot recall that. I find it very difficult to think back to a conversation I had six weeks ago. I cannot recall but that does not mean to say, of course, that such a statement was not made but I really cannot recall it. It does not sound like the sort of thing I would say.'

Or this from Labour's Andrew MacKinlay : 'You were aware that [the dossier] was signed off by the JIC chairman, that is correct, is it not?' Dr Kelly could have said 'yes'. Something stopped him: 'I am aware that the Joint Intelligence Committee was involved in the final compilation, yes.'

Or this from Bill Olner, another Labour member: 'So there

was no, if you like, feeling within the security services that this was a piece of work that had been "sexed up" and it was going to be rubbished at the end of the day?' Only Dr Kelly knew what exactly he intended not to say with his answer: 'I think there were people who worked extremely hard to achieve that document and the calibre of the document that was produced.'

But it was the final moments of his appearance that were most alarming. New Labour's Andrew MacKinlay put the question we were all thinking. And did so with a bluntness that was unsettling: 'I reckon you are chaff; you have been thrown up to divert our probing. Have you ever felt like a fall-guy? You have been set up, have you not?'

Dr Kelly's reply was not so blunt. But it was even more unsettling. He seemed elsewhere: 'That is not a question I can answer.' MacKinlay pressed: 'But you feel that?' Dr Kelly's words meant one thing, his posture and demeanour another: 'No, not at all. I accept the process that is going on.' His words trailed away.

The chairman Donald Anderson asked again whether he felt used: 'You have already asked that question. I accept the process that I have encountered.'

• • •

The committee now wanted to speak to Gilligan again. I'd intended him to go to Washington. I was keen to get him back working normally, something he hadn't done for six weeks.

Even after Dr Kelly's appearance, we still weren't confirming that he was Gilligan's source. We could do no other. That seemed to get under the skin of some of the MPs, in particular the committee chairman, Donald Anderson. We'd written that it was 'a necessary principle of free journalism' that Gilligan shouldn't reveal the identity of the person he met and whose allegations he subsequently reported. Anderson snapped back that Gilligan must answer the question: 'On what date, and at what time, did the meeting with this source take place?' And he reminded us that Gilligan's refusal to reveal his source – a refusal that we all thought non-negotiable – was the first in modern times where 'a journalist has refused to reveal a source which formed the basis for an allegation made in evidence before a committee'.

When Gilligan appeared before the committee again, this time in a private session on Thursday 17 July, it was incredibly hostile. Inexplicably so. It was a personal assault. And while I might have cheerfully slapped Gilligan myself, the session with the MPs was brutal. Ill-informed, partisan and vindictive.

Donald Anderson, comprehensively rebuffed over his ill-advised attempt to winkle out more information about Gilligan's source, warned of the 'considerable' powers the House of Commons had if Gilligan continued to refuse to disclose anything about his source. He did refuse. Another New Labour member, Gisela Stuart, who'd been absent for his first appearance, began with three attacks on Gilligan's record for accuracy over the previous twelve months, not one of which had anything to do with the matter in hand.

Some of the MPs seemed unfamiliar with their own report published just ten days earlier. Some were poorly briefed, confused about the number of sources Gilligan had. Some preferred Campbell's misleading, reformulated version of the allegations to the ones actually reported, unable to grasp that Campbell had denied allegations never made.

Given the nonsense that the MPs were throwing at him, Gilligan was remarkably calm and self-possessed. Only one member of the committee, Andrew MacKinlay, the member who two days earlier had put Dr Kelly on the spot, seemed to understand why he was there and what he was talking about. Struggling against his colleagues and especially the committee chairman, he came up with an intriguing thought. That both Gilligan and Campbell 'could be correct'. The scenario he set out was the only sense heard in that committee room that day.

He imagined that:

a request comes from No. 10 Downing Street, perhaps conveyed by Campbell, to the security intelligence community ... The backdrop of this is the fact that the Government believe they are right, the Prime Minister believes he is right, and so on. He has made a policy decision, which he is entitled to make, he wants to put into the public domain intelligence to back this, to build on his case that he is presenting to Parliament and to the people.

The request/demand which he is entitled to make is conveyed to the intelligence community ... then at the top echelon somebody is really irritated, pissed off, aggravated, either by the manner, the presumption, or the 'demand'? ... that irritation is conveyed to other parties, it becomes currency in the senior echelons...

The Thomas a Becket argument comes in, that when Campbell or No. 10 legitimately demanded the intelligence community produce some stuff, quite rightly, for the Prime Minister to put into the public domain, which everyone accepts is perfectly proper, the people in a high echelon decided they wanted to do their master's bidding and they were overzealous, they cut corners to please the master.

It may well be that people in the community feel that things are being over-egged, exaggerated, things are being put in. They would not know who has demanded this and so on, but they genuinely are concerned and, indeed, in some cases they have been proved to be correct.

Is there not a scenario whereby your sources, your source, are professionally aggrieved, they think things are going in without health warnings or whatever ... those are going in, but they do not know that the carelessness, the recklessness, does not lie with the politicians, No. 10, or Alastair Campbell – the recklessness lies with the senior echelons of MI6? ...

It could be that the higher echelons have been dilatory, they tried to please their master, the Prime Minister, who are the consumers of the stuff. If we accept that the chairman of the Joint

Intelligence Committee signed this off ... I do think that it is not impossible that there is a more complicated explanation than simply that Alastair Campbell is lying or that Gilligan is lying.

There are only three possible explanations for MacKinlay's insight. Pure chance, divine guidance, or a damn good source who'd seen something similar to Dr Kelly in the way the dossier had been produced.

• • •

While all this was happening in central London, Dr Kelly was leaving his house in Oxfordshire for the last time.

He walked about five miles from his home to the edge of a wood close to Harrowdown Hill – it was a walk he often took.

When he hadn't returned by the evening, his daughters first went to look for him. When they found nothing, they called the police just after midnight.

His body was found, slumped against a tree, a little after nine o'clock the following morning.

I happened to have a routine hospital appointment that morning and was waiting in outpatients when my phone rang. It was someone from the *Today* office. A body had been found close to Dr Kelly's home. 'Do we know...' my voice trailed off. 'No,' was the answer.

I went into the clinic, had some blood taken and caught a cab back to TV Centre.

On the way, my phone rang again. 'We don't know for sure ... but it looks like it's Kelly. He went missing yesterday.'

I felt desperately sad. But somehow not surprised.

CHAPTER EIGHT

HOW HUTTON FAILED

ῥεχθὲν δέ τε νήπιος ἔγνω
When [evil] has been done, even a fool realises it.

Homer, *The Iliad*

With Dr Kelly's death, what had been no more than a grubby political and media game suddenly became real.

Blair, who was out of the country in the Far East, announced an inquiry. His Lord Chancellor, Lord Falconer, was asked to find an appropriate senior judge and lay down the broad terms of that inquiry. Unusually, he also decided that there should be no separate inquest, that whoever he appointed should conduct both inquiry and inquest, a decision that led, in time, to any number of conspiracy theories.

Perhaps it was because of the speed of Blair's decision to hold an inquiry that it seemed to take some time for the Downing Street media team to understand the full import of Dr Kelly's death. Tom Kelly, my former deputy at *The World at One* and now one of Alastair Campbell's deputies in Downing Street, told journalists that Dr Kelly had been a 'Walter Mitty character'. Another in Campbell's press team briefed reporters that he had a 'serious heart condition', implying that might be a reason for him to take his own life.

The skill, as far as governments are concerned, in setting up inquiries is first to appoint the right judge, then to lay down the right terms of reference. For the *Inquiry into the Circumstances*

Surrounding the Death of Dr David Kelly CMG the terms of reference were quite narrow. With a judge who was so minded, they might become narrower still.

With hindsight, Lord Hutton was without doubt the man for the job. The late Philip Gould, one of the Prime Minister's most trusted advisors, was overheard telling a colleague 'we appointed the right judge'. What exactly he meant by that he took to his grave. But you don't need to search too far to see why he was right.

Hutton's career up to the summer of 2003 had shown an exaggerated respect for authority, especially the authority of the British government. He'd shown little sympathy for whistleblowers and for independent, critical journalism when it and government had come into conflict. He was not only cautious, but those who knew him or had appeared before him described him as the kind of judge who was 'more inclined to focus on the narrow point than to indulge in grand claims or unnecessary generalisation'. The last thing the government wanted was a judge who would drift off into broader questions such as why there were no WMD in Iraq when the dossier and the Prime Minister had assured us that there were. Or whether the intelligence that had gone into the dossier actually *meant* what Campbell and Scarlett's text told us it did. Or whether Dr Kelly was right to share with more than one journalist the concerns in the intelligence community.

As Brian Hutton QC, he first made headlines at the inquest into the Bloody Sunday killings. That inquest returned open verdicts on the fourteen civil rights protestors shot dead by British paratroopers during a march in the city on 30 January 1972. The Londonderry City coroner, Major Hubert O'Neill, accused the British army of 'sheer, unadulterated murder'. He added: 'These people [the civil rights protestors] may have been taking part in a parade that was banned but I do not think that justifies the firing of live rounds indiscriminately.'

Hutton, appearing for the Ministry of Defence, didn't just

dissent. He rebuked both the coroner and the jury in language that can only be described as high-handed: 'It is not for you or the jury to express such wide-ranging views, particularly when a most eminent judge has spent twenty days hearing evidence and come to a very different conclusion.'

That 'most eminent judge' was Lord Widgery. His report, which exonerated the soldiers of the Parachute Regiment, was widely discredited even as it was published because of its inconsistencies and absence of eyewitness testimony. Hutton must have known about the controversy. But that didn't deter him from holding it up as a paragon, not to be questioned by a mere coroner or jury who'd done nothing other than listen to the evidence. Thirty-seven years later, in June 2010, Prime Minister David Cameron apologised for the 'unjustified and unjustifiable' killings, echoing coroner O'Neill's judgment.

Five years after chiding those who doubted the discredited Widgery, Brian Hutton was appearing for the British government again. This time before the European Court of Human Rights, defending the so-called 'five techniques'. These were 'techniques' most ordinary people would recognise as torture. The British security forces used them to extract information and confessions from Northern Irish internees.

They included standing internees 'spread-eagled ... with their fingers put high above the head against the wall, the legs spread apart and the feet back, causing them to stand on their toes with the weight of the body mainly on the fingers'. They also included hooding, noise, sleep deprivation and refusing food and drink. The Lord Chief Justice of England, Lord Parker, had already found the techniques illegal under British law. The European Commission of Human Rights had gone further and determined that they amounted to torture.

Britain appealed to the European Court of Human Rights and Hutton led the government's defence. Hutton won. But it was a Pyrrhic victory. The court ruled that the 'five techniques' didn't amount to torture; they were merely 'inhuman and degrading treatment'.

In 1997, Brian Hutton became Lord Hutton. A Law Lord. Two controversial cases defined his time on the red benches. The first, the extradition proceedings against the former Chilean dictator, Augusto Pinochet. The second, an appeal that centred on a whistleblower's right to plead that he acted in the public interest.

In 1998, Pinochet arrived in Britain for medical treatment and was arrested under an international warrant issued by a Spanish judge, Baltasar Garzón. The warrant sought to put Pinochet on trial in Spain for the alleged torture of Spanish citizens and the murder of a Spanish diplomat. Pinochet claimed immunity from prosecution, and therefore extradition, as a former head of state. A panel of five Law Lords rejected his claim three to two. But it turned out that one of the Law Lords on that panel, Lord Hoffmann, had strong and active links to Amnesty International, which had been campaigning for Pinochet's extradition and trial.

The panel's ruling was overturned. And in overturning it, Lord Hutton was uncompromising: 'I consider that the links … between Lord Hoffman and Amnesty International, which had campaigned strongly against General Pinochet and which intervened in the earlier hearing to support the case that he should be extradited to face trial for his alleged crimes, were so strong that public confidence in the integrity of the administration of justice would be shaken if his decision were allowed to stand.'

The second important case came just eighteen months before Lord Falconer chose him to head the inquiry into Dr Kelly's death. It was the Shayler case.

David Shayler was a failed journalist who somehow managed to persuade MI5 to give him a job. According to his own account, he worked first in counter-subversion. That included monitoring leading Labour politicians including Jack

Straw, Harriet Harman and Peter Mandelson before the 1992 election. He also claimed to have discovered a number of shady British intelligence operations abroad, including a failed attempt to assassinate Colonel Gaddafi.

In 1997, a year after he left MI5, Shayler sold some of his stories, along with supporting secret documents, to the *Mail on Sunday*. There were legal battles, injunctions imposed and lifted. Shayler fled the country but returned in 2000 to face trial on charges under the Official Secrets Act. He was convicted and sent to prison. But not before Lord Hutton had intervened. Shayler had indicated he would plead a public interest defence. Effectively arguing that he was a whistleblower drawing attention to serious illegality on the part of the state. And that, he argued, warranted protection from prosecution. The Official Secrets Act 1989 included no such explicit provision and the trial judge ruled initially that Shayler couldn't rely on that defence. Shayler appealed on the narrow point, his appeal went all the way to the House of Lords and, in March 2002, Lord Hutton was one of four Law Lords who rejected his application.

Hutton's opinion on the Shayler case foreshadowed his thinking at the Dr Kelly inquiry, placing the interests of the state above those of the public or a whistleblower guilty of trying to tell the public what was being done in its name. The Official Secrets Act, he wrote, '[does] not permit a defendant to raise a defence that the information which he disclosed without lawful authority was disclosed by him in the public interest'. That is indeed the letter of the law. But the narrative of his opinion shows him hostile to whistleblowing full stop. And he states clearly that anyone working in the secret services who has concerns, no matter how serious, should share them with their boss or some other authorised Crown Servant or seek permission to voice them publicly.

Otherworldly, to say the least. But a clear indication of the way he was likely to lean in an inquiry that had at its heart a whistleblower speaking the truth to journalists.

Few of us in the media, few outside Downing Street, looked as closely at Hutton's background as we might and should have done. Had we done so, we might have had very different expectations. Instead, there was a broad feeling that he and the inquiry might be Blair's nemesis. 'HUTTON WILL REVEAL THE TRUTH' was a typical headline. The polls at the time told us that more than two-thirds of voters thought Blair's government dishonest and untrustworthy and blamed the culture of deceit and spin in Downing Street. Almost half were saying they simply didn't believe a word the Prime Minister said and 40 per cent blamed the government directly for Dr Kelly's death.

Judges in general had become unaccountably popular, based on their apparent readiness to give governments a bloody nose. The press routinely portrayed Hutton as some kind of wise being, sitting above the tawdry politics of the whole thing, who would doubtless turn over every small detail to get to the truth. And once Lord Hutton had appeared in public, his patrician appearance and curiously reassuring speech underlined that impression.

For all those who distrusted Blair and the political culture he and Campbell had created, here was the kind of judge who would finally call a halt. We thought.

• • •

It didn't occur to me until halfway through Lord Hutton's inquiry that I wouldn't be called to give evidence in person. Until then, the middle of that hot August, it had seemed obvious that I'd have to spend at least a morning or afternoon in the box. I'd made the decision to put Gilligan on air; I'd decided his source was reportable; I'd decided his allegations fitted with everything else I knew; I'd decided my private sources offered enough corroboration; I'd made sure the government knew about the allegations, that they'd had and had made use of their right of reply; I'd checked Gilligan's notes and passed his script; and I'd played my part in the row with Campbell.

Obvious.

The idea of appearing didn't appeal to me hugely, though. Accountability was one thing. The media circus the inquiry was bound to become, another. The more so since during August there would be little other news around. I expected some of the players, Campbell and probably Gilligan too, would enjoy the show of it all. The manly stride through the scrum of photographers, cameramen and reporters outside the Royal Courts of Justice. The defiance in the witness box. The idea of it made me feel physically sick.

I knew, too, that it would be a hindsight festival. There'd be the inevitable questions such as 'but if you thought that, why didn't you...?' To which the answer, 'it looks like that now, it didn't at the time...' is somehow never satisfactory. There was always the risk that someone as lofty as a judge simply wouldn't understand the grubby realities of a 24-hour newsroom. Nor how tough it had been for nearly a decade to get behind the 'truths' that the most cynical media outfit in British political history had 'created'.

Since it was so obvious I'd have to give evidence, I just had to get on with it. And once I was into the all-encompassing practicalities of being prepped by the lawyers, I had no time to think of anything else, including how disagreeable the whole business was. It was a dog of a job.

First, I had to dig out every computer file and piece of paper that had anything to do with Gilligan's story or the row with Campbell. There were hundreds, and every time I thought I'd found the last one, another file turned up. Then I had to forward them all to the legal team that was rapidly assembling in one of the BBC buildings in west London. Then, a few days later, on the hottest day of the year so far, I was summoned to a stuffy, airless, windowless room to meet a young member of Greg Dyke's staff who happened to be a lawyer, Magnus

Brooke. He would have made a brilliant journalist. Later, I tried to persuade him to join the *Today* staff as a kind of *consigliere* to work with our investigative reporters.

Brooke explained that now the job was to trawl through every email, note, document, script, fax and to make a comment on every one that was relevant. Oh .... and not just the ones I'd dug out from my own files. He patted the pile of six box files on the floor by his chair. They contained paperwork I'd never seen but might have some comment on in the light of events. Start with these, he said, and make sure you miss nothing; we're disclosing everything.

I'd already cancelled the family holiday. Not for the first time but that came with the job. And the loss of a few weeks in the Med was nothing compared to what the Kelly family had lost. How long have we got, I asked? A couple of days, Brooke said. He wanted to start writing the witness statement by the end of the week and that could take another five days or so, depending on how much I had to say.

It was unnerving. Looking over emails and notes I'd written months before, assuming every one of them would remain private. I wondered whether a judge could ever understand why I'd said what I'd said. Some were angry. Others frustrated. Yet others were quick notes I'd dashed off reflecting what I knew at the time. Many I'd forgotten about completely. Most were opaque or ambiguous. And with some, memory told me I'd meant one thing when the words on the page clearly said something quite different. But by the end of the week, I was done. And as the temperatures outside climbed higher and higher, we started putting together something that would make sense to a judge who'd never been near a newsroom.

It was exhausting. We worked up to ten hours a day in that windowless room deep inside the BBC's White City building, a silver ziggurat beside the M40. Outside, the temperature was ninety degrees plus. Inside, Brooke was quizzing me over every word. What did I mean by that? Why is there no reply to this? What conversation came before you wrote this? He wrote fast on an A4 pad that seemed to get magically typed up without me knowing quite how. Each evening, around seven, I'd emerge from White City into the humid blanket of a well-used summer's day. And each evening, I'd feel more remorse for the Kelly family, more responsible for everything that had happened.

After about a week, we were done. We finished on a Saturday, I think. I can't remember clearly. All the days had started to run one into another. But the one thing I do remember vividly was the sudden feeling that now, once I'd written that statement, I was alone. An outsider. I couldn't work out why.

In the days that followed, I went over a couple of times to the legal team's office in the White City building. In one room, the BBC's counsel Andrew Caldecott QC and the team of lawyers sat at tables set against the walls, surrounded by boxes, files, papers, speaking infrequently to each other in sharp half sentences, dipping into an obscurely complex narrative only they knew. In another room, a long table was covered in corporate snack food. Sandwiches, samosas, crudités, taramasalata, crisps and prawn tails deep fried in batter. Permanent lunch.

Neither time did I feel especially welcome. The first time, I assumed it was the pressure to get the work done. The second, there was an atmosphere. It seems that the legal team were having problems with my witness statement, though none of them mentioned it at the time. Years later, I learnt that some felt my testimony was 'toxic'. That it raised difficulties for the strategy they intended to run. And that it raised difficult questions for anyone who knew nothing about news and newsrooms: why hadn't I foreseen the impact the story would have; why hadn't I put it through a 'special' process, more like a *Panorama* than a daily news programme; why hadn't I called Gilligan in and grilled him like the inquiry inevitably would; why had I let him on air at all; and why had I reacted so aggressively to Campbell's first complaints?

All good questions. But, to me, only with hindsight. And only after Campbell's calculated decision to re-ignite the row had turned the story into something that it had never been, the allegations into something they never were.

The 'toxicity' emanated from that draft of Gilligan's appraisal that I'd sent to my immediate boss on 27 June, the 'good investigative journalism marred by flawed reporting' memo. It raised obvious questions: if I'd thought Gilligan's trouble with words was a 'millstone', why did I ever let him on air? Why, indeed, was he working for the BBC? Did other more senior BBC executives share my view? If they did, why had they defended him so forcefully? Why hadn't we admitted that, in one broadcast, he might not have reported the allegations exactly as he intended, exactly as he'd scripted? There was the risk, too, that a routine appraisal intended to prod Gilligan into correcting long-term problems would be misunderstood as a list of things that went wrong on a single occasion. The fear was, I discovered many years later, that I'd be 'ripped apart' in cross-examination.

The second time I went over there, I went into the lunch room and ran into Gilligan. 'It's surprising what you find out about people at times like this,' he said. Archly. I asked what he meant. It was the 27 June memo. I shrugged: 'But you knew that's what I think, I've told you often enough. You know it's true, too.' I wasn't going to apologise for the truth. Nor was I going to hang about dipping breadsticks into stale taramasalata while he and the legal team treated me like botulinum.

Hutton formally opened his inquiry on Friday 1 August promising that it would not be 'a trial conducted between interested parties who have conflicting cases to advance. I do not sit to decide between conflicting cases.' Judging between conflicting cases, in the event, was exactly what he did.

He said, too, that 'evidence may be given of decisions and conduct on the part of individuals which may subject them to criticism ... I will notify the relevant persons of possible criticisms which I consider might be made of them.' Something else that didn't turn out quite as promised. I was subject to any number of criticisms both during the inquiry and in Hutton's final report. Yet he never notified me nor gave me the opportunity to rebut them.

With the inquiry under way, I wasn't absolutely sure what I was expected to do. And no one seemed ready to tell me. Sit tight, I supposed. Follow the inquiry through the transcripts on the website, I guessed. Plus, I still had the business of running *Today*, though it was hard to focus on that. I assumed I'd get a couple of days' notice before I was needed. So I sat tight.

And the days got hotter and hotter.

I wasn't called and, as August drew on, the BBC's strategy began to alarm me. We seemed to have decided to admit mistake after mistake. Some we could have conceded from the very start. Others were mistakes Gilligan had admitted to the inquiry but not to Dyke, Sambrook and me during the row with Campbell. He told the inquiry that Dr Kelly hadn't used the phrase 'sexed up' unprompted, for example. That wasn't something he'd told us. He admitted to Hutton, too, that Dr Kelly had never said the government 'probably knew' the 45-minute claim 'was wrong'. That he'd never said the claim wasn't in the dossier's early drafts *because* it was single sourced: it wasn't in the early drafts *and* it was single sourced ... but the first wasn't the consequence of the second. Nor had Dr Kelly ever used the phrase that 'Downing Street ordered more facts to be discovered'. It didn't matter that some of Gilligan's inferences turned out to be true. His error was to attribute them to his single, anonymous source.

It would have helped, too, if he hadn't varied his descriptions of his source: 'involved in' or 'in charge of' the dossier. And if he hadn't tripped over phrases like 'intelligence community' or confused it with 'the agencies'.

It was right to admit these mistakes. It's what you would expect of the BBC. But we were also 'admitting' mistakes which had never been made, most of which, it seemed, were being laid at my door. That Gilligan had no script, an 'admission' that carried with it the implication that I hadn't properly considered what Gilligan intended to say. We even implied that it was only after Gilligan's 'live and unscripted' first broadcast and Downing Street's denial that we realised we'd made a mistake which we 'corrected' an hour later. That was completely untrue. So was the 'admission' that we hadn't contacted the government about the allegations the evening before.

By the end of August, what was coming out of BBC witnesses seemed to me to be drifting so far from what I knew to be the truth that I tried to persuade the lawyers to put me in the witness box. I knew it was damaging me and, probably, the BBC too.

It never occurred to me that the corporation's interest and mine might no longer be the same.

•••

It's impossible to know why Lord Hutton didn't think it necessary to hear my evidence. It meant he never understood the 'editorial system' at *Today* and that his conclusions about it were flawed. It's difficult to understand, too, why the BBC didn't insist he hear from me.

The legal team said at the time that we'd have our worst days when our own people were in the box. That turned out to be true. Gilligan's appearances were devastating, Gavyn Davies's not always helpful.[†] Witnesses, under the pressure of

---

† For example, under cross-examination, Gavyn Davies said 'there is a higher bar of certainty to get into, for example, a news bulletin. One thing I would like to add … is if it appears on a news broadcast in the voice of a BBC newscaster, then the bar of certainty is higher. And it is interesting to me in this case that what was said on the news broadcast at 6 o'clock was actually somewhat different from what was said at 6.07.'

the occasion, have a tendency to fall over themselves, appear self-contradictory and stutter out apparently incriminating half-truths.

Some senior BBC executives shared with me another theory. One told me he believed the decision to keep me out of the box was a calculated one. Everything, he told me, could then be heaped on me: failure to control Gilligan; failure to consider what he was intending to say; failure to put the DG and others in the picture about his shortcomings; failure to approach the government with the allegations. But it could only work, his theory was, if I never had the opportunity to give my account.

I don't happen to believe any of that. But I do believe that when the decision was made to 'admit everything', its consequences for me weren't high on anyone's list of things to think about.

Whatever, it meant that the only defence of *Today*'s 'editorial system' came from the Head of News, Richard Sambrook, even though he could only be expected to know it in outline. He was put in a position, too, where he was required to explain that 27 June 'toxic' memo – a bizarre turn of events since it was part of the BBC's case that no one in the hierarchy above my immediate boss, Steve Mitchell, had seen it before it was disclosed to the inquiry. Even so, both Hutton and the BBC thought it acceptable that Sambrook should be asked to speculate on what I'd meant and why I'd written it.

He did the best job he could under the pressure of cross-examination and I'm grateful to him for that. He was helped at first by the incomplete preparation of the government's counsel, Jonathan Sumption QC. He began with the incorrect assumption that the memo had been addressed to a completely different 'Stephen', the Controller of Editorial Policy at the time, Stephen Whittle, and not my immediate boss, Stephen Mitchell. Then he wanted to know whether Sambrook had 'discussed with Mr Marsh his views as reflected in this document?' That was a tough one given the strategy. But Sambrook wasn't going to mislead anyone.

'I had discussed, before this document, in broad terms, his views of Andrew Gilligan as a reporter and indeed with Stephen Mitchell, yes.' It was the best he could do. And he made a precise point that Hutton ignored. For dull, boring, bureaucratic reasons the memo never made it up the hierarchy. It was never intended that it should. It did no more than capture a view of Gilligan that was already well known and much discussed.

'Should he have seen the memo?' Sumption wanted to know. 'I think if Kevin Marsh or Stephen Mitchell had had real concerns about the nature of his reporting … I would have expected them to bring those to my attention. I am not clear that this email necessarily represents serious concerns.'

What Sambrook meant by that was the kind of serious concerns that would have meant dealing with the row with Campbell in a different way. Concerns that went beyond those that we all already shared. But the phrase 'serious concerns' attracted Hutton's attention straight away. 'You think it does not represent serious concerns?' he intoned. It was a bad moment.

Sambrook tried to explain that the email was actually a bog standard draft appraisal note, setting out 'how things should be managed in the future'. That, too, was a hostage to fortune. But for the time being, Sumption was keen to hammer the point home: 'Is it not a source of concern if grave allegations are made against public figures on the basis of loose use of language and lack of judgement in the phraseology?'

The only truthful answer to that question was 'yes'. But that was why I'd insisted Gilligan write a script. But the decision to 'admit' Gilligan had no script for the 6.07 two-way blocked that response. Sambrook bit his lip and did his best: 'If that is their view, then it would be, yes.'

He tried once more to explain the point of the email. That Gilligan was capable of sniffing out good stories but could be a shambles on air. 'The view I had had for a considerable period of time and which was certainly partly informed by Mr Marsh and by Mr Mitchell which was that Andrew Gilligan was in some respects a good reporter.'

'There are two aspects to journalism,' he went on. 'There is the finding out of the information and there is then how you present it. My view from some time would be that Andrew Gilligan is extremely good at finding out information but there are sometimes questions of nuance and subtlety in how he presents it which are not all they should be.'

Back in April, Sambrook had given a similar account to the governors. Then, he'd said Gilligan 'painted in primary colours'.

Sumption hadn't finished but it was absurd. A conversation between two men about a note of which neither was the author and whose meaning and significance had been changed entirely by the circumstances in which it was now being read.

Sumption characterised the rest of the email as 'lessons to be learnt'. That was misleading, but it was an idea he stretched to the furthest possible point, inferring, incorrectly, that it must represent what had gone wrong prior to Gilligan's broadcasts.

Again, Sambrook's hands were tied by the masochism strategy: 'No. I do not think you can necessarily draw the conclusion from these proposals that they are things that failed to happen on this occasion. I think they are simply an encapsulation of what Kevin's view of good practice would be.'

Sumption wasn't to be deterred: 'He is not outlining good practice in the past, he is proposing changes to the future. All these bullet points are proposed changes which represent lessons learnt from what had actually happened over these broadcasts.' That was wrong. Sambrook tried to explain why. But he was the wrong person to do that.

Sumption asked: 'Does it look as if he did not discuss this piece in good time, face to face, with Gilligan?' In fact, something better than that had happened, though not face to face. Gilligan had discussed his story with the day editor. She'd then discussed it with me. I'd asked questions. She'd gone back to Gilligan. I'd asked more questions … and so on. Something similar had happened with the night editor, too, who'd also been the first to look over Gilligan's script, filed in the middle of the night. In other words, there were several separate minds testing Gilligan's story. The point wasn't that his story hadn't been discussed in good time. It was that, once again, I'd had to strong-arm him into it. That was what I wanted to change. In future, I wanted him to take responsibility for bringing his stories to me rather than me having to chase him down.

Sumption went on: 'Does it not look as if no explicit credibility tests had been passed at editorial level before the piece was broadcast?' Again, a reading that seemed to me to be calculated to make the editorial process look as shabby as possible. The truth was, I knew more about Gilligan's source for this story than almost any other source whose allegations I'd ever broadcast. And the source passed every test. But again, we'd had to squeeze that out of Gilligan and again it was something I had wanted to change. I had wanted him to volunteer that kind of information in future.

And then the most damaging of all, to me and to the BBC. Sumption read out another bullet point from the memo: 'that we agree on a core script or on core elements of a script that he does not subsequently vary. That was clearly something that did not happen in the case of the 6.07 broadcast.' Sambrook had few options. The strategy was to 'admit' there'd been no script, not that there'd been a script and Gilligan had drifted off it. 'That is true,' he said. Sumption closed in: 'And [it] had particularly serious consequences in the light of what was actually said?' Again, Sambrook had no choice: 'As it appears now, yes.'

I was more than alarmed now. I was angry. The 'no-script' myth had got out of control. It was hurting us. It would hurt me, I knew that.

It had begun with one of Gilligan's many surprising moments in the witness box. On the first morning of BBC evidence, when Gilligan was giving his evidence in chief, Hutton's counsel, James Dingemans, asked: 'Was this contribution to the programme scripted?' Gilligan replied: 'No, it was not.' He didn't quite realise that wouldn't be understood in the way he intended.

Dingemans then asked: 'So this was you speaking from the studio or from home?'

Gilligan: 'From home. I have an ISDN line at home because it is an early morning programme. This is me speaking live and unscripted.'

Hutton's ears pricked up: 'You are speaking?' Gilligan: 'Speaking live and unscripted.' Dingemans: 'Live and unscripted.' Gilligan: 'Yes.'

Then, when Gilligan was forced to concede that Dr Kelly hadn't told him 'actually the government probably, erm, knew that that 45-minute figure was wrong, even before it decided to put it in' he added: 'With the benefit of hindsight, looking at it now with a fine toothcomb, I think it was not wrong, what I said, but it was not perfect either, and in hindsight I should have scripted that too ... it would be better if I had scripted that item.'

Whatever Gilligan intended, the impression he gave was that he was speaking off the top of his head. That no preparation had gone into what he intended to say. That he hadn't discussed it with anyone and that there was no script of any kind. But the truth was, he had worked out the way he was going to report the allegations and he'd captured that in his script. My night editor had seen it first, then I'd seen it and passed it for broadcast. There were other scripts too – one for the news bulletins which he'd sent to the newsroom – all of which were part of the process of working out exactly how to phrase the allegations. And by dawn on 29 May, when he made the first of his broadcasts, Gilligan knew exactly how every BBC editor planning to run his story, including me and the overnight editor at *Today*, expected him to word those allegations. We'd all considered carefully the words he *intended* to use. But once the mic was live for his first appearance of the morning, for a host of banal reasons, he went off-piste.

To someone who's never worked in broadcasting, that phrase 'live and unscripted' seems pretty unequivocal. 'Live' is clear enough. It means 'not recorded'; the listener is hearing the words as they're actually being said. 'Unscripted' isn't quite so clear. It's a format in which the reporter doesn't sound as if they're reading the words from a script. It's more chatty and there will often be some banter between the presenter and the reporter. But it never means the reporter is talking off the top of his or her head or making it up as he or she goes along. They'll always have worked out what they want to say and, where the precise words matter, they'll have worked out carefully and precisely the wording they intend to use.

On *Today*, the vast majority of 'live and unscripted' two-ways in the first hour of the programme are tasters for a substantive report later on. That's how it was with Gilligan; his substantive piece was due to be broadcast at 7.32. In all these cases, the reporter writes the substantive script first, especially if it's contentious or relies on precise quotations. Once it's written, a producer and then the output editor checks it. There'll be some discussion, parts may be rewritten and, eventually, it will be passed for broadcast.

That, then, is the 'story'. That's exactly what you expect to hear on air, certainly any key quotes and allegations, both in the substantive piece and in the early two-way. For the substantive piece, the reporter will read or record the script verbatim. And that script will be the basis, the 'core script', for the two-way. Some will even rewrite that 'core script' in the form of a two-way, handing the presenter the questions to ask. Many court reporters on *PM* used to do exactly that. Whatever the approach, though, 'unscripted' doesn't mean what Hutton was allowed to believe. It doesn't mean 'without forethought and prior editorial approval'.

I expected Gilligan to have his script in front of him for that 6.07 two-way. I expected to hear the allegations expressed exactly as they were in the script. I certainly didn't expect him to use different words, changing both meaning and attribution.

I would have liked to have explained this to Lord Hutton.

• • •

The absence of evidence from me had another consequence for the BBC's case. It undermined the argument that the BBC wasn't making allegations itself but reporting those of a credible, authoritative source. It was a line of defence based on an emerging area of media law – the so-called 'Reynolds Defence' – a defence firmly based on the diligence and responsibility of the journalism that went into reporting those allegations.

It's been argued that Lord Hutton misunderstood the law. But it's also the case that even a judge who was on top of media law would have found it difficult to see diligence and responsibility in the image the BBC allowed to be formed of the journalism that had gone into Gilligan's broadcasts.

In his conclusions, Lord Hutton said starkly: 'False accusations of fact impugning the integrity of others, including politicians, should not be made by the media.'

On the face of it, that seems a reasonable enough thing to say. It's obvious that false accusations impugning the integrity of others tend not to help the world go well. Nor does any ethical journalist set out to write or broadcast something they know to be false. But journalism isn't quite that simple. It never has been and never could be unless it were never to report anything disputed or contentious.

All journalists know that there are some areas of life where their reporting is protected by the law precisely so that they can report allegations that may well turn out to be false but which impugn the integrity of others. The courts, for example. During every trial, claims and counter-claims are made of criminality and wrongdoing. Many are false – that's inevitable in an adversarial system. Yet lawyers and witnesses who make such allegations have absolute protection, or 'absolute privilege'. They can't be sued for defamation. And to ensure justice is seen to be done, journalists who report such allegations made in court are protected by 'qualified privilege'. The qualification being that their reporting must be accurate, fair and contemporaneous.

Something similar is true of Parliament. MPs and peers can throw whatever allegations they like, true or false, across the floor of either house knowing that they enjoy 'absolute privilege'. The law can't touch them, nor the journalists who report their words accurately, fairly and contemporaneously.

Towards the end of the last century, media organisations started to argue that some types of political argument outside the narrow confines of a legislative chamber should attract a similar 'qualified privilege', as should some kinds of responsible investigative journalism. And the Law Lords tended to agree. So long as the journalism was demonstrably careful and responsible. The idea was to protect serious-minded journalism done in good faith which reported allegations the journalist believed to be true at the time, based on the evidence they had. Which included reporting the allegations of a credible, authoritative source.

It became known as the 'Reynolds Defence' because it sprang out of a libel action that the former Irish Prime Minister, Albert Reynolds, brought in 1994 against the *Sunday Times*. It was a highly contentious action, full of complex appeals and counter-appeals that went, eventually, to the House of Lords.

The *Sunday Times* had argued that they were simply reporting a vicious political argument, including allegations of misleading the Irish Parliament. They were making no allegations of their own but faithfully reporting allegations made by those involved in the argument. Their lawyers argued that such reporting was protected by 'qualified privilege' in much the same way it would have been if the allegations had been made in the Irish Parliament. And that they'd only lose that privilege if they knew at the time the allegations were false, or didn't care one way or the other or if they published the allegations out of spite or some other improper motive.

The *Sunday Times* lost the substantive action. Reynolds was awarded damages of just one penny and faced with also paying his own costs. He appealed. The *Sunday Times* cross-appealed. They lost again. Reynolds won both a retrial and a ruling that the newspaper couldn't depend on 'qualified privilege' at the new trial. The *Sunday Times* appealed and the question went to the House of Lords.

Five years after the original action, in October 1999, the Law Lords led by Lord Nicholls of Birkenhead rejected the *Sunday Times*'s attempt to extend 'qualified privilege' to all political argument. But they did decide that there was already sufficient flexibility in the law to ensure that 'interference with freedom of speech ... be confined to what is necessary' and that a court could give 'appropriate weight, in today's conditions, to the importance of freedom of expression by the media on all matters of public concern'. And Lord Nicholls set out ten considerations that might be used to arrive at that 'appropriate weight'. These included:

> The seriousness of the allegation; the nature of the information, and the extent to which it's a matter of public concern; the source; the steps taken to verify the information; the status of the information, especially if it's already been the subject of an investigation which commands respect; urgency; whether comment was sought from the person against whom the allegations are made – though an approach to the plaintiff [claimant] will not always be necessary; whether the article contained the gist of the plaintiff's [claimant's] side of the story; the tone of the article, whether it simply raises queries or calls for an investigation; the circumstances of the publication, including the timing.

In other words, news organisations might now argue that their journalists had a degree of legal protection if they reported an allegation that they couldn't know beyond all doubt was 'true', perhaps even turned out not to be true, but did it diligently, responsibly, without malice and in the public interest. In the years following Hutton, other cases made their way to the House of Lords which fleshed out the 'Reynolds' principle, all making more clear the circumstances in which journalism has this protection.

Hutton took a very much more restricted view, however. It's worth reading his conclusion in full:

> Counsel for the BBC and for Mr Gilligan were right to state that the communication by the media of information (including information obtained by investigative reporters) on matters of public interest and importance is a vital part of life in a democratic society. However the right to communicate such information is subject to the qualification (which itself exists for the benefit of a democratic society) that false accusations of fact impugning the integrity of others, including politicians, should not be made by the media. Where a reporter is intending to broadcast or publish information impugning the integrity of others the management of his broadcasting company or newspaper should ensure that a system is in place whereby his editor or editors give careful consideration to the wording of the report and to whether it is right in all the circumstances to broadcast or publish it.

As far as the second part of that goes, Hutton heard no evidence of the 'system' that was in place 'whereby his editor or editors give careful consideration to the wording of the report and to whether it is right in all the circumstances to broadcast or publish it'. He therefore assumed there was no system. Had he asked, I could have explained both the system and what had happened on the day.

But it's the first part that is both wrong and ill thought out. To support his reading of the Reynolds principles, Hutton quotes from three of the Law Lords who delivered that final judgment. But those quotes are selective and give the appearance that Lords Nicholls, Cooke and Hobhouse took as repressive a view as he did. They did not.

Hutton prefigured his eventual view during the BBC counsel Andrew Caldecott's closing speech to the inquiry. As he advanced the argument that the BBC had reported Dr Kelly's allegations, not made them itself, Hutton interjected that 'as regards the person who is the object of the criticism it matters little to him ... that the report does not directly allege the misconduct on his ... part'.

Caldecott countered: 'To the person criticised it will still remain a serious charge even if it is not adopted as true ... a hearsay charge can still be very serious in its consequences.' But, he went on: 'In the context of public interest issues there is a quite separate consideration as to the value of the material in the public interest ... it is very important that publishers make clear whether it is their conclusion after thorough investigation or whether it is merely the conclusion of the source which they are reporting.'

But here was another drawback to this line of argument. We knew and had conceded that Gilligan hadn't maintained the distinction between reporting his source and his own inferences during that that sleepy 6.07 two-way. It wasn't the only weakness.

To make the defence stick, we needed to produce the strongest evidence we could that we'd satisfied most if not all of Nicholls's 'ten points'. Without my evidence, that was impossible.

Take the 'steps taken to verify the information'. The only evidence that Hutton heard was Gilligan's account of the steps he took to decide whether or not to offer his story to the *Today* newsdesk. But he was allowed to think they were the only steps taken. They were not. Once Gilligan had offered his story, I had to decide whether or not to broadcast it. But Hutton knew nothing about that. The omission was fatal to this part of the BBC's case. But it was compounded by those 'admissions' of mistakes that weren't made. Together, they suggested that where there should have been careful, responsible journalism and editorial diligence there'd been a vacuum.

CHAPTER NINE

HOW THE DOSSIER WAS WRITTEN

If the cause be not good, the king himself hath a heavy reckoning to make ... if these men do not die well, it will be a black matter for the king that led them to it ...

Henry V, Act 4, Scene 1

It wasn't in Lord Hutton's remit to find the 'truth' of the September dossier. Many hoped he would, though, especially those who'd always opposed the war and those who believed we'd gone into that war on a false prospectus. They were disappointed.

It was his remit, however, to investigate the circumstances surrounding Dr Kelly's death. And it's hard to see how it was possible to do that without understanding why it was that Dr Kelly felt moved to share with journalists concerns within the intelligence community about the dossier. There's an unbroken thread that connects the way intelligence was used, the way the dossier was written and the conversations Dr Kelly had with those journalists in private and the pressure he came under once his name had become public.

Hutton made it his business, though it was never his remit either, to judge that the allegations Gilligan reported were 'unfounded' and that the journalism that went into reporting those allegations was shoddy and unreliable. That the 'editorial system' was 'defective'. Again, it's hard to see how it was possible to come to that conclusion without carefully comparing Dr Kelly's allegations and Gilligan's reports with a critical assessment of the way Alastair Campbell and John Scarlett produced the dossier.

He threw an extraordinary amount of energy into drilling down to the detail of Gilligan's reporting – including a wholly irrelevant diversion into the internal clocks and file structures of the Sharp personal organiser on which Gilligan claimed to have made the notes of his meeting with Dr Kelly – while accepting the government's account of the dossier's production without serious question.

Perhaps because Lord Hutton was so incurious, millions of words have been sacrificed since to finding the 'truth' of the dossier and the way it used intelligence. Some in official inquiries and reports. Many more in newspaper articles, academic studies and on campaigning websites. The former Head of the Home Civil Service, Lord Butler, looked specifically at how intelligence was used in the run-up to war. Sir John Chilcot has covered similar ground. And the Intelligence and Security Committee of MPs took a closer look at the dossier in their 2004 annual report.

The fact is, there'll never be a definitive account of how the dossier was produced. Indeed, it's not always clear what exactly those using the word 'dossier' actually mean. Do they mean it to refer to the many documents and drafts that had been in production from the beginning of 2002? Or only to the work begun and completed during September? Do they mean the entire document published on 24 September 2002 – including the foreword drafted for the Prime Minister by Alastair Campbell? Or do they mean only the executive summary and main body – the parts 'owned' by the JIC?

As to the production process itself, as Lord Butler found, much business in Blair's Downing Street went unrecorded. 'Sofa government' it was called. Plus, all that was recorded in memos, memoirs and diaries was inevitably subjective, often contradictory and never more than a tantalising snapshot. Not because things were being deliberately concealed but because that's the way the world is. As time has passed, the accounts of all those involved have tended to be burnished and revised. And there has been, inevitably, a degree of convergence.

It's been too easy to fill in the blanks with preconceptions and prejudices. To 'prove' Campbell and Blair lied. To 'prove' those 'lies' nudged the country into an illegal, ill-judged war. To 'prove' Blair was always intent on invasion, that he'd signed 'a deal in blood' with President Bush. To 'prove' the diplomacy and the search for a UN Security Council resolution in the winter and spring of 2002–3 was deception. And, to cover it all up, to 'prove' that Dr Kelly was murdered. Many theories lurk at the furthest reaches of what is credible. Some beyond it. All of them assume, as conspiracy theorists tend to, that an evil, all-knowing, controlling mind and hand directs political events.

I don't believe a word of any of these theories. Real life isn't like that.

At the same time, serious-minded dogged campaigners, Freedom of Information researchers and investigative journalists have laboured with a determination that few of us could ever muster to uncover and analyse documents that take us as close to the truth as we're likely to get. Even now, more are revealed almost every week.

From their work and from other sources, a picture emerges of the attitudes and mindsets inside Downing Street. How minds were made up and fixed, even when the facts changed. Most importantly, how it was that Blair's belief that Saddam was a real and present danger trumped any evidence to the contrary.[†] And how those around Blair developed a faith that

---

† Tony Blair writes in *A Journey* (p.407): 'The overall impact of the intelligence was not that he had given up on his programme but that he was hiding it from the inspectors. I was specifically told this intelligence confirmed his WMD programme. So far from being a warning to desist, it confirmed the need to persist ... The truth is, we believed without any doubt at all that Saddam had an active WMD programme.'

the Prime Minister was right, though the facts said he was wrong. We see how that faith caused those at the very top of intelligence and government to chop and shape the intelligence to justify Blair's beliefs. It was that chopping and shaping that some in the intelligence community thought was wrong. This picture is fundamental to understanding the circumstances surrounding Dr Kelly's death.

We all owe these journalists and researchers a huge debt of gratitude. Theirs is a monumental public service and their determined, detailed scrutiny has probably ensured that no government will ever attempt such a deception again.

For what it's worth, I never believed the dossier was a 'lie', nor did I or anyone else I know at the BBC ever say that it was, in spite of Campbell's constant accusations. Nor did I ever use the phrase that many others did, that 'we went to war on a lie'. Apart from anything else, the September dossier was only a small part of a huge, complex and nuanced debate. A political prop.

That said, it *was* a deception. Not because it made the case for war – Blair had every right to do that. He had every right to persuade us that his beliefs about Saddam were justified, even to tell us why his reading of the intelligence led him to those beliefs. What was not legitimate was to present to MPs and the public a dossier that included questionable intelligence in order to appear to support the Prime Minister's beliefs. The sad thing was, it was nothing exceptional, well within the norms of what we'd come to expect from New Labour's 'truth creation'.

The Prime Minister took us to war because he *believed* Saddam was an urgent threat. He *believed* Saddam had a current and growing WMD programme. He may even have *believed* he'd seen intelligence that endorsed his beliefs. But all the evidence now available suggests that there was no corroborated intelligence with a secure reporting line that said Saddam had such an active programme and plenty to suggest he might not have.

He told MPs the intelligence in the dossier was 'extensive, detailed and authoritative'. That intelligence 'concludes that Iraq has chemical and biological weapons, that Saddam has continued to produce them, that he has existing and active military plans for the use of chemical and biological weapons, which could be activated within forty-five minutes ... and that he is actively trying to acquire nuclear weapons capability'. He was asking MPs and the public to trust the intelligence agencies if the idea of trusting him stuck in their craw.

This isn't just pedantry. It was the gap between the dossier, its language and messages, and the language and messages of the intelligence that caused the concerns in the Defence Intelligence Staff, the concerns Dr Kelly described to journalists. That caused him to tell Susan Watts, the *Newsnight* journalist, that the dossier had gone over a line. 'You must realise sometimes that's not actually the right thing to say.'

Lord Hutton's conclusion on the dossier echoed that first Downing Street non-denial denial: 'Not one word was not the work of the Joint Intelligence Committee.' Downing Street was wrong to say that of the published dossier. 'The dossier was prepared and drafted by a small team of the assessment staff of the JIC...' he concluded. Again, that's not quite true of the published document. There was such a team but it wasn't the only team or group with its hands on the text. And that JIC assessment staff team never went near Blair's foreword. Campbell drafted that.

'Mr John Scarlett, the chairman of the JIC, had the overall responsibility for the drafting of the dossier...' That's true, but it hides more than it reveals and again raises the question of what is meant by 'the dossier'. In the early months of 2002, Scarlett was not responsible for any of the many attempts to put a dossier together. And when he finally took overall responsibility, he had no hand in the foreword, which he thought a purely 'political statement'.

'The dossier, which included the 45-minute claim, was

issued by the Government on 24 September 2002 with the full approval of the JIC...' Again, not untrue – but less than the full story. The JIC never met as a body to approve the dossier. The MI6 chief, Sir Richard Dearlove, even delegated reading the final text to a subordinate. And changes were made in Downing Street after the JIC members had seen it for the last time.

'The JIC, the most senior body in the Intelligence Services charged with the assessment of intelligence, approved the wording in the dossier...' That doesn't seem to have been the case. The JIC chairman, John Scarlett, was involved in determining the wording of that part of the published dosser that he 'owned'. But the agencies whose heads sit on the JIC were less concerned with the precise wording than with avoiding any risk of it jeopardising their people or operations. And the wording changed after they'd seen it for the last time.

'The 45-minute claim was based on a report which was received by the SIS from a source which that service regarded as reliable...' Yet MI6 had doubts about the 45-minute claim from the moment it came in. The immediate source was 'reliable'. But the claim came initially from a sub-source that MI6 knew little or nothing about. How likely is it that that Downing Street knew nothing about these doubts?

'Ten Downing Street wanted the dossier to be worded to make as strong a case as possible in relation to the threat posed by Saddam Hussein's WMD...' That's the contradiction at the heart of the dossier. The contradiction that meant the JIC chairman, John Scarlett, may have been 'subconsciously influenced ... to make the wording of the dossier somewhat stronger than it would have been if it had been contained in a normal JIC assessment'. Hutton could have, and perhaps should have, appreciated that what 'transformed' the dossier wasn't just what went into it. It was also what was left out or taken out – its conclusions, for example, or the qualifications and uncertainties attached to the questionable intelligence.

Only with those omissions was the dossier 'somewhat stronger then ... a normal JIC assessment', apparently supporting Blair's beliefs.

The contradiction and the omissions that were necessary to deliver the dossier Blair needed caused very serious concerns amongst the analysts in the Defence Intelligence Staff. One of their senior managers, Dr Brian Jones, an old friend and colleague of Dr Kelly, told Hutton about these concerns. Hutton concluded that they 'were considered by higher echelons in the Intelligence Services and were not acted upon...' They certainly weren't acted upon. But that was less because they were considered, more because they were trumped by the sudden production of a piece of mystery intelligence they weren't allowed to see.

Hutton appeared not to see how vital it was to understand how the dossier had been produced if he was also to understand how Dr Kelly came to take his own life. Indeed, when his counsel was able to question some of the senior figures who'd been central to writing and producing the dossier, he failed to ask a significant question about it. Did Hutton regard this as outside his remit?

• • •

At the turn of the millennium, Blair's government fretted, but no more than that, about 'rogue states'. North Korea was on track to develop nuclear-tipped ballistic missiles. Libya and Iran had weapons of mass destruction, saw themselves as 'outlaws' and had a record of supporting terrorists, even engaging themselves in state terror. Iraq's psychopathic dictator, Saddam Hussein, seemed to some to have the lot: chemical and biological weapons that he'd used on his own people, a recent history of invading neighbours, a nuclear weapons programme. His activities had been curtailed, however, by a system of UN weapons inspections put in place after the 1991

Gulf War. The inspectors had since been withdrawn but still, the state of alarm over the 'rogue states' was set at 'watch' rather than 'act'.

The 9/11 attacks changed all that. Something indefinable became urgent. What had been, until then, tolerated was now intolerable. The fear was that WMD, 'rogue states', global and state terror would come together with consequences even more devastating than those suffered by lower Manhattan and the Pentagon.

At first, though, it wasn't a 'rogue state' that rose to the top of the West's to-do list. It was a failed state. Afghanistan. Its ruling regime, the Taliban, had given support to Osama bin Laden and al Qaeda. And though the 9/11 hijackers were mostly Saudi, as was Osama bin Laden, it was Afghanistan that had to be dealt with.

It was. Quickly.

'Operation Enduring Freedom', mounted by the US and Britain in tandem with the Northern Alliance of local tribal powers, toppled the Taliban in a little over five weeks.

Policymakers in London and Washington were already assuming that regime change in Afghanistan was just a prologue. Bush said as much. In his 'Axis of Evil' speech, his State of the Union address to Congress on 29 January 2002, he captured the certainties and anxieties of the moment. He reported that 'the American flag flies again over our embassy in Kabul. Terrorists who once occupied Afghanistan now occupy cells at Guantanamo Bay. And terrorist leaders who urged followers to sacrifice their lives are running for their own.' But there were questions, too. In Afghanistan itself, there was a long way to go and no road map. As for the other rogue states … what?

Few thought the US, with or without allies, could intervene in Libya, North Korea, Iran or Iraq as swiftly and decisively as they had in a basket case like Afghanistan, though it wasn't off the White House agenda. Bush told Congress his purpose was to 'prevent regimes that sponsor terror from threatening

America or our friends and allies with weapons of mass destruction'. That could mean anything from inspection regimes and sanctions to full-scale land invasion.

And top of his list was Saddam Hussein's Iraq. Here was a man who'd 'plotted to develop anthrax and nerve gas and nuclear weapons' and led a regime that 'has already used poison gas to murder thousands of its own citizens'.

Cue the major chords. 'States like these, and their terrorist allies, constitute an axis of evil ... America will do what is necessary to ensure our nation's security.'

'An axis of evil.' Any speechwriter would have clapped their hands at the phrase. Originally, Bush speechwriter no. 1, David Frum, had it as 'axis of hatred'. It was speechwriter no. 2, Michael Gerson, who burnished it from 'hatred' to 'evil'.

Blair shared Bush's new sense of urgency and, in the light of that urgency, he commissioned a briefing paper. One that was never supposed to emerge into the light outside Downing Street. It drew on every available source and tried to explain the new sense of urgency over North Korea, Iran, Libya and Iraq.

Blair liked it, in the sense that it was a powerful, rhetorical capture of the new sentiment in London and Washington. And even though much of it was based on secret intelligence, he floated the idea of publishing it. Or something drawn from it. He wanted to tell the British public why sentiments had changed and why he now thought something had to be done about the 'rogue states'. Why he wanted to turn the dial from 'watch' to 'act'.

This was where the idea of a dossier was born. At the beginning of 2002 and in the shadow of 9/11.

From the purely political point of view, the idea was persuasive. Share a version of the intelligence that was shaping Blair's beliefs, or at least the government's assessment of that intelligence. It came and went until the following autumn. But in the spring, when the idea was still fresh, a section of the Cabinet Office called the Overseas and Defence Secretariat (ODS), headed by Blair's foreign policy advisor Sir David Manning, picked up the work and set out to prepare what was called a 'four nations paper'.

At the end of February, the first draft – called 'WMD Programmes of Concern' – was circulated to the agencies, MI5, MI6 and the Government Communications Headquarters (GCHQ), to the technical analysts who made up the Defence Intelligence Staff, to the Foreign Office and to Downing Street. It was unclassified, though not public. Again, Blair liked what he saw and since the idea of publishing something was still current, Julian Miller, the head of the Joint Intelligence Committee's Assessments Staff, was asked to produce a second draft.

Miller and his team went about that draft in much the same way they produced their routine intelligence assessments for the JIC, assessments that went up to ministers to inform policy. It was careful, almost academic. The debates were finely detailed as regional, military and technical experts on North Korea, Libya, Iran and Iraq disputed and corrected each other's facts, nuanced judgements and honed the language. There were even some who wondered, why these four rogue states? By 6 March, the second draft was ready.

At the same time, Manning's ODS was working on a paper for Blair that looked at options on Iraq only. It hit Blair's desk two days after the 'four nations paper', on 8 March, and walked the Prime Minister through options that, in the event, he took. It's a very important paper, but Hutton didn't know about it. Downing Street never disclosed it – they were very much more selective in their disclosures than the BBC. And while Lord Hutton's counsel James Dingemans questioned Manning closely on Dr Kelly's role in the production of the dossier and about what was right and proper in an 'intelligence' dossier that was made public, he showed little curiosity about Manning's role in influencing Blair's beliefs nor his role in the September dossier's many precursors and 'feeder' documents. This March paper was one of those and was very influential.

Manning was close to Blair, who'd hand-picked the career diplomat to take on the role of his Foreign Policy advisor in September 2001, just before the world changed. He was close, too, to the head of MI6, Sir Richard Dearlove, partly through the agency's 'new weight' in the system. They travelled regularly together to and from Washington.

It's almost comical, now, to read the transcript of the questions Manning was asked about his own role in the dossier. After he'd confirmed that he was foreign policy advisor to the Prime Minister and also the head of the Overseas and Defence Secretariat in the Cabinet Office, Dingemans asked:

Q. So you were in post effectively at the time that the dossier was being written and prepared?

A. Yes, I was.

Q. Did you have anything to do with the preparation of the dossier?

A. I was aware of the preparation surrounding the dossier. I was not actually involved in drafting it.

Q. Right. And you had nothing to do with any of the intelligence aspects to it?

A. No. I would have seen some of the intelligence that went into the dossier but I was certainly not involved primarily with the intelligence.

And that was it as far as Manning's own role in the dossier was concerned. What did he mean by 'primarily'?

It seems clear that Hutton saw any investigation of Manning's role as beyond his remit. And that lack of curiosity helped him form the impression that the dossier began its life on 3 September 2002, rather than stumbling uncertainly into existence, as it did, over the six months before that.[†]

---

† Alastair Campbell writes in his diary for Thursday 24 September 2002: 'Dossier day after months of waiting'.

We know about Manning's March paper because it was one of six documents leaked to the *Daily Telegraph*'s Defence Correspondent Michael Smith in September 2004. It is as direct as it was intended to remain secret. There is, it says, nothing to suggest that Saddam is any greater threat at the beginning of 2002 than he had been for the previous decade. Intelligence was patchy, but in spite of that Manning states unequivocally that Saddam continues to develop WMD. And what marked him out from other dictators was the fact that he was the only one who'd ever used them. And he could do so again, Manning writes, if he felt his regime threatened – that might include delivering 'chemical and biological weapons by a variety of means, including its ballistic missile warheads'.

It's impossible to know for certain how much this assessment of the threat from Saddam influenced Blair and shaped his beliefs. It certainly reflected attitudes in Washington, attitudes that Blair had himself heard there. And it represented a strand of thinking that carries all the way through to the September dossier.

Manning's paper also sets out options for dealing with the threat. He writes that there are two in theory, but only one in reality. It was a theoretical option to toughen containment: press to get weapons inspectors back into Iraq and hold Saddam to a disarmament regime. But, Manning argues, that's a stop-gap measure; it wouldn't reintegrate Iraq into the international community and Saddam would remain an outcast if not an outlaw. The US has moved on, too, he reported. The Bush administration has lost faith in containment. For those around Bush, regime change is the only option – they'd been talking about it since the day after 9/11. The swift initial military success in Afghanistan, Washington's distrust of UN sanctions and inspection regimes, and the feeling since 1991 that Iraq was 'unfinished business' were all part of that thinking.

So at the beginning of March 2002, a month before Crawford, a month before Blair used the phrase 'regime change' in public for the first time, Blair's closest and most trusted foreign policy advisor is telling him that's the only realistic option. If he wants to stand shoulder to shoulder with Bush, that is.

There are three ways of bringing regime change about, Manning writes. Covert support for an uprising or coup; air support for opposition groups; or full-scale invasion. The last of those is 'the only certain means to remove Saddam and his elite', though, he adds, there's no legal justification for it. Manning closes by advising 'a staged approach ... establishing international support, building up pressure on Saddam and developing military plans. There is a lead time of about six months to a ground offensive.' And in that six months 'sensitising' the public is vital.

It would be too simplistic to see Manning's paper as a 'first draft' of the September dossier. But it absolutely is a first draft of the mindsets that went into making it. In it, we see attitudes in Downing Street taking shape; beliefs developing that Saddam continues to develop WMD, even though there's no intelligence to suggest it and all that they have is 'patchy', 'sporadic' and 'limited'; that regime change, almost certainly by invasion, is the only realistic option but presents a legal problem; and that the diplomatic, political, military, legal and propaganda strategies will all have to move in step. Especially propaganda – 'sensitising' the public.[†]

In the meantime, on 6 March, Miller had sent round his assessment team's second draft of the 'four nations' paper for more comments. He was now working on the assumption that something from it would definitely be made public and that brought important questions to the fore. There was very little 'real' intelligence to put in it. The Foreign Office thought that the intelligence they had on Iraq was 'weak' and that it was

---

† Less than a month after the September dossier was published, Vladimir Putin wryly told Campbell that it 'could be seen as a propagandistic step to influence public opinion'.

much stronger on, say, Libya. There were questions, too, about how exactly it should be presented to the public. Miller, an intelligence man through and through, noted that 'it may be buffed up somewhat by the presentational experts'.

The agencies had reservations, too. How should a public dossier acknowledge those judgements that drew on intelligence? Was it wise to publish material that could only have come from intelligence sources? And was there a risk of pushing intelligence assessments to show that the intelligence suggested that there was a new urgency about dealing with rogue states? That was, after all, the point of a public document.

The Joint Intelligence Committee chairman, John Scarlett, wrote that Alastair Campbell was 'standing ready to advise' on presenting the 6 March paper to a wider public. He noted, too, that in any public dossier, different sections would deal with facts and judgements differently. So, for example, the 6 March paper set out the main concerns and conclusions 'in very accessible form in the opening paragraphs. But the supporting detail is drafted a little more formally, to convey the sense that these difficult issues have been given authoritative treatment'. It was a pattern the September dossier was to follow. Particularly that line about 'conveying the sense of authoritative treatment'. That would be a huge plus in a political document issued by a government that fewer and fewer people trusted.

Campbell thought the 6 March draft was 'on the right lines' but suggested 'more detail'. Manning, who'd just completed that 'Iraq Options' paper for Blair, wanted the drafting team to take a hard look at the section on Iraq. While the Foreign Secretary, Jack Straw, put his finger on the main problem: that 'the paper has to show why there is an exceptional threat from Iraq. It does not quite do this yet.' Nevertheless, he felt that if a 'four nations' paper was to have impact, Iraq should come first.

The 'four nations paper' was close to completion. The

agencies still had reservations and the analysts at the Defence Intelligence Service were still finding factual errors, especially in the section dealing with Iraq's chemical weapons programme and its efforts to conceal it. But the plan was to finalise a text on 14 March and send it up to No. 10 the following day.

The final version was tweaked to highlight some of the 'unique features' of Saddam's threat but it was possible to highlight Iraq even further. In the covering note Scarlett sent to No. 10, he put it to Sir David Manning that: 'You may still wish to consider whether more impact could be achieved if the paper only covered Iraq. This would have the benefit of obscuring the fact that in terms of WMD, Iraq is not that exceptional.'

Around the end of March, someone killed the 'four nations paper'. No one seems to remember who. Campbell argued that there was such a focus on Iraq in the current debate that a paper that included Libya, Iran and North Korea would be trying to do too much. Or, as Scarlett might put it, would make it plain that, in terms of WMD, Iraq was not that exceptional. And the important thing Blair needed was a document that showed Saddam and his WMD *were* exceptional.

No one seems to have told everyone who'd been working on 'a dossier' that the idea was on ice, either. In the last two weeks of March, some officials were still expecting they'd have to produce something probably in the week between Easter, 31 March, and Blair's summit with Bush at his Crawford ranch on 6 and 7 April. But in that week, the dossier idea cooled to freezing point.

Publicly, Blair said that publishing a dossier then, just before the summit with Bush, would raise rather than lower the temperature. That was true. It would inevitably have cranked the debate up to maximum heat. But it's also true that, much as the Foreign Office and others were warning, there was very little to put in it that would make a compelling case. Peter Ricketts, the Political Director at the FCO, wrote that

Saddam's WMD programmes were worrying, 'but have not, as far as we know, been stepped up'. And in political terms, there was a risk that any attempt to single out Saddam and portray him as a unique and imminent threat would increase scepticism rather than swing opinion behind the government.

Just before the idea of a public dossier was put on ice, the Head of the Non-Proliferation Department at the Foreign Office, Tim Dowse, wrote down his thoughts on a troubling piece of work that had emerged from the intelligence analysts on the Defence Intelligence Staff (DIS). Those thoughts give an interesting insight into the relationship between the presentation of intelligence to the public and the content of that intelligence. An interesting insight, too, into the sense of what was permissible and what was not. During their work on the various papers over the spring, the DIS analysts had taken another look at all the available intelligence to re-calculate one of their estimates, the quantity of chemical weapon precursors they thought Saddam still had. This was an important figure since it could give some indication of the state of Saddam's weapon stocks, the extent of concealment as well as some pointer to the ease and speed with which Saddam could resume production.

When the analysts ran through the numbers again, they came up with an estimate that was lower than before. That was bad news for a dossier intended to show Saddam was an imminent and increasing threat. Dowse realised that changing the 'public line' would be unwelcome. But he had an idea how they could 'finesse the presentational difficulty'. Why not drop the measure they'd used so far, 'tonnes of precursor chemicals'. That would make it more difficult to make comparisons with previous DIS estimates. Instead, change the measure to 'precursor chemicals sufficient to produce X thousand Scud warheads/aerial bombs/122mm rockets filled with mustard gas/the deadly nerve agents tabun/sarin/VX'. Dowse admitted it wouldn't 'hoodwink a real expert, who would be able to reverse the calculation and work out that our assessment of precursor quantities had fallen. But the task would not be straightforward, and would be impossible for a layman. And the result would, I think, have more impact on the target audience for [an] unclassified paper.'

In the last two weeks of March and in the run-up to the Crawford summit, policy hardened. And so did the determination to stand 'shoulder to shoulder' with Bush. On 14 March, Manning reported back to Blair that he'd reassured President Bush's National Security Advisor Condoleezza Rice that Britain supported regime change in Iraq. Though he'd warned them, too, that the press, Parliament and public opinion would need careful management.

Three days later, on 17 March, the British Ambassador in Washington, Sir Christopher Meyer, told the US Deputy Secretary of Defense, Paul Wolfowitz, that his government intended to produce a dossier that they hoped would swing a critical mass of parliamentary and public opinion behind joint UK/US military action against Saddam. Though at the time, the idea was already cooling.

Not everyone was uncritical of the hardening stance. The Foreign Secretary, Jack Straw, warned the Prime Minister that the rewards of forcing regime change in Iraq would be few but the risks high. Both politically and personally. Straw was concerned that there was little enthusiasm and certainly no majority in the Parliamentary Labour Party for war. And while no Labour MP doubted Saddam was evil and would have preferred a world in which he didn't exist, there was a long way to go to convince them that regime change achieved by war was the answer. Many of them doubted that regime change by force could ever be legal and didn't think it would guarantee a compliant, law-abiding replacement regime.

Straw told Blair that, to win the argument, he must realise that 'the whole case against Iraq and in favour (if necessary) of military action needs to be narrated with reference to the international rule of law.' That meant a careful sequence of events leading to Saddam either accepting or refusing a new round of unrestricted weapons inspections. Straw genuinely believed there was mileage in the policy of containment and continued to do so until the very eve of war. He kept pushing for a new UN Security Council resolution – the 'second resolution' of journalistic shorthand during the rest of 2002 – backed by the threat of force and was convinced it could be negotiated. Straw never gave up on the idea that diplomacy could reduce and contain the threat from Saddam. But if Iraq remained defiant, a 'second resolution' would provide legal justification for war and swing enough opinion inside the Parliamentary Labour Party to give Blair the political support he would need.

By the week before the Crawford summit, however, Straw and his officials in the Foreign Office were increasingly out of the loop that mattered. One official who was at Straw's right hand throughout recalls that he and his boss believed at the time that they were seeing all the policy papers and communications with Washington in the normal way. But neither he nor, he believes, Straw saw any of the emails or direct communications between Downing Street and the White House. And that was where policy was really being made. Increasingly, Straw and the Foreign Office found themselves working on a policy parallel to the main one. Some insiders even saw Straw's efforts at the UN as no more than the erection of a tripwire.

Crawford was a turning point – but not the one it seemed at the time. Not because of the alleged 'deal in blood'. Blair had already turned to favouring regime change; he didn't need to go to Texas to be persuaded of that. His own foreign policy advisor had all but convinced him already. Nor was his commitment to stand shoulder to shoulder with Bush quite as simple-minded and poodle-esque as his critics have portrayed it. Crawford certainly firmed up the policy, but only along the lines that Manning had already mapped out.

Soon after Crawford, those around Blair started to recognise that the most important motivation driving Blair on was his belief. Manning, Powell, Straw and even John Scarlett kept telling him that the intelligence on Saddam was 'patchy'; that Saddam was a threat no bigger than he'd been for a decade; that his WMD would be a danger at some point ... but not right now. But lack of evidence for what he believed troubled Blair no more than the lack of evidence for 'The Creation' troubles a religious zealot. He answered his critics with an explicit or implicit 'trust me'. Many did trust him, but regretted it afterwards. 'He was right before when we didn't believe him' became a refrain. Increasingly, disbelief was suspended. Wise counsel went unoffered.

The day after Crawford, Monday 8 April, Blair delivered a speech at the George Bush Senior Presidential Library in Washington. In that speech, he used the phrase 'regime change' publicly for the first time: 'We must be prepared to act where terrorism or weapons of mass destruction threaten us ... If necessary the action should be military and again, if necessary and justified, it should involve regime change.'

There's no reason to think Blair wasn't honestly representing the way he saw possible support for Bush and military action. Inevitably, though, that phrase 'regime change' fed the 'deal in blood' theory, even though the idea of regime change had been rattling around Downing Street since the end of 2001. Nor was it synonymous with war. A diplomatic solution might force regime change. It's often forgotten, too, that in the US, regime change in Iraq was neither a neo-con obsession nor even controversial. It was a bipartisan policy and had been since 1998, when Clinton was in the White House.

The real impact of this speech though was its barely concealed plea to 'have faith and trust me'. Shortly after that reference to 'regime change', Blair reminded his audience that he'd been involved in three conflicts which had led to regime change. 'Milosevic. The Taliban. And Sierra Leone'. And that those interventions grew out of the stance he set in his famous Chicago speech, the speech that set out his 'post-modern' foreign policy. It was a reminder, and not a very coded one, that he'd been right to act decisively, in the Balkans for example, when all around were urging caution. There, Blair's belief in his judgement was vindicated. As one insider remembers: 'Throughout the military campaign there were serious, expert voices saying it could not or should not be done. He was, I think, proved right.'

The same insider went on: 'That vindication was still a recent memory when he decided his Iraq policy was equally right. I thought at the time that what he had done in Kosovo had set a precedent for justified intervention, and that Blair's judgement was sound.'

That mindset, that faith in Blair's judgement and belief, became critical. It meant, apart from anything else, that dozens of middle-ranking FCO officials who had serious doubts about Blair's certainties, the kind of contrary voices any organisation needs in order to avoid groupthink, kept their mouths tightly shut. While those who shared Blair's faith were happy to silence or discount those who did venture a sceptical 'yes, but'. It was critical to the dossier's eventual assertiveness.

After Crawford, the idea of publishing a dossier remained on ice but work on a text continued. Two new pieces of intelligence came in. They were written up and added to the draft. The call went out for recent photographs. More work was done on Saddam's human rights record. But the pressure to publish was off.

During the early summer the Coalition Information Centre (CIC) worked up a version of a possible dossier, adding itself to the already impressive number of groups with a hand in the project: Sir David Manning's Overseas and Defence Secretariat, John Scarlett's Joint Intelligence Committee, Julian Miller's Assessments Staff, the Defence Intelligence Staff and the agencies.

The CIC, which was to produce the February 2003 'dodgy

dossier', was directly answerable to Campbell. Its involvement was at his behest, an indication that if there was to be a public dossier, it was in Campbell's mind that the CIC would write it. During the spring and early summer, they worked on a paper called 'British Government Briefing on Iraq'. By 6 June, they'd finished their paper and the Cabinet Office circulated it. It was largely a reformatted version of the paper that Miller's assessments team had drafted back in the middle of March. The CIC had made a few changes, moving the section on Saddam's ballistic missiles to the end, adding pictures and, in one section, simplifying the numbers making them less precise. It was never published, however.

The significance of the CIC paper was twofold. It was the first overtly political stab at preparing 'intelligence' for public consumption. And it established the basic shape of a public dossier, a shape that later drafts built on.

The next important date was 23 July 2002, the day the Prime Minister chaired a Downing Street meeting with a stellar list of attendees. The Joint Intelligence Committee chairman John Scarlett was there. As well as Foreign Secretary Jack Straw; Defence Secretary, Geoff Hoon; Attorney General Lord Goldsmith; 'C', the MI6 chief Sir Richard Dearlove; and the Chief of the Defence Staff, Admiral Boyce, amongst others.

There are several, very different accounts of this meeting – two, though, matter more than any other. One was given to Lord Butler as part of his inquiry into the intelligence surrounding the Iraq war. The other was leaked. Hutton, perhaps owing to his understanding of his remit, remained unaware of the meeting, what it discussed and how it reflected the hardening mindsets in government and foreshadowed the way intelligence would be politicised in the production of the dossier.

The account given to Lord Butler reads like a very dull affair. A meeting chaired by the Prime Minister, involving 'officials primarily involved in UK policy formulation and military contingency planning'. It looked at the latest JIC assessment of Iraq's nuclear, biological, chemical and ballistic missile programmes. It noted that Iraqi capabilities were smaller in scale than those of other states of concern. It discussed the re-engagement of United Nations inspectors, considered the threat of force and commissioned work on legal issues.

All of that is true. Except the bit about it being a dull affair. Thanks to the leak of what's become known as the 'Downing Street Memo', published in the *Sunday Times* on 1 May 2005, we now have a much clearer account of that meeting.

Scarlett did indeed present the latest JIC assessment and it said little that was new. But he shared with the meeting his own judgement that the only way to overthrow Saddam was by massive military attack. Sir Richard Dearlove said that this was certainly the way the Bush administration saw it. He might have added that they had since 9/11. They thought military action was inevitable and President Bush had decided that a war to remove Saddam would be 'justified by the conjunction of terrorism and weapons of mass destruction'. Then he added one of the most cryptic sentences of the whole affair. In Washington, he said, 'the intelligence and facts were being fixed around the policy'.

Only Dearlove would know what he meant, assuming he actually uttered that phrase in exactly those words. Some believe the record, such as it is, was amended. And there's no clue to the precise context or tone of voice actually used. The most common interpretation is that his comment was proof that in the US the intelligence and facts were being manipulated to justify the policy. Others argue that he meant the facts and intelligence were falling into place as the policy required.

Now it was Straw's turn and he agreed that Bush seemed set on military action. But the case against Saddam, he said, was 'thin'. He was no threat to his neighbours and his WMD capability was less than that of Libya, North Korea or Iran. Indeed, of those 'four nations' offering any kind of threat, Iraq was fourth. Saddam lacked nuclear weapons. Straw wondered whether the issue really was WMD – or whether it was regime change. He thought it was WMD and favoured giving Saddam an ultimatum to let the UN weapons inspectors back in uncon-ditionally, the policy he pursued 'til the end. If he refused, then military action would have the legal cover it needed and public opinion would realise there was no other option.

Blair's response was telling. 'We have to be with the Americans ... I actually believe in doing this.'

The Attorney General, Lord Goldsmith, picked up the legal point. He warned that there were considerable legal obstacles to forcing regime change. There had to be a clear case for any military action. And even one based on self-defence or human-itarian considerations might not be enough. Authorisation from the United Nations Security Council was the only legally safe way to go.

For Blair, regime change was inextricably linked with WMD. It was the regime that was producing the weapons. It would make a big difference if the diplomatic route were tried and Saddam refused to accept unconditional inspections. If the political context were right, Blair said, people would support regime change. It was the Blair faith in action.

By the time of this Downing Street meeting, Bush was intent on invading Iraq from Kuwait and other surrounding states and from ships in the Gulf. The momentum was unstoppable but the precise plans, especially the timing, were 'still evolving' around two main ideas: a 'generated' start which involved a slow build-up over several months; or a 'running' start which foresaw a rapid start to hostilities, triggered by an Iraqi 'prov-ocation', followed by a quick build-up to the kind of force levels assumed in the 'generated' planning. Within those two options, the UK had any number of options of its own, and the choice that had to be made between them rested largely on the extent to which it wanted to offer support that was separate from or integrated into American plans. Playing no role in military action was not an option.

Off the back of the July conference, the Chief of Defence Staff, Admiral Boyce, put together a briefing on UK military options. He set out four, each successive option requiring more forces and time to prepare. He warned, too, about the problems that still remained, especially with a 'discrete' UK operation. There would be other demands on the army, providing cover for an expected Fire Service strike, for example. It would take six months to move tanks to the region and that couldn't be done secretly. There was uncertainty about transit routes and overflights, especially through and over Turkey. And the Chiefs of Staff were still unable to judge whether any of the options presented a 'winning concept'. Blair, in the meantime, gave an interview to *Prospect* magazine, promising: 'If the time comes for action, people will have the evidence presented to them,' and he was in no doubt what that evidence would say: '[Saddam] is certainly trying to acquire weapons of mass destruction, in particular a nuclear capability.'

Lord Hutton failed to discover how these events prior to September framed the production of the dossier because he failed to inquire about them in any depth. That was fatal to the validity of his inquiry. It simply ignored how the shift of focus from the 'four rogue states' to Iraq alone created a mindset around Blair that wanted, needed, to find justification for that focus. And that Bush's convictions and Blair's faith quashed scepticism at the heart of government. It was important, too, to understand how powerful Sir David Manning's March paper was in setting out a detailed road map which, amongst other things, prefigured the need for a dossier to 'sensitise' the public. Had he asked, he would also have understood the significance of one of Dr Kelly's allegations – that in the first half of 2002, the idea of a dossier stalled because there was nothing to put in it. Nothing that justified Blair's beliefs, that is.

Work on the dossier slowed during August while the pace of the politics quickened. Politicians and officials criss-crossed the Atlantic and their frenzied activity was matched by an equivalent frenzy in the press. Everyone's working assumption was that war was inevitable. Perhaps imminent.

Blair and Bush were due to meet again at Camp David on 7 September. Before then, they'd spoken by phone and decided it was time to 'get on with it'. For Bush, that meant finalising plans and starting to move his military into position. For Blair, it also meant more military planning as well as stepping up the pressure for a new 'disarmament and inspections' resolution at the UN, that 'second resolution'.

Blair also felt that he was losing control of the national and media debate, a debate that had become increasingly complex. He was more certain than ever that his beliefs about Saddam and WMD were justified and that something must be done. But he didn't wholly share Washington's hardening belligerence. He still thought the UN route worth taking but was determined it shouldn't become a way of avoiding real decisions and real pressure on Saddam to disarm. Public opinion and domestic political pressures were moving against him, too. And in spite of his belief, there was no clear answer to the question, 'Why now?'

It was time to revive the dossier. On 3 September, four days before Camp David, Blair announced in his Sedgefield constituency that he was going to 'present the evidence' that he'd promised at the end of July. The case for dealing militarily with Saddam and his WMD and doing it sooner rather than later.

That decision brought to the fore the contradiction at the heart of the kind of dossier Blair needed. He was certain that Saddam was the most serious and urgent threat and that he possessed and continued to develop WMD. He needed a dossier that made it clear why he believed that, one which justified his faith in his own judgement. And because he'd embraced this belief partly as a result of the intelligence he'd seen, he wanted the public to see some of that intelligence too. Intelligence that was 'real'. Apart from anything else, it would impart a credibility that Downing Street just didn't have.

But there was no conclusive 'real' intelligence. And what there was, the JIC's assessments staff had written up in language that was measured, full of qualifications and dealt in possibilities and balance of risk. Even Blair's chief of staff, Jonathan Powell, was wary of his boss's certainties. He thought the evidence thin and pointed to a threat that was real but distant.

Nevertheless, the following day, Wednesday 4 September, work restarted on the dossier. In Downing Street, Sir David Manning's Overseas and Defence Secretariat collected together all the existing papers; the aborted 'four nations paper'; its own earlier work on Iraq; the 6 March draft; the CIC's June reformatting and other material. At the same time, but separately, the JIC assessments staff started to bring its formal assessments of Saddam's WMD up to date. There was due to be a routine meeting of the JIC later that day. And Campbell agreed with Washington that they had to get the CIC up and running and on the case, an indication of who it was that he intended would write the dossier.

That same morning, Manning called Dearlove over at MI6 to try to resolve some of the spy chief's doubts about a public dossier. They'd almost certainly discussed these concerns before and there was a suspicion amongst some in No. 10 that MI6 might hold back the kind of material they needed to make the dossier as persuasive as possible. Dearlove agreed that it would be possible to put 'real' intelligence-based material into the public domain, so long as he had the last word on withholding anything that might reveal or compromise any sources. He also stipulated that any section of the dossier which drew heavily on intelligence should be under the control of the JIC. It's important to realise that Dearlove's concerns over the dossier were for the security of his sources and agents and the reputation of MI6. The precise wording of a published document was of little consequence in itself.

At the time of the call, Dearlove knew he had something that might turn out to be exactly what the dossier needed. A new piece of intelligence with a startling headline that suggested Saddam might still be producing WMD. Dearlove apparently said nothing about it to Manning at that time – it was still going through the assessment mill – but disclosed it at the routine JIC meeting later. It had come in, he said, too late to be included in the draft assessment they had in front of them at that meeting, an assessment called 'Iraqi use of Chemical and Biological Weapons – Possible Scenarios'.

That intelligence was the 45-minute claim.

It had come into MI6 on 30 August from a senior Iraqi military officer. He was a known source and believed to be reliable. MI6 judged that his role in the Iraqi military meant he knew what he was talking about when it came to the deployment of chemical and biological weapons. They were taking it seriously, though they were aware it came originally from a sub-source unknown to them.

This scrap of intelligence seemed to offer the sparest possible glimpse of the current state of Saddam's WMD and his deployment plans. It was sparse and said that it took the Iraqi military 'on average twenty minutes' to move chemical and biological munitions into place for attack. The maximum response time was 45 minutes.

Like much secret intelligence, it raised more questions than it answered. It could be no more than an assumption that it referred to military planning that was current. Similarly, it was only an assumption that it was a serious insight and not a mere anecdotal aside. But as far as MI6 was concerned it was the only recent piece of intelligence from Iraq that had anything quantifiable in it. And it was possible to infer from it that Saddam was continuing to produce chemical and biological munitions in sufficient quantities to feed such a deployment.

But there was nothing to corroborate it. Nor did it fit into any known pattern of intelligence. Dearlove suggested to the JIC that the assessments staff should use the new piece of intelligence to work up a new assessment. And that meant letting the analysts at the Defence Intelligence Staff get their teeth into it.

As soon as they saw it, the DIS analysts thought it was 'weak'. They and the JIC's assessments staff struggled with it. They weren't sure what it actually meant. What segment of the command and control procedure it actually referred to. Or what kind of munitions.

Was it small-scale battlefield munitions? Larger scale munitions? WMD warheads for ballistic missiles? If the weapons were in such a state of readiness, where were they held? Current thinking was that Saddam had dispersed his WMD to avoid detection. So where might they be moved to and from in so short a time? Nor could anyone readily identify any Iraqi weapons system that could be assembled in under 45 minutes.

The best they could guess was that it was about moving battlefield munitions from storage sites close to the front line to the military units themselves. But no one knew. They could only guess. It was 'questionable' to say the least.

The JIC assessments staff had a first stab at a line of text that went out to JIC members the following day, 5 September. It read: 'Intelligence also indicates that from forward-deployed storage sites, chemical and biological munitions could be with military units and ready for firing within forty-five minutes.'

The Defence Intelligence Staff and MI6 didn't like it. Miller's assessments team had gone too far. The line about 'forward-deployed storage sites' might be a reasonable guess, but guess it was. It wasn't in the intelligence. They sent it back. Miller's team had another go and the following day sent round another draft which read: 'Intelligence also indicates that chemical and biological munitions could be with military units and ready for firing within 20–45 minutes.' A weak statement of weak intelligence, one former analyst said later. And while they didn't bury the 45-minute claim in their draft assessment, it wasn't headlined and didn't appear in the 'Key Judgements' section when it finally went up to the next regular JIC meeting on 11 September.

To the analysts in the Defence Intelligence Staff words were everything. If the intelligence was weak, so the language had to be. And they saw no reason to depart from their usual standards of care and precision this time nor any reason to subvert their usual ways of working. Careful analysis needed time and if, at the end of that time, their analysis was conditional and qualified, so be it. That's what 'real' intelligence was like.

In the meantime, at noon on 5 September, Campbell held his first formal meeting on the renewed dossier. There's no complete record of that meeting though there is a memo recording the 'action points'. Campbell and Scarlett both told Hutton that it was a meeting purely about presentation: what a public document would look like; the voice it would use to speak to its audience. They insisted there was no discussion of any intelligence-related matters, a nice point and only true in the narrowest possible sense. They did decide the dossier had to be 'revelatory', new insights into the 'bigger case'. The tone, if nothing else, was set – the only problem was they had nothing in front of them that was new though Scarlett and Miller were aware of the new intelligence, the 45-minute claim that was still being analysed and assessed.

As well as Campbell, the principals at that meeting were Scarlett, Miller, Manning and Straw's media chief, John Williams. It was obvious to everyone, especially Campbell and Williams, that they didn't have the makings of a dossier they could publish. Scarlett warned that on nuclear weapons, for example, they had very little. They didn't even have a credible draft. Campbell decided they needed to 'restructure' what they had, a process Miller interpreted as 'a degree of cutting and pasting' of the papers that already existed. They decided, too, that the draft needed new material on Saddam's human rights abuses and the way he wielded his power.

Campbell decided the dossier should comprise seven sections and divided the work of assembling them between the Foreign Office and the JIC assessments staff. The FCO was to take care of the first two and the last sections: the bloody nature of Saddam's regime, his misuse of power, and 'why we should act now'. The assessments staff were to take care of the sections on the UN's resolutions, the effects of WMD and ballistic missiles and the all-important section on the current state of Iraq's WMD. While the Foreign Office's Non-Proliferation Department were to write the section on the history of weapons inspections. They decided, too, that the dossier needed more 'real' intelligence. Someone was going to have to find some.

They didn't decide, though, who would actually write the dossier. There had already been dozens of hands and an alphabet soup involved in all the papers and drafts to date: the ODS, the JIC, the CIC, the FCO, the DIS as well as No. 10. Scarlett admitted that no one in intelligence had any experience of writing documents for public consumption. There would have to be a 'golden pen'. He turned to Williams, but Campbell ignored the hint. He had other plans.

Williams was sceptical about the whole idea of a dossier. He thought it was a mistake and had even written a note to his boss, Jack Straw, urging him to persuade Blair to drop the idea. He thought a dossier would take the pressure off Saddam, a tactical error. And he was beginning to regret he hadn't voiced his opposition more loudly and earlier. But that moment was gone.

At the end of the meeting, Williams asked Campbell who was going to be the 'golden pen'. Who would actually write the dossier. Campbell said he was inclined to give it to the Strategic Communications Unit in No. 10.

The prospect of Campbell and his team writing the dossier alarmed Straw and his most senior officials at the Foreign Office. They were adamant it should be a Foreign Office production, if it were to happen at all, and that Williams would write it. Williams was prepared to take it on, in spite of his instincts that it wasn't a good idea: 'We were where we were and the dossier was going to happen,' he thought.

And although his and Straw's priority was the imminent UN General Assembly and the 'second resolution', Williams rolled up his sleeves, asked Scarlett for the material that he intended to use and prepared to put together a quick draft which, at the very least, would show how to turn the raw material into a publishable dossier.

For Williams, this kind of job was 'routine'. As a former tabloid political editor, he had an eye for a story and how to tell one, plus a way with words. He was also a 'straight shooter'. Some distance from the type of spin doctor that had become the norm in New Labour. Of all those involved in producing the dossier, he was one of the few who seemed to understand that it could be intelligence and underwhelming or political rhetoric and alarming. It couldn't be both, not 'real' intelligence *and* alarming.

Over the weekend of 6–7 September he bashed out a draft that was, indeed, 'underwhelming'. There was still nothing much new in it, nothing very different from what had been around the previous March when the idea of a dossier was dropped. And however you pushed and pulled the structure about, it couldn't be turned into the document Blair needed.

Some journalists and campaigners have identified Williams as the 'real author' of the dossier. They argue that his work that weekend and the final product are strikingly similar except for the 45-minute claim. And that since he and other media specialists were on the drafting group, the dossier was an exercise in 'spin' just like any other.

That last is undoubtedly true, but Williams was in no sense the 'real author' of the dossier. He may well have expected to be. Straw was prepared to let him devote himself to it full-time. And Williams himself referred his work over that weekend as '*the* media friendly editorial job'. The notes he scrawled on his text, queries about details and requests for more information, suggest strongly he was looking ahead to writing the next draft.

Downing Street insiders, with the exception of Campbell,

seem to have seen it that way, too. Many of the first round of comments from those insiders are written in a way that implies it was their understanding that this was the text to look at. But the documentary evidence and Williams's own account show he became marginal to the dossier after 9 September. Apart from anything else, his focus shifted with that of his boss, Jack Straw, to the UN General Assembly later that month. His text, however, clearly did influence the final dossier, in assertiveness, structure and media-friendliness if nothing else. The reason for that is simple – it's how documents like the dossier get written. Previous documents are absorbed, resonant lines borrowed; framings and structures that seem to work get preserved and provide the framing for new content as it comes in.

In this case, though, there were two very different types of document, two different streams. The political stream and the intelligence stream. The essential characteristics of each stream meant that reconciliation in a single document was never possible. One would always be subservient to the other.

Lord Hutton allowed Campbell to dismiss Williams's work over that weekend as no more than just trying to be helpful, something he did off his own bat and no part of writing and producing the dossier. That seemed implausible. Hutton could and should have inquired further. Such was his and his counsel's lack of curiosity on the point that when Williams appeared as a witness on 14 August, he wasn't asked a single question about his role in the production of the dossier.[†] Nor was he recalled after Campbell's and Scarlett's evidence. Apparently, Lord Hutton believed it was beyond his remit to

---

† Intriguingly, during that evidence Williams said 'the Foreign Office, MoD, No. 10 were all collectively responsible for policy on Iraq, for the dossier, for the conflict, for its aftermath.' What did he mean by that? It appeared to contradict the argument that the JIC was in charge and Downing Street officials merely commenting 'above their pay grade'. And at the end of his evidence, Williams even volunteered some details of his role in the production of the dossier during September but Hutton did not take the bait.

discover more about how Williams's work shaped the final dossier, in particular its assertive 'capping' piece that strongly influenced the kind of document the dossier became and its absorption of previous drafts and pieces of political work. The Coalition Information Centre's paper, for example. His text ran to almost thirty pages, covered the whole subject and went out for review to No. 10 insiders as well as Miller's drafting team. Had Hutton or his counsel been more forensic, they might also have ·discovered Campbell's initial intention to have the dossier written inside No. 10, evidence that would have been difficult to reconcile with Scarlett's insistence that he went away from that first planning meeting with 'complete control' of the draft.

The weekend that Williams was doing 'the media friendly editorial job', Blair was at Camp David where the timetable for the military build-up was taking shape. His media briefings on the way out focused on an International Atomic Energy Agency report that pointed to potential activity at nuclear sites. It wasn't the only briefing of journalists, though. A 'No. 10 official' also briefed two senior correspondents travelling with Blair, telling them that the agencies, meaning MI6, weren't coming up with the goods for the dossier. One of those journalists was the *Daily Telegraph*'s diplomatic editor, Anton La Guardia, well respected and positioned very much at the serious, almost academic, end of journalism. La Guardia reported, as did the *Financial Times*, that 'officials have expressed frustration over the reluctance of Britain's intelligence community to release fresh information'. He quoted his source as saying: 'The secret services live in a world of their own and don't understand why the information should be released in public ... Ministers are breathing down their necks to release the evidence.'

Fighting talk. And briefings like that don't happen for no reason. Someone in Blair's entourage intimately involved in the dossier wanted to send a message to MI6 in the only way he knew how that he thought they weren't playing the game.

They were holding back. And if they carried on like this, he was prepared to blame them publicly for a dud dossier. It looked, smelled, walked and talked like a major row between No. 10, or someone senior in No. 10, and MI6.

The following Monday morning, 9 September, the day Miller's drafting group was due to hold its first meeting, MI6 top brass demanded an urgent meeting with Campbell, irked by those pieces in the *FT* and *Daily Telegraph*.

The MI6 chief, Sir Richard Dearlove, was close to Blair and fully understood his need for more 'real' intelligence to put in his dossier. He wasn't against the idea in principle but he wanted to be absolutely certain, as he'd made clear to Manning the previous week, that the JIC, of which he was a member, should 'control' any part of the dossier that drew heavily on intelligence.

However frustrated he may have been, Campbell knew he needed MI6 onside. They were the only possible source of the intelligence, should any exist, that would create headlines, endorse Blair's beliefs and persuade a sceptical public. Scarlett's 'owning' the dossier or substantial parts of it had not been his initial inclination, but at least it was better than if it were to become a Foreign Office production. But he had little choice. Satisfied at the 'clarity' he'd achieved, Dearlove said he and the MI6 chiefs were now content to co-operate on the dossier. Meanwhile, at the Foreign Office there were muted cheers when they learnt Scarlett and not Campbell was 'in charge'.

Off the back of his meeting with MI6, Campbell wrote to Scarlett, with copies to the MI6 chiefs, setting out 'the process by which the dossier will be produced': 'This must be, and be seen to be, the work of you and your team … its credibility depends fundamentally upon that.' 'Be seen to be' was the important phrase there.

> The media/political judgement will inevitably focus on 'what's new?' and I was pleased to hear from you and your SIS colleagues that, contrary to media reports today, the intelligence

community are taking such a helpful approach to this in going through all the material they have. It goes without saying there should be nothing published that you and they are not 100 per cent happy with.

It comes across as the sort of letter written to respond to the demand 'and I want that in writing', its last sentence a master-piece of New Labour ambiguity.

There were two other important meetings that Monday 9 September, either side of the session with MI6. In the morn-ing, Campbell held another planning meeting, while in the afternoon, Miller's drafting team held their first session. That team included a number of communications specialists: Daniel Pruce from No. 10, and Paul Hamill and James Paver from the FCO. Williams was thanked for his work over the weekend but stood down. Scarlett was now in charge, though still with-out that 'golden pen'.

That team met for three hours and produced a draft which they sent round the following day. Like Williams's draft, it was chunky, beginning with a foreword, followed by an executive summary and then by the main text. Its language was asser-tive, more assertive in its judgements than was usual in a pure intelligence document.

It was at this meeting that the communications special-ists first saw the 45-minute claim. And though it had been understated in the assessment, they recognised a piece of 'real' intelligence at last. Revelatory and capable of making head-lines. To the intelligence experts, it was no big deal. Military units would often hold armaments at zero notice, never mind 45 minutes. And anyway, the analysts thought it was probably wrong.

Campbell insisted to Hutton that while he knew the 45-minute claim was fresh, he knew nothing of its provenance nor anything about the tussles there'd been between the analysts and the assessment team over the wording. Only that it came via the JIC. Yet he'd told the Foreign Affairs Select Committee the previous June that he'd seen the secret Joint Intelligence Committee assessments on which the September dossier was based and discussed them with MI6. Those assessments pointed to the limitations and qualifications of that intelligence. And they were considerable. After the war, a Tory MP and former Grenadier Guardsman, Adam Holloway, claimed that the agencies knew the sub-source was a taxi driver who'd overheard Iraqi military officers gossiping in his cab two years earlier. And that a footnote was appended to the intelligence, warning that it was 'verifiably false'. How improbable is it that there was not a word exchanged between Campbell and Scarlett about the reliability of such an exciting, but difficult, piece of new intelligence?

The wording of the 45-minute claim that finally appeared in the JIC assessment was: 'Intelligence also indicates that chemical and biological munitions could be with military units and ready for firing within 20–45 minutes.' The dossier drafting team changed that to read: 'Recent intelligence ... indicates that Iraq: attaches great importance to the possession of weapons of mass destruction and that Saddam Hussein is committed to using them if necessary; it envisages the use of weapons of mass destruction in its current military planning, and could deploy such weapons within forty-five minutes of the order being given for their use'.

Scarlett thought the change was 'not significant'. The analysts in the DIS disagreed. They thought it unacceptable. Nor was it, to them, simply some arid academic debate about the meaning of words. The analysts' most important customers were men on the battlefield with guns in their hands. Men whose lives might depend on unambiguous, accurate, precise assessments of intelligence. Over-or under-interpreted intelligence could be lethal. And it was as important to them to spell out what the intelligence didn't tell them as what it did.

To the analysts, the word 'average' in the original intelligence was very important. They reasoned that if it took twenty minutes *on average* to move chemical and biological munitions into place for attack, then some could be ready in *less* than twenty minutes. That meant the intelligence almost certainly referred to battlefield munitions and not WMD – something you might quite like to know if you were a soldier in battle facing the possibility of a chemical or biological shell coming your way. The only way the intelligence could apply to WMD would be if the programme were so vast and ready to hand that it couldn't have escaped detection. Taking out the 'twenty minutes on average' line made it easier by sleight of hand to associate the 45-minute claim with WMD.

Something else bothered the DIS analysts. The drafting team hadn't just hardened the wording of the 45-minute claim beyond the JIC assessment they'd agreed to. It was also used, by juxtaposition, to give a more threatening edge to the judgement that Iraq 'envisages the use of weapons of mass destruction in its current military planning'. It gave a new, alarming twist to old information. Made it sexier.

This draft went out for comment. To the officials in No. 10, it looked like a new take on Williams's draft. Some still thought he was the 'golden pen'. One of those who made comments was Daniel Pruce, the FCO press officer seconded to Downing Street who was one of the media specialists on Miller's drafting team. Hutton's belief that the drafting team was drawn only from the JIC assessments staff was wrong, incidentally.

Pruce made some comments on presentation: 'voice' and 'ownership'. Others about content. He recommended portraying Saddam as a 'bad and unstable man' and personalising the whole thing. Identifying 'Iraq' with 'Saddam'. He wanted the next draft to 'bring out' the impression that Saddam had been 'relentlessly pursuing WMD'. Politically, that made sense. But there was next to no intelligence to support it. Another of those commenting, Godric Smith, the PM's official spokesman, confined himself to presentation. It was, he thought, 'a bit of a muddle' and needed 'more clarity' about what was old and what was new. While Philip Bassett, one of the Prime Minister's senior advisors, wanted a style that was more 'officialese'. He wanted the content to be 'at least as good as IISS', the International Institute for Strategic Studies dossier that had just come out. He wanted more intelligence. 'It's intelligence-lite,' he wrote. It needed 'better intelligence material ... more material ... more convincing material'. It also, he thought, needed 'a conclusion ... making a case which *is* compelling'.

The significance of all these comments, and those that came later, is that their very existence reveals the kind of document Downing Street insiders thought the dossier was and was going to be. A political, rhetorical document. Intelligence-based, perhaps, but political nonetheless. They clearly saw the point of the whole exercise was to produce a dossier that endorsed Blair's beliefs.

Campbell insists he never saw any of these comments. When Hutton asked him about them, he brushed them off as 'well meaning', much as he did Williams's text. Contributions 'above their pay grade' by people 'not involved in the process', even though Pruce and, initially, Williams were on Miller's team drafting the dossier. Hutton inquired no further.

There was another comment, too, on this draft. It came from Dr David Kelly. It showed the attention to detail that he, and the analysts in the DIS, expected in intelligence-based documents. And as far as they were concerned, if the dossier was going to contain intelligence, it had to be no different from the kind of work they were used to producing. They were at the other end of the politics/intelligence spectrum from the Downing Street insiders.

Dr Kelly was troubled by a paragraph which said that 'UN inspectors could not account for up to twenty tonnes of growth media' – the growth media for biological weapons, that is. It was wrong and over-hyped. 'In fact', Dr Kelly had said, '2.456 tonnes was missing', an eighth the amount the draft claimed. UNSCOM, he explained, couldn't account for a further 15.457 tonnes which Iraq claimed it used in BW work.

But 'Iraq has not revealed its production documents therefore this amount is unaccounted for. The existing wording is not wrong – but it has lots of spin on it.'

On 10/11 September, a 56-page draft drawing heavily on previous documents and papers was circulated which included the 45-minute claim, worded in two distinct ways. In the body of the draft, it read: 'Within the last month, intelligence has suggested that the Iraqi military would be able to use their chemical and biological weapons within 45 minutes of an order to do so.' In the executive summary, it said that Saddam 'envisages the use of weapons of mass destruction in its current military planning, and could deploy such weapons within 45 minutes of the order being given for their use'. It was the only new, striking piece of intelligence in the whole document and it's evident already from the hard assessment in the executive summary how much was being hung from this one, questionable, intelligence insight.

After the 10/11 September draft, Scarlett sent round a 'last call for any items of intelligence that agencies think can and should be included'. Apart from anything else, it would be ideal to dig out something to corroborate the inference the dossier was drawing from the 45-minute claim. That Saddam had continued to produce, was continuing to produce, chemical and biological agents in large, military quantities.

On 11 September, as if to answer Scarlett's and Campbell's prayers, a new piece of intelligence came in that was, apparently, perfect. It said that Saddam's production of chemical and biological agents had been accelerated and that he was also building new production facilities. It was 'corroboration' that could override the analysts' objections to the wording of the 45-minute claim and take both the language and inferences in the dossier to the limit.

When Dearlove briefed Blair about the new intelligence, he told him that the intelligence they had was real, that it hadn't been planted by someone with an agenda of their own. He also set out his view that while Saddam was determined to retain whatever WMD he had, it was to assert regional power rather than threaten the West. He didn't want the intelligence itself to appear in the dossier, but if Blair, Campbell and Scarlett wanted, they could assert it or include their own assessment based on it. And while that worked rhetorically, Campbell was concerned that a dossier that relied too heavily on assertion and revealed too little 'real' intelligence would lack credibility. The following day, Campbell met Miller to talk about the latest draft and share with him that worry.

The analysts in the DIS were told about the new intelligence. And that it allowed Scarlett and Miller's drafting team to dismiss their concerns over the 45-minute claim. But they were never allowed to see it or put it to the test. It was too sensitive, they were told. Very few people have ever seen it. The MPs on the Intelligence and Security Committee did in 2003 and concluded, cryptically, that they could understand why it had the effect on thinking that it did. A conclusion that falls some way short of an endorsement. Since then, it's disappeared. The agencies had to acknowledge it was wrong and withdrew it just before Hutton began his inquiry in August 2003. Neither Dearlove nor Scarlett thought it worth mentioning this. And Hutton showed no curiosity about it whatsoever.[†]

---

† Lord Butler wrote of this in July 2004: 'In mid-September 2002 SIS issued a report, described as being from "a new source on trial", on Iraqi production of chemical and biological agent. Although this report was received too late for inclusion in the JIC assessment of 9 September, it did provide significant assurance to those drafting the Government's dossier that active, current production of chemical and biological agent was taking place. A second report from the new source, about the production of a particular chemical agent, was received later in September 2002. In July 2003, however, SIS withdrew the two reports because the sourcing chain had by then been discredited. SIS also interviewed the alleged sub-source for the intelligence after the war, who denied ever having provided the information in the reports. We note, therefore, that the two reports from this source, including one which was important in the closing stages of production of the Government's September dossier, must now be treated as unsafe.'

With the analysts now back in their box, Miller's team produced another draft on 16 September which went out to JIC members the same day and to No. 10 the following day. It was during this phase of its production that the dossier lost its downbeat conclusion, written by the JIC drafting team, and gained its foreword, drafted by Campbell. The 45-minute claim was there in this draft, in the executive summary and twice in the main body of the text but, significantly, not in the conclusion. That read:

1. Four themes dominate even the most sober account of Saddam Hussein's rule in Iraq:

- Brutality as exercised against his own people,
- Aggression against neighbouring states,
- Cynicism in dealing with the Iraqi people, regional states and the International Community; and
- Single minded pursuit of military power and above all weapons of mass destruction as the most effective means of exercising that power.

2. This paper has set out our assessment of Saddam's current holding of chemical, biological and nuclear weapons and ballistic missile systems as well as his programmes for their development. Although our knowledge is partial, the paper concludes that he possesses mass destruction weapons and the means to produce them and to deliver them. His development programmes continue. An analysis of what he will do with these weapons now and in the future, must rest upon his record and our current information, including intelligence.

It is reasonable to conclude that he will use whatever weaponry he has to hand to protect his power and eventually to project it when he feels strong enough to do so.

John Williams, the author of the 'media friendly' shot at a dossier over that first weekend in September, wrote to John

Scarlett on 17 September that: 'The new draft of the dossier now looks like a paper that will persuade those who have an open mind...' though he thought the section on nuclear weapons was weak and predicted that the reaction from some journalists would be that there was 'no basis for action because the sanctions are working perfectly well'. He went on:

> I understand why you have chosen an unrhetorical tone, but it would be possible to carry the argument more vigorously in the executive summary without a complete change of approach ... The conclusion is counter-productive; it serves no purpose that is not already served by the executive summary; and if taken alone, particularly by a sceptical broadcaster holding it up to a camera, it could be portrayed as 'all we've got'; I would drop it.

He wasn't the only one who thought that. Campbell asked a Downing Street special advisor, Jo Nadin, to look over the draft. Like Williams, she thought the section on nuclear weapons was not very convincing – as did Campbell. He wrote to Scarlett suggesting a number of changes; some re-ordering, but some hardening of language, too: 'radiological devices in months: nuclear bomb 1–2 years with help; five years with no sanctions'. He wanted more on Saddam's concealment plans and commissioned the CIC, the 'information' unit directly responsible to him, to write a paper on that, just in case. And he wanted a tougher executive summary. He wanted it to say that despite sanctions and containment, Saddam had made real progress in developing WMD.

The following day, Wednesday 18 September, as Campbell was to record and retain in the published version of his diaries, Scarlett was 'keen to keep in the very downbeat assessment'. Most downbeat of all was that conclusion – though presumably, since it was written by the JIC drafting team, it represented their considered view. The next day, Nadin had some more thoughts about the draft which Campbell put through. Most important of all, though, he 'agreed' to drop the conclusion – implying there'd been some discussion in Downing Street which led to him sharing Williams's view that 'we'd end up convincing those who wanted to be and not those who didn't'.

Blair and Campbell had already made another important decision, too. They decided that there'd be a foreword where Blair would set out his beliefs, in his voice – though drafted by Campbell, of course – and above his signature. It was no small decision. Everyone would read a foreword. It would probably be the only part most people would read. Certainly the only part most would remember. The media would pick it up and it would shape the headlines – especially now the downbeat conclusion had gone. And a Prime Ministerial foreword would, inevitably, shape the rest of the dossier too. Drawing its content and assessments towards it like a magnet.

Campbell's first shot at putting Blair's beliefs into words read: 'In recent months, I have been increasingly alarmed by the evidence from inside Iraq that despite sanctions, despite the damage done to his capability in the past, and despite the UNSCR's [United Nations Security Council resolutions] expressly outlawing it, Saddam Hussein is continuing to develop WMD.'

Clearly, the rest of the dossier had to deliver. Scarlett, the guardian of the intelligence, saw no problem. The foreword was simply a 'policy statement' by the Prime Minister. That 'policy statement' went from hard to harder still under Campbell's pen. For example, in that first shot at the foreword, he writes: 'The case I make is not that Saddam could launch a nuclear attack on London or another part of the UK (he could not).' By the final draft, that sentence had gone along with anything else that suggested Saddam's WMD were anything other than an imminent threat. A classic example of 'sexing up' by omission.

By the third week of September, the pace was quickening. MPs had been called back from their holidays to hear a Prime

Ministerial statement on Iraq and debate the dossier on 24 September. It was an immovable deadline and the dossier had to meet it. With just a week to go, the Prime Minister's official spokesman, Godric Smith, told lobby journalists that the dossier 'had been moved onto a faster track than originally intended and that had caused some difficulties ... It was expected to take up until the morning of 24 September to get the dossier ready.' The 'faster track' meant that the tried and tested processes that ensured intelligence assessments were made as meticulously as possible were overridden or short-circuited. It also meant the dossier couldn't go to a full JIC meeting. The next one in the diary was the day after the dossier was due to be published.

On 19 September, Miller's team produced the main text and executive summary of what was very close to the final dossier, the text that was to be bolted on to Campbell's foreword. The 45-minute claim was in it three times and Campbell added it a fourth time in that foreword. Around this time, the DIS experts were getting very concerned about the 45-minute claim. Not just at the way it was worded and the way the qualifications and careful language they thought essential were being eroded, but also at what else the drafters were hanging from it. The assertion that Saddam was continuing to produce chemical and biological weapons. The 'faster track' was making considered analysis impossible.

The DIS, while part of the 'intelligence community', are slightly off to one side. They're not an 'agency' in their own right but are part of the Ministry of Defence. They were represented on the JIC by their chief, Air Marshal Joseph French, and their expertise was vital to intelligence assessments. But the agencies, especially MI6, dismissed them as 'dweebs'. They didn't do the glamorous stuff with agents and dead-letter drops and duplicity. They were the ones that sat in airless rooms, analysing the intelligence MI6 and others had gathered. And they knew careless analysis and language cost lives.

They were heavily involved in the spadework of producing the dossier, not just during that September but over the years during which much of the intelligence content had been assembled. They had an encyclopaedic knowledge of Saddam's WMD history. They were the group that brought expertise in chemical, biological and nuclear weaponry to the table. They saw, checked, corrected and commented on all parts of the dossier, especially the section that dealt with Saddam's current WMD capabilities. The only part based on 'real' intelligence.

On 17 September, they'd put their concerns in writing to Miller's drafting team. Amongst other things, they highlighted the wording of the 45-minute claim in the executive summary. That draft read: '[Iraq] has military plans for the use of chemical and biological weapons, some of which could be ready within 45 minutes of an order to use them.' The DIS staff thought it 'rather strong since it is based on a single source'. They also thought the assessment in the summary that Iraq has 'continued to produce' chemical and biological agents was too strong.

Miller's team toned down some assessments in the dossier in the light of their concerns. Others were left as they were. It was less than satisfactory, the analysts thought. Plus, there was a rising volume of grumbling amongst them at the rapidly increasing workload and what they saw as an increasingly chaotic way of working.

It was into this atmosphere that one of the DIS senior scientists, Dr Brian Jones, returned from holiday, on Wednesday 18 September. Dr Jones was the branch head in the Scientific and Technical Directorate of the DIS. He managed the scientists and engineers who analysed the intelligence on chemical and biological warfare.

Dr Jones had left on his holiday at the end of August, before Blair announced the revival of the dossier project. When he came back three weeks later, his section was working frantically on revision after revision of a dossier that was just hours from its final form. On that first day back, he ran into Dr Kelly who, while not on the DIS payroll, was a frequent visitor. Dr Jones had known him since 1986 and had often drawn on his expertise in biological warfare. Dr Kelly even had his own pass to the DIS offices in the Old War Office on Whitehall. On that day, he happened to be looking over the latest draft of the dossier. He'd read it all several times, with a special interest in the section on chemical and biological weapons, his area of expertise. He told Dr Jones that, on the whole, it was a good piece of work.

But as Dr Jones spoke to more people, it became clear that not everyone took the same view. His chemical weapons specialist, for example, thought that there was no reliable intelligence nor any other evidence to show Saddam had continued to produce chemical weapon agents. It was a possibility, even a probability, that there were *programmes*. But it wasn't known if they were active. And the condition of any raw materials, precursors or agents wasn't known, either. It was far from certain any were being produced at all, yet that's what the dossier drafts were saying in ever more certain language. Worse, when these concerns were passed up the line, they seemed to be ignored.

He learnt, too, about their concerns over the 45-minute claim. They thought it raised more questions than it answered. They'd rather it wasn't there at all, but if it had to be, they'd rather it read: 'intelligence *indicates...*' or '*suggests...*' They'd managed to get the main text changed, but not the executive summary. That was edging ever closer to Campbell's assertive wording in the foreword. There, Campbell was planning to say that the dossier 'discloses' that Saddam's 'military planning allows for some of the WMD to be ready within 45 minutes of an order to use them'. Wording with which the analysts could never agree.

They were worried, too, about the source. Or rather the source's source. As far as they could tell, nothing was known about the sub-source. Was he reliable? Did he have an agenda to influence rather than inform? Did he know or understand what he was talking about? It seemed not. Anyone who did know what they were talking about would know how important it was to differentiate between chemical and biological munitions and agents. A truly credible source would have known that the figure of 45 minutes from order to launch is irrelevant for biological warfare agents but might be important for chemical munitions.

Plus, no one amongst the analysts or anyone they spoke to, including Dr Kelly, could think of any weapons system Iraq was known to have that could be assembled in 45 minutes. A credible source would also have known how important it was to indicate the scenario in which the munitions might be used.

None of this meant that the intelligence couldn't be accurate. Nor did the single sourcing matter on its own. But taken together, all the doubts did mean that, at the very least, any assessment should be cautious, ditto the language used. Especially in a document for consumption by a public that would have no access to the raw intelligence or JIC assessments.

Late in the morning of 19 September, just before the shutters came down on the drafting process, Dr Jones chaired a small, rushed, get-together of experts and analysts to try to draw together the various views. Dr Kelly, who happened once again to be in the office, came along and repeated his view that the latest draft was overall good, though he still had over a dozen changes he'd like to see, some of fact, some of language.

The get-together went over most of the WMD section of the draft dossier but inevitably they kept coming back to the 45-minute claim. Everyone felt it was problematic and the questions kept proliferating. Did it, in fact, refer to a technical process? Or was it purely a command and control process? What were its real implications? Most took the view that if the claim led to so many questions, it shouldn't be included. Certainly not as a bold, bare statement of fact.

They were bothered, too, that in the rush to produce, their careful, considered routines had gone out of the window. In more normal times, if the DIS and the agencies didn't agree on an assessment, they tried first to work it through informally. If that didn't work, it went up the line and more senior figures would try to resolve it. And if they couldn't agree, the disagreement would go to the weekly routine JIC meeting where it would be resolved one way or another.

That wasn't what had been happening. As far as Dr Jones could tell, their concerns weren't going through these stages and up to the full JIC. There wasn't time. He decided to have one last try. With the final draft in the can and just three days before the dossier was due to be published, the DIS urged a rethink on 'a number of statements which are not supported by the evidence available'.

Campbell's foreword, for example, which read: 'What I believe the assessed intelligence has established beyond doubt is that Saddam has continued to produce chemical and biological weapons…' This might well be what Blair believed and what he wanted the dossier to say, but in a note circulated to Defence Intelligence chiefs on 20 September, the stark judgement was that 'the intelligence available … has NOT established beyond doubt that Saddam has continued to produce chemical (and biological) weapons'. And the note's author questioned the way the 45-minute claim was worded. But the last-minute effort was in vain.

Not all last-minute suggestions went ignored, though. There were still some very important changes to come – from Downing Street. On 19 September, after the deadline had passed for JIC members to object to anything in the final draft, Blair's Chief of Staff Jonathan Powell realised something that, until then, no one else seems to have noticed. On page 19, the text read: 'Saddam is prepared to use chemical and biological weapons if he believes his regime is under threat.'

That was, Powell wrote, 'a bit of a problem. It backs up the … argument that there is no CBW threat and we will only create one if we attack him.' He had a point. The implication of that sentence was that Saddam wasn't much of a threat to anyone unless attacked. But it was the text that the JIC had, silently, signed off. A text that was, presumably, 'consistent with the intelligence'.

'I think you should redraft the para,' Powell suggests. 'My memory of the intelligence is that he has set up plans to use CBW on western forces and that these weapons are integrated into his military planning.' Scarlett made the change Powell asked for, insisting later that there was intelligence to support it. If there is or ever was such intelligence, it was never revealed to the MPs on the Intelligence and Security Committee. Hutton seemed not to realise that this meant the JIC did not approve the final published dossier in its entirety, though its chairman, acting alone, did.

There was another intervention that day, too. It came from Sir David Omand, Blair's Security and Intelligence Coordinator. Omand was a career civil servant who'd been Director of GCHQ before taking up his post in September 2002. He was a senior member of the JIC and, effectively, Scarlett's line manager.

Omand was intimately involved in writing the dossier and in daily conversations with Scarlett, Blair and Campbell. Yet when he appeared before Lord Hutton, questioning over the dossier was minimal. He told Hutton that his main concern was that 'the whole exercise was conducted in a way that did not endanger our intelligence'. He was, he said, 'anxious to produce as strong a document as possible, consistent with the protection of intelligence sources and methods'. He saw no problem, however, with the Prime Minister making a case based on intelligence: 'we mustn't be too precious about [it].' But he warned that the case should be separated from the intelligence. And that it was dangerous to elide the two.

On 19 September, he saw Campbell's final draft of the dossier's foreword and judged it had crossed the line. Scarlett had already changed one of Campbell's earlier drafts, which had claimed that the dossier was 'the work of the JIC'. Scarlett changed it to *based in large part on* the work of the JIC'. Now, a matter of days before publication, Campbell found another of his misleading assertions punctured. He intended the dossier's opening line to read: 'The document published today is based, in large part, *on secret intelligence, as assessed by* the Joint Intelligence Committee (JIC).' Omand struck out 'on secret intelligence, as assessed by' and changed the opening to read: 'The document published today is based, in large part, on the work of the Joint Intelligence Committee.' He also changed the foreword's concluding paragraph, which Campbell wanted to read: 'I believe that faced with the information available to me *by the JIC* over the past three years, the UK Government has been right to support the demands that this issue be confronted and dealt with.' He took out the phrase 'by the JIC'.

There was one other last-minute tweak, too. Just before the dossier went off to the printers, the title changed from 'Iraq's *Programmes* for Weapons of Mass Destruction' to 'Iraq's Weapons of Mass Destruction', the title under which it was published.

In the final dossier, all the bold assertions that the Defence Intelligence Staff had complained about remained. The two contentious assertions they believed could not be supported by the intelligence were there, unqualified. 'What I believe the assessed intelligence has established beyond doubt is that Saddam has continued to produce chemical and biological weapons, that he continues in his efforts to develop nuclear weapons, and that he has been able to extend the range of his ballistic missile programme.' The dossier 'discloses that his military planning allows for some of the WMD to be ready within forty-five minutes of an order to use them'.

The day before publication, Blair told his Cabinet ministers that the dossier brought together all the evidence there was, some based on historical information already in the public domain, some based on intelligence, that Saddam was building up his WMD. He told them, too, that something must be done. That he believed in getting rid of dangerous dictators like Saddam Hussein. That it would be folly to go against the US on this one. That he was prepared to go down the UN route, but if that failed, there'd have to be some kind of military intervention to force Saddam to disarm.

The dossier was exactly the prop Blair needed for the grand piece of theatre the following day, 24 September: the recall of Parliament. After that, it could be forgotten.

It was published that morning and captured the public's imagination. Demand was overwhelming; websites offering downloads crashed. And though the military and diplomatic experts who reviewed it for the morning news outlets saw little in it that was new, apart from the language, by lunchtime Campbell was purring. Coverage was 'massive' and the dossier was 'leading almost every bulletin in the world'.

CHAPTER TEN

WHAT DR KELLY SAID TO ANDREW GILLIGAN
– AND WHY

In the light of the uncertainties arising from Mr Gilligan's evidence and the existence of two versions of his notes made on his personal organiser of his discussion with Dr Kelly on 22 May it is not possible to reach a definite conclusion as to what Dr Kelly said to Mr Gilligan.

Lord Hutton, 28 January 2004

In many ways, this was the most important of Lord Hutton's conclusions.

It raised the prospect that Dr Kelly might not have said to Andrew Gilligan what he later reported. Or that what he said was materially different from what Gilligan later attributed to him. That Gilligan might not simply have tripped over his words in that one 6.07 two-way but that everything he reported that day might not have been allegations first levelled by Dr Kelly.

On the precise point, Lord Hutton was correct. Of course it was impossible to reach 'a definite conclusion' about the precise words Dr Kelly used to Gilligan – it's impossible to reach that conclusion about what any source says to any journalist unless the conversation is recorded. But Gilligan had also conceded that Dr Kelly had not used some of the phrases he'd attributed to him. And it was true that his notes turned out to be less than ideal. Those he'd made on his personal organiser were sketchy and incomplete. Nor was it clear exactly when they were written. And the 'transcription' he presented to me and to my day editor turned out not to be as 'verbatim' as he'd claimed.

But the real significance of this conclusion was that in raising doubts over what Dr Kelly might have said to Gilligan, Lord Hutton absolved himself of the duty to inquire why he might have said it. Crudely, his thinking seems to have gone: we can't trust this man Gilligan, therefore we can't know what Dr Kelly's allegations really were, therefore I don't need to inquire further whether they reflected justifiable concerns in the intelligence community. Yet that was the key to understanding the circumstances surrounding Dr Kelly's death.

Even if Hutton couldn't 'reach a definite conclusion' about what Dr Kelly had said to Gilligan, he could be absolutely certain of what he'd said to another journalist. He'd heard the tape *Newsnight*'s Susan Watts had made of one of her conversations with him. And that tape showed beyond argument or doubt the concerns there were over the dossier and the language Dr Kelly had used to share them with at least one journalist. And that when you strip out Gilligan's inferences, over-interpretations and loose language, you find something too similar to dismiss as peremptorily as Lord Hutton did.

• • •

Lord Hutton's fascination with Andrew Gilligan's notes and his personal organiser was as baffling as it appeared misdirected. It demonstrates how little he understood of journalism. Even the BBC found itself sidetracked, commissioning a report from the manufacturer that failed to conclude definitively that Gilligan had or had not written his notes when he said he had.

Hutton spent hours investigating the internal clocks and file structures of an obsolescent piece of electronic equipment, trying to establish exactly when Gilligan wrote the sketchy phrases and half-sentences that he said were a partial, contemporaneous record of his conversation with Dr Kelly. Whatever else it did, it cast a further shadow over Gilligan's reliability and, by extension, the BBC's.

It was a red herring. Hutton seemed to think he should treat Gilligan's notes in the way a criminal trial judge treats a police officer's notebook. And while, in an ideal world, a reporter's notebook should be crammed full of verbatim quotes written at the time of any event, the real world of journalism isn't always like that.

Gilligan's personal organiser and any notes there may have been on it played no part in my decision to put him on air. Nor should it have. I didn't even know about it and didn't need to. Reporters make notes to remind themselves of what their sources say. But those notes can never be 'proof' of anything. A clear, definitive, dated note of a fabrication or mishearing is a bad note – worse than no note at all. And one of the sights that always used to make me laugh at big events was the press pack gathering after some public figure had spoken, comparing notes to make sure all their quotes agreed – not necessarily with what had actually been said, but with each other.

In an ideal world, all sources would go on the record. And in broadcast journalism, that means delivering their opinions or testimony or making their allegations in their own words, in their own way, in their own voice. For fairly obvious reasons, some sources will be reluctant to go on the record, or to go on air themselves. If they're revealing something that others, especially those in power, would rather remained secret, then going on the record might well endanger them or their career. If you broadcast their allegations, you have a clear duty to protect their identity. For a broadcaster, using a reporter to give an account of an anonymous source's testimony is always a poor second best. Sometimes, though, it's a second best we have to settle for if we're going to break meaningful stories based on whistleblowers' accounts.

When we do, verbatim notes that the reporter makes at the time with fast, accurate shorthand are the ideal. That, or taping the conversation for note-taking purposes, much as *Newsnight*'s Susan Watts did with Dr Kelly. Documentary evidence, a report or a draft of a document, is good, too. But it's not always convenient or even possible for the reporter to whip out a notebook and make complete and verbatim notes as if taking dictation. And it's rare for a source who wants to remain anonymous, a whistleblower, to be happy to speak into a microphone, even with the assurance that it will never be broadcast. Often, too, a reporter stumbles on a new story while talking to a contact about something completely different, as happened with Gilligan and Dr Kelly.

When that happens, reporters will usually try to do what Gilligan described. Take out a notebook or device or even grab a napkin and ask 'do you mind me taking notes?' The reporter can then, at the end, check usable quotes with the source. Sometimes, though, it's just not possible or not a good idea. You might be standing around at a reception, balancing canapés and a lukewarm grape-based beverage. You might have bumped into your source unexpectedly. Or perhaps the source has let something slip. Then, whipping out a notebook would guarantee he or she clammed up. Dealing with confidential sources is rarely calm and well ordered, rarely like covering a court case or a news conference or conducting a set-piece interview. Or, indeed, noting an interview like a police officer might.

Imperfect notes made at the time, notes made soon after the event or even no notes at all don't mean in themselves that you don't have a story. I'm a habitual note-taker and tend to keep a small notebook in my pocket just in case. But once I stumbled on a good story at a Christmas party when there was no piece of paper anywhere around. Lord Heseltine told me that Tories must change the party rules to avoid electing a right-wing 'dog whistler' as leader. I couldn't make a note of what he'd said for several hours, but that didn't mean it couldn't be reported. Many political stories ('sources close to' or 'friends of') start life like that. Or as a couple of sentences culled from a lunch or a chance meeting in a corridor. Then, memory is all you have to go on, assisted by a quick note made as soon afterwards as possible.

Hutton also castigated BBC management for failing 'to make an examination of Mr Gilligan's notes on his personal organiser' once Alastair Campbell had decided he needed to re-ignite the row at the end of June. He continued: 'When the BBC management did look at Mr Gilligan's notes after 27 June, it failed to appreciate that the notes did not fully support the most serious of the allegations which he had reported in the 6.07 a.m. broadcast, and it therefore failed to draw the attention of the governors to the lack of support in the notes for the most serious of the allegations.' It's a conclusion that lacks logic.

Whatever the status of those sketchy notes, they strongly support the allegations Gilligan intended to report, the story in his script: that the dossier was 'transformed' the week before it was published 'to make it sexier'; that 'the classic' was the 45-minute claim; that 'most things in the dossier were double sourced but that was single sourced'; that the 45-minute claim was 'misinterpreted'; that 'most people in intelligence weren't happy with it because it didn't reflect the considered view they were putting forward'; that the dossier contained 'real information' but included it 'against our wishes'; that it was 'Campbell' who was responsible; that when he saw the 'original draft' it was 'dull' and he 'asked if anything else could go in'. Gilligan may have fallen over his words in one broadcast, but contrary to Hutton's assertion, when we looked at those notes they did, in fact, support all that Gilligan intended to say. That doesn't excuse Gilligan's mis-reporting, but it does make a nonsense of Hutton's conclusion.

• • •

Before Gilligan went to meet Dr Kelly in the Charing Cross Hotel, just off Trafalgar Square, on 22 May 2003, he'd been in Baghdad for most of the winter and spring of 2003, covering the war. No one, least of all me, had been hugely thrilled at the idea but he'd engineered himself a visa and, for a while, was one of the few people the BBC was able to get into Iraq.

He'd come back to the UK at the beginning of May and one of the first things he did was call Dr Kelly and arrange a meeting. They'd met two or three times previously and he was someone Gilligan respected and admired.

Gilligan had no agenda for the meeting, except to talk a little about Iraq, something about Saddam's WMD and perhaps something about the weapons inspectors' next steps. Dr Kelly was one of the UK's top biological weapons experts who'd also developed an expertise in chemical weapons and he was due to go back to Iraq as part of the Survey Group. The two of them had also spoken about the September dossier before and Gilligan knew Dr Kelly had been involved in its production.

Gilligan remembers he was fifteen minutes late, bought a Coke and an Appletiser and kicked off their conversation with complaints about trains. He didn't take notes to begin with and they spoke in general terms about Iraq. Out of politeness and, perhaps, genuine curiosity, Dr Kelly asked about and showed interest in Gilligan's time in Baghdad. As they talked, Gilligan wondered out loud why Saddam's troops hadn't used biological or chemical weapons. The conversation went back and forth with Gilligan asking why Dr Kelly thought coalition forces, six weeks after the end of the war, still hadn't been able to find a trace of current production or stockpiles held at 45 minutes' notice, as the September 2002 dossier had said. He wondered, too, how the claim had ever got into the dossier. It was a startling claim and, as he reminded Dr Kelly, when they'd last spoken in the spring of 2002, he'd said the dossier wasn't 'very exciting'.

'Yes, that's right,' Dr Kelly replied, 'until the last week it was just as I told you. It was transformed in the week before publication.' We can't be certain those were his precise words but we can be certain that was the sense of what he said.

'To make it sexier?' Gilligan suggested.

'Yes, to make it sexier.' Dr Kelly didn't volunteer this phrase but he did pick it up once Gilligan had used it.

Gilligan asked for examples. The 'classic' was the 45-minute claim: 'Most things in the dossier were double sourced but that was single sourced.' Gilligan wondered how those involved in the dossier felt about the transformation. Dr Kelly replied that 'most people in intelligence' weren't happy with it because it 'didn't reflect the considered view they were putting forward'.

Gilligan pressed. How did the transformation happen? There followed, according to Gilligan, a one-word reply: 'Campbell.'

Why had the claim been included if people in intelligence were unhappy about it, Gilligan wanted to know. 'For impact.' Dr Kelly said he'd always doubted the 45-minute claim. He knew of no weapons system that could be assembled for use within 45 minutes. And while he acknowledged that he didn't know the intelligence behind the claim, he thought it was unwise to include it in the September dossier.

'We believed that the source was wrong,' Dr Kelly said. The intelligence had been 'misinterpreted'.

'Campbell made it up? They made it up?' Gilligan asked, sensing something truly astonishing. But Dr Kelly disappointed him: 'No. It was real information and it was in the dossier against our wishes.'

Then they talked about other problems with the dossier. The claim that Saddam had tried to buy uranium from Niger, for example. And then on to highly technical aspects of Iraq's weapons and inspections.

That, more or less, is Gilligan's account of the meeting, almost all of it supported by the notes on his personal organiser. But whatever doubts Hutton may have had about those notes, it wasn't the only evidence he had of what was on Dr Kelly's mind at the time.

On 16 July, two days before Dr Kelly's body was found on the edge of an Oxfordshire wood, he gave his own account of his meeting with Gilligan to the Intelligence and Security Committee (ISC). Two of his bosses, Brian Wells and John Clarke of the MoD, were there as observers. Otherwise, the evidence was taken in secret.

Dr Kelly's recollection differs from Gilligan's in many key respects. And though it's difficult to pick up his tone from a written transcript, it seems that he felt discomfort similar to that we'd seen the day before when he gave evidence on live TV to the Foreign Affairs Select Committee.

He told the ISC that he couldn't recall saying the dossier had been 'transformed'. Nor naming Campbell as the culprit. He could recall discussing the 45-minute claim, but not in the context of the dossier; it was a 'possibility' that it was 'unwise' to include the claim in the dossier for 'impact'. And that he might have used the word 'sexier'. But he told this committee, as he had the Foreign Affairs Committee, that he doubted he was the sole source for Gilligan's story.

But he was the only source. And in order to accept his account of his meeting with Gilligan we must also accept a major improbability. That the conversation he had with Gilligan was substantially different from the one he had with *Newsnight*'s Susan Watts, the conversation she taped.

As it happened, Watts had spoken to Dr Kelly a fortnight before he met Gilligan. She hadn't recorded that conversation, though she did make full notes. They'd spoken, amongst other thing, about the 45-minute claim. Dr Kelly had told her that it was 'a mistake to put it in'. That it was 'Alastair Campbell' who'd seen 'something in there', something in the 45-minute claim. But, Dr Kelly told Watts, while the claim looked good on paper, it was single sourced and not corroborated.

Watts made nothing of it. She saw it as a gossipy, speculative aside. But once Gilligan had broadcast his report, Watts called Dr Kelly again, unaware that he was also Gilligan's source, wondering whether she'd 'missed a trick'. This time, she had a tape recorder running.

Watts reminded Dr Kelly about the 45-minute claim in the dossier. Dr Kelly replied that 'We spoke about this before of course ... I think you know my views on that.' Watts said she did and added: 'You were more specific than the source on the *Today* programme ... in fact you actually referred to Alastair Campbell in that conversation.'

Dr Kelly did not demur. It would be reasonable to conclude, then, that it's Gilligan's rather than Dr Kelly's recollection of that part of their conversation that's more accurate. That Dr Kelly did indeed name Alastair Campbell.

The recording goes on. Dr Kelly declines to call himself 'part of the intelligence community', though he was across the arguments about the way the 45-minute claim had been used in the dossier. And, he told Watts, he reviewed the dossier in its entirety.

'I knew the concern about the statement...' So, there was concern then. Or at least Dr Kelly thought there was and told at least one journalist, Watts, about it. 'It was a statement that was made and it just got out of all proportion ... they were desperate for information ... they were pushing hard for information which could be released ... that was one that popped up and it was seized on and it was unfortunate that it was.'

Why unfortunate? Because it was questionable. Because the analysts thought it was wrong. 'I was uneasy with it ... I mean my problem was I could give other explanations which I've indicated to you ... that it was the time to erect something like a Scud missile or it was the time to fill a 40-barrel, multi-barrel rocket launcher ... there are all sorts of reasons why 45 minutes might well be important.'

Dr Kelly's difficulties with the 45-minute claim also came from the way in which the intelligence had been gathered: 'I have no idea who debriefed this guy … quite often it's some-one who has no idea of the topic and the information comes through and people then use it as they see fit.'

Gilligan had reported that Dr Kelly told him the dossier had been 'transformed in the week before publication … to make it sexier'. He told Watts something similar:

> It was an interesting week before the dossier was put out because there were so many things in there that people were saying 'well we're not so sure about that…' or in fact they were happy with it being in but not expressed the way that it was because, you know, the word-smithing is actually quite important, and the intelligence community are a pretty cautious lot on the whole … but once you get people putting it, presenting it for public consumption then of course they use different words.
>
> I don't think they're being wilfully dishonest I think they just think that that's the way the public will appreciate it best … [but] in your heart of hearts you must realise sometimes that's not actually the right thing to say.

'Not actually the right thing to say'. That's such a key phrase. Gilligan conceded to Lord Hutton that Dr Kelly didn't say to him that 'the government probably knew it [the 45-minute claim] was wrong.' It was an inference and a serious mis-attribution to an anonymous source. Had Gilligan said in that 6.07 two-way: '*and I think* the government probably knew it was wrong…' he would have been on much safer ground. It's not unreasonable to think, though, that Dr Kelly may well have shared a thought similar to 'not the right thing to say' with Gilligan. Something that brought the word 'wrong' to the front of his mind when he went on air.

On Watts's tape, she could be heard finally putting Downing Street's denials of Gilligan's story to Dr Kelly. 'It's a matter of perception isn't it…' he replied. 'People will perceive things and ... they'll see it from their own standpoint and they may not even appreciate quite what they were doing.'

Hutton heard all of this, yet still felt entitled to conclude that he couldn't 'reach a definite conclusion' about what Dr Kelly said to Gilligan. That was a classic example of judicial abdication. Based on Watts's evidence alone, he could have found to a high degree of probability that Dr Kelly had levelled allegations to at least one other reporter that were exceptionally close to those Gilligan reported. To assume that he might have said something totally different to Gilligan would be highly improbable.

But Hutton had more than just Watts's tape and evidence to go on. He also heard from Dr Brian Jones, one of the senior men in the Defence Intelligence Staff. Dr Jones had described what Dr Kelly thought about the dossier when it was published in September 2002, that it was a 'good' piece of work and a decent summary. He didn't share all Dr Jones's and the DIS analysts' reservations about the 45-minute claim, but he knew about them and had discussed them many times. He was around the DIS offices during the last week or so when the dossier was being drafted and saw for himself the 'transformation'. He saw, too, the pressure the analysts were under. The heavy and increasing workload, the ever tighter deadlines. He heard their grumbling about the way their reservations were apparently disregarded. Their growing frustration and unhappiness at what they were being asked to do.

Like the analysts, he cared about language. Like the analysts, he would debate to the point of exhaustion precise words to express a precise assessment. Words, the meaning of words, the possible ambiguities that words could hide mattered to them. An inexact word in the wrong place could cost lives.

Dr Kelly disliked oversimplification too and that was his main personal criticism of the way the 45-minute claim had been worded in the dossier. We know this from a confidential article he'd drafted on his home computer. An article that tried to answer the question why, three months after the end of the war, no WMD had been found. The same question Gilligan had asked at their meeting in the Charing Cross Hotel.

'Fuel has been added to the debate', he wrote, 'by the ferocious row between the BBC and No. 10' over the 'famous warning that Iraq's WMD could be deployed within 45 minutes ... both sides, at the time of writing seem prepared to go the mat on the issue. What is the probable truth?'

Not the claim as it appeared in the dossier, apparently. That, according to Dr Kelly, was 'risible to anyone who knows how the weaponry works'. That's not to say Saddam had no WMD programme and was no danger. He just wasn't the real and present danger the dossier portrayed. If all the evidence of dispersal, development and concealment were taken together, Dr Kelly wrote, 'it points inescapably in one direction only'.

'The irony is', he concluded, 'it never needed "sexing up".'

And that reflected Dr Kelly's distaste for spin. An unidentified senior official in the DIS wrote to him, lamenting that 'you and I should have been more involved in this than the spin merchants of this administration'. It was a reflection, too, of the view amongst the analysts that the dossier had been round the houses several times to try to find words to make the content fit the politics and to allow the politics to masquerade as intelligence.

There was one final oddity about Hutton's conclusions over what Dr Kelly had said to Gilligan. He accepted that Dr Kelly did use the phrase 'sexed up' to describe what he believed had been done to the dossier. Dr Kelly didn't initiate the phrase but he did pick it up once Gilligan had used it. He'd told the Intelligence and Security Committee as much. And though there could be no dispute over that, there could be one over what the phrase meant. Hutton placed on it a meaning that was most favourable to the government's case and least favourable to the BBC's.

The phrase 'sexed up' was 'capable of two different meanings', he concluded. 'It could mean that the dossier was embellished with items of intelligence known or believed to be false or unreliable' or 'it could mean that while the intelligence contained in the dossier was believed to be reliable, the dossier was drafted in such a way as to make the case against Saddam Hussein as strong as the intelligence contained in it permitted'. Hutton decided it must mean the first. That made him a member of a very tiny club.

The phrase 'sexed up' is, of course, capable of very many more than two different meanings. Hutton's preferred meaning never occurred to me when I passed the story for broadcast. I never thought that's what the phrase meant and was clear what I thought it did mean. The meaning Gilligan intended, the meaning Dr Kelly intended when he picked it up and the one that any fair-minded listener would understand.

To accept Hutton's meaning, you also have to accept, as he did, that the dossier was a pure intelligence document, written by the JIC and the agencies in isolation from Downing Street, that landed, perfectly formed, in Campbell's in tray. And that Dr Kelly and Gilligan had alleged Campbell had taken that 'pure', carefully measured text and inserted intelligence he knew was false. That isn't what happened at all, nor is it the allegation Dr Kelly made.

The dossier as it was published was a Downing Street inspired, political document whose production had had Campbell at its centre. It had been 'dull' – an on/off affair because the kind of 'revelatory' intelligence that might justify Blair's beliefs about Saddam's WMD didn't exist. Shortly before publication, it was 'sexed up' to make sure it was the kind of dossier Blair needed by including – not 'inserting' – 'sexy'-looking intelligence and removing from it the qualifications essential to understanding it.

In other words, it was 'sexed up' for impact and to make 'the strongest possible case' for war. In essence, it was no different from anything else that came out of Downing Street in the New Labour era.

CHAPTER ELEVEN

'THE PROCESS'

It is not necessary to accept everything as true, one must only accept it as necessary.

Franz Kafka, *The Trial*

'**G**et yourself a lawyer.'

I wish I could remember who'd first said that to me. I think it was Richard Sambrook, but it might not have been. Whoever it was, they were more aware of what was happening than I was.

It never occurred to me until after Lord Hutton reported that the BBC and I might not always have had the same interests during the inquiry. Within days of Hutton's report, I needed that lawyer. For something coyly called 'The Process'.

It was the acting DG, Mark Byford who announced the internal inquiry designed 'to rebuild trust in BBC news' – though opinion polling after Hutton suggested that trust in the BBC had risen rather than fallen. Byford was certainly right that there had to be some kind of process, if for no other reason than to show the BBC was taking its accountability to the public seriously and was prepared to be transparent about what it had learnt from the whole affair. What wasn't immediately clear was how 'The Process' that was announced was going to be that or do that. Lord Ryder, the acting chairman, had already accepted all Hutton's conclusions without reservation and he and Byford had apologised unreservedly for anything and everything anyone might or might not have done. If that was where 'The Process' was starting from, there was nothing left to say. Hutton had said it all.

Byford had a tricky time explaining the purpose of 'The Process' both inside and outside the BBC. He conceded on my old show, *PM*, that he was 'concerned' that Hutton had criticised my editing as 'defective' without questioning me. 'It makes me realise that we have to examine those findings, understand why he said that.' That seemed to me an odd phrase to use. Almost as if one aim of 'The Process' was to show that Hutton was right to condemn my editing as 'defective'.

He was uncomfortable again a few days later when he appeared on David Frost's Sunday morning show. Frost's questioning was cuter, Byford more coy than I'd expected. At first, he described 'The Process' as a kind of 'survey' that he would lead with the BBC's Director of Human Resources, Stephen Dando – a man who never seemed to me to have BBC blood running through his veins and who always spoke as if he was reading from the manual. Frost quipped that with the head of personnel there in 'The Process', 'It means you can actually interview the person and give him his cards at the same time.'

It was a much better question than I realised: 'We're not looking at … giving cards or anything like that … it will be done extremely professionally.' That wasn't how it looked to me over that first weekend after Hutton had delivered his conclusions. I needed to know more and decided to track Dando down and ask him what exactly he planned to do. After all, I still had a programme to run and that was pressured enough at the best of times. Now, added to that were the post-Hutton pressures and 'The Process'. But Dando wasn't easy to get hold of and it wasn't until 8.15 that evening that he finally called me back. I lost my outward cool, asking what that 'duty of care' Byford had talked about actually meant. And yelled at one point that what was happening was 'fucking hypocrisy of the worst sort'.

I may as well have been talking to his voicemail.

He repeated over and over that 'The Process' would begin as soon as possible and be completed as quickly as possible and that the BBC would exercise its proper duty of care.

It was obviously going to be uncomfortable. For all of us.

• • •

The following morning, Byford came to see me, apparently to reassure me about 'The Process'.

He loped through the far door of the news factory, tall and ungainly, carrying a small man-bag, his hair still recovering from a pledge to shave his head for the previous winter's *Children in Need*. He planted a bear paw on my shoulder and scooped me into the glass box that was my office. Thirty lip-reading pairs of eyes turned towards us as he began, in strictest confidence, to tell me about 'The Process'.

I was in a sour mood, still angry from the non-conversation I'd had the night before with Dando. And Byford called me by my first name throughout, something that – irrationally – has always annoyed the hell out of me. It didn't help.

'Now I know, Kevin, how important this job is to you...' That didn't seem the best place to start. 'I know how much you've dreamed about being editor of *Today*...' Being told what I was thinking never amused me much either. 'You'll see this as a knock-back...' I wasn't really listening now. I was already working out how to handle 'The Process' – whatever it turned out to be.

Byford painted a benign picture of 'The Process' adding what, I'm sure, he meant to be reassuring words of encouragement. Then, we were done. I stood up, bracing myself for the Byford bear paw that I knew would smash down onto my shoulder in a show of comradeship. Later that day, the letter arrived telling me that I was now subject to 'disciplinary procedures'. 'The Process' was going to be no benign 'survey', as Byford had described it on air. It was 'disciplinary procedures'.

It was grotesque and I was angry again. Not only had the BBC failed to ensure my voice was heard at the inquiry; not only had it allowed Hutton to think I was responsible for mistakes no one had made; it was now going to put me through the disciplinary mill like someone who'd fiddled his expenses or hit the boss.

Then that voice: 'Get yourself a lawyer.' That evening, I did.

• • •

David Price is now one of the leading media lawyers in the country. Back in 2004, he'd already established a reputation on high-profile media cases and was, in a good way, fashionable. He'd just moved to new offices in Fleet Street, a little down the road from the Royal Courts of Justice. And he was a good man to have on your side.

I'd consulted him before, in 1997. To fire a warning shot across the bows of Charlie Whelan, the Chancellor of the Exchequer Gordon Brown's boorish press chief, after he'd libelled me. It was in a fly-on-the-wall documentary about the New Labour Treasury team. Brown had invited Scottish Television, the TV company both Gordon and his brother John once worked for, to follow him and Whelan around for a few days. It wasn't the best idea either of them had ever had. At best, it was narcissism and throughout both Brown and Whelan seemed oblivious to the damage they were doing to themselves.

They were shown cynically manipulating news stories, including Brown's plan to take away from the Bank of England its role regulating, amongst other things, pensions. In one scene, Whelan is seen briefing John Fryer, then a BBC correspondent, predicting that 'they', the Bank, would 'go mental' if they found out he'd been talking to journalists. Whelan clearly thought that filming the briefing and showing it on TV was one way of keeping it secret. Brown, too, appears the ruthless 'truth creator' you had to be to survive at the top of New Labour. He warns that the story headline could become 'BANK ATTACKS LABOUR MOVE' if they're not careful. Whelan's answer is the standard New Labour one: 'make sure people in advance know that isn't the story'. Make it seem the Bank is whining in defence of their vested interest.

It worked. It made headlines such as the BBC's: 'THE CHAN-CELLOR OF THE EXCHEQUER ORDERS A MAJOR SHAKE-UP OF THE FINANCIAL WORLD TO GIVE INVESTORS GREATER PROTECTION' while pundits pointed out that 'the new regulatory regime ... followed automatically' on the heels of independence for the Bank. Brown's team gloated that some journalists 'bought the whole bloody lot'.

But the documentary began with Whelan steering Brown into the BBC's Millbank Studio to do a live interview with Nick Clarke on *The World at One*. Between him leaving the Treasury and arriving at Millbank, a new story had broken and I'd put an interview with Michael Heseltine at the top of the running order. I told Whelan that I'd dropped Brown down to second and he'd have to wait a few minutes.

Brown was visibly irritated and the two of them briefly wondered out loud whether we'd realised the Tories weren't in government any more. Then, casually, Whelan tried to reassure Brown: 'Don't worry about it, Gordon. The editor is a Tory.'

I knew nothing about it on the day. I was in the studio at Broadcasting House driving the programme, not out in the corridor with the STV documentary team. But the week before it was due to go out, I got a call from a friend who'd seen it at a media preview in Scotland. He wanted to know if I'd seen it, too. I said I hadn't. Did I know what Whelan had said about me. I said I didn't. He told me. I was irritated. It looked like yet another New Labour front opening on me. First Mandelson, then Campbell. Now Whelan who, bizarrely, in opposition had been a free-flowing source for *The World at One*.

In any other circumstance, I'd have let it go. Journalists

don't sue or even threaten to. They answer back. But I wasn't allowed to answer back. The press office, my boss, my bosses' boss all told me not to go public. They didn't want another slanging match over political bias on *The World at One*. I didn't either. But I did want STV to take the line out of the documentary, at the very least. I knew that if they didn't, it would end up in the cuttings and would be trotted out when every lazy journalist wrote about me and *The World at One*. The BBC shrugged. They couldn't be seen to make the request, they said. It would reflect badly on the corporation. They were perfectly happy, on the other hand, to have one of their biggest frontline editors branded, libellously, a Tory. Biased.

So I told the BBC that I was going to sue Whelan and STV unless they cut the line from the documentary. I would use my own lawyer and there was nothing they could do to stop me. After some dithering, they realised there was indeed nothing they could do. I asked around for the best libel lawyer and someone pointed me towards David Price, then a young solicitor-advocate who already had his own practice and had authored a textbook on libel: *Defamation: Law, Procedure and Practice*. He seemed a good bet.

He was. A couple of letters later, STV had taken the line out of the documentary and I'd had a letter from Whelan apologising and promising not to do it again. It was a trivial victory but it made me smile and Whelan deserved it.

So, when I decided to get myself a lawyer to steer me through 'The Process', Price was the obvious choice. I went to see him that same evening down at Fleet Street. His new offices were still only partly furnished and freezing cold. We sat on uncomfortable wooden chairs, coats buttoned up and I explained the whole thing. About the row, about Hutton and about the way I felt the BBC was now behaving. Price listened. Said he'd think. I went home. Fed up.

Wondering what was really going on.

Price phoned me the following day. He'd read up on Hutton

and thought I was absolutely right. I had grounds for a judicial review and we could talk about it later that day if I wanted to. Meantime, he'd asked for an expert opinion on my position as a BBC employee and that 'duty of care' business and was recommending me to meet a barrister, Jon Turner of Monckton Chambers, for a full opinion on any action I could take against the BBC or against Hutton.

'You know, you should have had your own lawyer right at the start,' Price said. As far as he could see, he said, my interests and the BBC's were going their different ways from the moment Gilligan started giving evidence on the second full day of the inquiry.

'I know you trusted them. You thought you were all on the same side … but you weren't.' It was brutal. And I didn't like to think about what it meant. 'At the very least, they should have given you the option of your own lawyer … you've got a case against the BBC. Of course, you'd have to resign to pursue it.'

I said nothing. I couldn't quite think through the consequences of that.

'And you could always sell your story.'

I didn't like the sound of that last bit. But it was the conversation I needed. It injected realism and energy back into my determination to fight. I said OK to the legal opinion and to the meeting with the barrister. Great, Price said. And he didn't hang about. Delays of minutes annoyed him and if there were decisions to be made, he wanted them made there and then. He'd call and arrange meetings for half an hour's time. He always seemed to be available when I needed to talk. And I spent much of February 2004 shuttling at short notice between the BBC in west London and his offices on Fleet Street.

• • •

'The Process' turned quickly into an embarrassment. Senior journalists and executives made it public that they were disgusted. One called it 'the BBC's Guantanamo' and more than one denounced it as 'not the BBC I joined'. Later, as it dragged on, three of the most senior executives in the corporation, Jana Bennett, Director of TV; Jenny Abramsky, Director of Radio; and Alan Yentob, Director of Drama called for it to be stopped. It was, they said, 'tearing staff apart'. Even Gavyn Davies's successor, chairman designate Michael Grade, let it be known that he intended to ask Byford if he was 'happy' with what was happening.

The embarrassment was evident in Dando's letters summoning me and the rest of us involved to the first round of hearings. Mine invited me to a 'discussion about the management and circumstances of Andrew Gilligan's broadcast ... [and] the handling of the complaint'. In my case, that was to include 'the reports you made to ... your senior managers'. And then, in what read like a shamefaced afterthought, cleared its throat and mumbled that it was a 'formal meeting under the BBC's agreed procedures'. Disciplinary, that is. It didn't use the word. Whatever justification there might have been for what was happening, there was no excuse for this kind of evasion about what it actually was.

Those 'agreed procedures' said we had to be given 'full details of the alleged misconduct or unsatisfactory performance'. That meant not just the charges but also the full evidence allegedly supporting them. For the best part of a month, I tried to get those charges and that evidence out of Dando and Caroline Thomson, then the Director of Policy and Legal whom Byford had nominated to take his place in 'The Process'. But the most I got was the question thrown back at me. What was it that I needed clarifying? I wrote a final snarky note to Dando telling him that 'I was ready to take part in a full and open discussion about any lessons from the Hutton report. However, I do not believe any constructive discussion can take place under the disciplinary procedure ... [which was] damaging to individuals and the BBC.' I reminded him, too, that the way 'The Process' was unfolding, the 'agreed procedures' had been so subverted that any adverse outcome would be 'an abuse of process'.

But once again, it was like talking to his voicemail.

• • •

Almost all of what I had to say in 'The Process' was already down on paper. In my witness statement, prepared for Hutton and gathering dust on a BBC lawyer's shelf somewhere.

I worked through it all again with Price. My focus was almost entirely on 'The Process' but he and Jon Turner were also thinking about something else. Something much more ambitious. A judicial review of the whole Hutton Inquiry.

Price and Turner were very different characters, though both had extraordinarily retentive and precise legal minds. Price's, though, was restless and worked at several times the speed of a normal person's. Turner was much more deliberate, much more determined to think through all the options before moving on, and often had to bring Price back to the question the rest of us were still working on rather than the one he'd moved onto, several stages ahead.

By the middle of February, Turner had read everything: the Hutton report, the BBC's evidence, my witness statement, my contract with the BBC and the BBC's 'agreed procedures' and was ready with his opinion. It was impressive.

Hutton's 'adverse findings' about me, Turner wrote, 'were reached in ignorance of relevant facts that might well have pointed towards different conclusions'. Had my evidence been heard, 'Lord Hutton's findings might well have been different, or at least would have been significantly qualified.'

Turner's opinion wasn't confined to Hutton, however. His opinion on the way the BBC's case had, in his view, left me high and dry was pretty damning: 'the manner in which the BBC presented its case … led … at a certain stage to a divergence of interests between, on the one hand, certain of the

BBC's senior executives, and, on the other hand, the *Today* programme staff.'

'The BBC's conduct of its case ... involved admissions of editorial failings ... that were based on an incomplete or misleading account of the procedures' that I followed. That account hadn't been incorporated elsewhere in the BBC's case, either. 'This approach was calculated to seriously damage the degree of trust and confidence which Kevin Marsh was reasonably entitled to have in his employer.'

I guess I just hadn't been able to admit to myself that that's exactly how it was. Turner concluded the point: the failure to offer me 'independent legal representation ... at the stage where the BBC's interests and/or the interest of the senior executives who gave evidence diverged from those of Kevin Marsh, appears to have been in breach of the duty of mutual trust and confidence which is implied in his contract of employment'.

And then the big one. As far as Hutton's findings went: 'those findings are vitiated by a material error of fact and/or by a failure to take relevant evidence into account; to that extent, the report may be susceptible to challenge by way of judicial review.'

I knew it was Price's and Turner's job to be on my side but at last, I thought, someone other than me was looking at all of this and seeing it the way I should have been. I'd been too ready to accept everything that had happened.

But all of this still left me with the problem of how to handle 'The Process' since I had no idea what it was thought my 'disciplinary' offences had been. That left me with no option but to deluge Dando and Thomson with everything that could possibly be relevant.

In the meantime, I had to decide what to do about Hutton. Whether or not to launch that judicial review. Price wanted a decision now. I needed time. I managed to put it off for a few days, fixing a mega conference for the following week.

It was a sunny, early spring afternoon when that conference

came around. We held it at Turner's Monckton Chambers on the north side of Gray's Inn and 'yes' or 'no' to judicial review was the only item on the agenda. Taking it would be a massive step. Intimidating. Almost as intimidating as the group gathered that afternoon round Turner's conference table.

I was used to chairing meetings at the BBC where most are bigger than they need to be, bulked out by people no one really knows, who are there for reasons no one really knows either. But there's also a casualness about BBC meetings. Late arrivals, spilled drinks, a lot of lip and backchat. Being in the chair is often little more than being abusee in chief. Actually, I rather like that sort of meeting. And usually, out of the chaos, lack of preparation, personal rivalries and vituperation something new, original, brilliant emerged.

This was very different.

When I arrived at Monckton Chambers, a hyper-neat, hyper-efficient assistant took my coat, showed me to an ante-room – a large room with white-painted, panelled walls, antique furniture and a view over Gray's Inn gardens. She poured me coffee and gave me a pen and pad with the chambers' logo.

There was the buzz of people arriving in the next-door room. No one was going to be late, that was clear. After a while, moments before the appointed time, I was shown in, too. A lot of people I'd never met sat in tall leather-covered chairs around a large, dark wood conference table. David Price on one side, Jon Turner on the other with their various assistants at either side. As I came in, they all fell silent. The hyper-assistant gestured to the chair at the head of the table.

This was not like a BBC meeting at all. Price and Turner casually flicked through their papers. They'd prepared. The juniors and specialists looked intently at me; they were not going to be lippy, spill drinks or answer back. For the first and last time in my life, I was too over-awed to say a word. I sat. And waited.

Price kicked off. 'We need you to make a decision whether to go ahead with judicial review...' That was clear enough. But

before I did, he said, I might want to think about the consequences and about other options.

It all seemed suddenly very real. Turner tried to go about it
systematically, or would have done if Price hadn't jumped in
on the most contentious questions. I wondered if they were
always like this. I felt completely out of my depth as they
batted the legal jargon back and forth across the table and
assiduous assistants took copious notes.

It boiled down to this. Both Price and Turner felt I had a
very strong case to challenge Hutton one way or another. I
could do it informally, writing to him, via Turner, to express
my concerns and setting out the reasons his findings were
flawed. This, they said, would be the cheapest and quickest
way of getting some kind of public redress. But, they felt sure,
Hutton would argue *functus officio*. That's to say, that he had
completed his task and, in layman's terms, there was nothing
more to be said or done.

At the other extreme was judicial review. Again, they were
confident I'd have a strong chance of success. I suppose at this
stage lawyers always are. That would have maximum impact,
but it would take a long time, probably as long as the original
inquiry, be fiendishly complex and would cost a fortune. And
there was an added complication. Part of that judicial review
would have to look at the way the BBC conducted its case.
How, according to them, it failed to show an employer's 'duty
of care' towards me and protect my interests when they and
those of the BBC diverged.

And I couldn't really do that from the inside – I'd have
to resign.

'What are your instructions?' Price asked.

Everyone fell silent. Legal pens poised over legal pads. Nothing
in their faces. This really was my decision and mine alone.

Emotion told me to go for it. Now that my lawyers had
opened my eyes to what had been happening at Hutton, I felt
even angrier than I had the day Ryder and Byford had offered

their 'unequivocal' apology. The BBC whom I'd trusted had let me down. Hutton had trashed my reputation unjustly and unfairly and without allowing me a hearing.

Reason told me no. That I would have to have been a very different person to say yes. It would have meant becoming the very thing I hated most. Becoming even more a piece of public property than I was as editor of *Today*. There would be weeks of press and broadcasting coverage. Some of the same grandstanding there'd been at Hutton. More than anything else, though, I would still always feel responsible for setting in train the events that led to Dr Kelly's death.

I told the conference that we wouldn't be going ahead. Everyone smiled, packed their things away and trooped out. When they were gone, I told Price that what I really wanted was the clearest possible win in 'The Process'. I didn't want the attention judicial review would bring. I did want to force out of the BBC the admission that its case at Hutton had been flawed and that those flaws had damaged me. An admission, too, that Ryder and Byford had been wrong to accept Hutton so comprehensively and apologise so readily and unreservedly.

I expected Price to be disappointed. He wasn't. Or if he was, he didn't show it.

'Let's get on with it then,' he said.

• • •

One of the weird conventions of disciplinary hearings in the BBC is that you're allowed to take someone with you so long as they can't help you in any way. Like a lawyer.

I reckoned that didn't matter hugely though. I had Price's help and guidance outside so I bowled along to that first 'interview', as they'd coyly called it, with several hundred pages of notes and a shorthand writer.

Dando and Thomson appeared to know little about Lord Hutton's inquiry or his conclusions and no matter how often

I asked which part of my employment contract they thought I'd violated they wouldn't tell me. It was very unsatisfactory and later, when they sent me their record of the interview as they were required to do, it read like the notes of a completely different meeting.

I decided to change tack. Everyone else being questioned as part of 'The Process' had taken along with them the most senior 'friends' they could find and pressed me to do the same, if for no other reason than to make it clear what senior executives thought about 'The Process'. I called Helen Boaden, at that time the Controller of Radio 4. She'd replaced James Boyle after he'd been squeezed out for doing exactly what he'd been asked to do. He'd been treated abominably, I thought, but that wasn't Boaden's fault. She changed little of Boyle's schedule but cranked up programme commissioning a gear while chucking in the odd brilliant new idea, like turning over the entire network one Boxing Day to an eight-hour reading by Stephen Fry of *Harry Potter and the Philosopher's Stone*.

I wasn't as close to her as I'd been to Boyle, but I trusted her. I'd known her since she'd been a current affairs reporter working out of Manchester. She said she'd expected me to call her. I said she probably knew why I'd called and she said she probably did. We agreed that neither of us knew what being a 'prisoner's friend' entailed and she said shall I just sit there and look senior and I said that was probably the best way to start.

The other part of the new tack was to say nothing in direct answer to Dando and Thomson's questions. Instead, I'd find the most appropriate part of the hundreds of pages I'd worked on with Price and say 'I refer you to the following…', reading the appropriate paragraphs into the record. That way, there could be no doubt or misunderstanding over what I'd said.

When Boaden and I arrived at the next 'interview', she asked just before we went in: 'Has anyone told you that you've been set up?' They had, of course. But part of me still didn't want to think it was possible.

Boaden sat quietly by my side during all the rest of the 'interviews', patient and assiduous occasionally underlining phrases that needed underlining, reinforcing impressions that needed reinforcing. By the end of the business, I'd read hundreds of pages into 'The Process', recording everything that had happened before, during and after Gilligan's story went out, not one word of which Hutton had heard, much of it correcting what he had.

There was never any question 'The Process' would have to vindicate me. They found that, contrary to Hutton's conclusion, I *had* considered what Gilligan was intending to say; that I'd correctly assessed his source, following the BBC Editorial Guidelines to the letter; that Gilligan had a script but veered off it at 6.07. They also concluded that the memo that had so alarmed the BBC legal team and so entranced Hutton, that 'good investigative journalism marred by flawed reporting' memo, *did* reflect my bosses' thoughts too. All of it directly contradicted Hutton and implied that the BBC's temporary leadership, Lord Ryder and Mark Byford, had been wrong to accept his conclusions as they had.

They concluded, too, that the BBC had bungled its case by admitting 'mistakes' that hadn't been made. 'Admissions' that led to Hutton trashing my reputation.

But any satisfaction at the outcome was compromised. By the time it was all over, I'd been at *Today* for the eighteen months I'd originally set as my limit and wanted to move on. Much of the work I'd intended to do, I'd done. Boring but important stuff like getting the money and the people right and more interesting stuff like getting the journalism right and winning audiences back.

But I knew that if I got out now, there'd be the predictable snide comments in the press, quoting 'insiders', that I'd been 'quietly moved aside' or 'sidelined'.

That shouldn't have mattered but it did.

And I couldn't help the feeling that I was trapped.

POSTSCRIPT

Every word is like an unnecessary stain on silence and nothingness.

Samuel Beckett

Questions over the September dossier never went away. Lord Hutton's inadequacies saw to that along with the simple fact that no one was able to find any appreciable WMD in post-war Iraq. That was clear even as he sat down to write his conclusions. It meant the intelligence in the dossier had been wrong or misleadingly presented. Saddam had had no active WMD for a decade or more. He hadn't continued to produce them and didn't hold them at 45 minutes' readiness, if indeed he ever had.

'What went wrong with the intelligence?' was the question that needed an urgent answer. Less than a week after Hutton reported, on 3 February 2004, the Foreign Secretary Jack Straw announced yet another inquiry, specifically to examine:

> The accuracy of intelligence on Iraqi WMD up to March 2003, and to examine any discrepancies between the intelligence gathered, evaluated and used by the Government before the conflict, and between that intelligence and what has been discovered by the Iraq survey group since the end of the conflict.

It was the kind of remit an incoming government might give an inquiry to trawl through its predecessor's misdeeds. It meant going over in fine detail the roles of Alastair Campbell and John Scarlett in 'creating the truth' of the dossier out of the pre-war 'intelligence'. It meant asking how questionable the intelligence really was and how much Campbell and Scarlett knew about that when they wrote the September dossier.

The former head of the Home Civil Service, Lord Butler, chaired the new inquiry. But as if that wasn't enough, as he started his work, the Public Administration Select Committee of MPs also began an inquiry into inquiries themselves: 'Government By Inquiry', it was called. Naturally, they wanted to hear from Lord Hutton and, on 13 May, he appeared.

Those MPs who were less than wholly convinced Hutton had done a thorough job struggled to understand how he'd thought it reasonable not to consider any of the facts that lay behind the intelligence analysts' concerns. At first, he argued that the 'background facts' preceding Dr Kelly's death were 'reasonably clear', but then went on to describe how he intended the first part of his inquiry to establish those facts. At one point, he insisted that it was only when he'd completed that first part that he thought about the detail of his remit ... but later argued that his would have been 'a totally different inquiry' if he'd looked at the concerns over intelligence, and that would never have been 'appropriate' for 'a single judge sitting in public'. It was a muddle. On the one hand, he set out to consider 'matters and events which had affected [Dr Kelly's] mind and also events which had affected the minds of those who had dealings with [him]'. On the other, he decided not to think at all about the 'matters and events' that motivated Dr Kelly that had anything to do with intelligence. The committee chairman, Tony Wright, found it was 'almost incomprehensible', 'inexplicable' that Hutton had not 'cast [his] net slightly wider' when the death of Dr Kelly 'turned so much on the reliability of the intelligence information that was being put out and on whether the intelligence community were being asked to deliver, for political purposes, a document that they would not otherwise have produced in that way'.

Hutton gave one answer that was startling. One of the DIS analysts' most important doubts about the 45-minutes intelligence was whether it referred to WMD – as Campbell and Scarlett had unequivocally stated in the dossier – or to small-scale, battlefield munitions. 'It seemed to me', Hutton told the MPs, 'that that did not relate to the circumstances of Dr Kelly's death *because neither Dr Kelly nor Mr Gilligan had referred to that distinction.*' Yet Lord Hutton had read, as we all had, that Gilligan noted Dr Kelly telling him that the source of that intelligence had said 'it took 45 minutes to construct a missile assembly and it was misinterpreted to mean that WMD could be deployed in 45 minutes. What we thought it actually meant was that they could launch a conventional missile in 45 minutes.'

Gilligan had 'referred to that distinction' on air, too. At 6.07 he said, 'the intelligence agencies … thought the person making the claim had actually made a mistake … had got mixed up'. Ninety minutes later, at 7.32, he'd said 'they actually thought it [the intelligence] was wrong, they thought the informant concerned had got it wrong, they thought he'd misunderstood what was happening.'

It wasn't surprising that when the MPs reported, they recommended that in future, judges shouldn't sit alone 'in politically sensitive cases' and that future inquiries should have terms of reference 'drawn up in a way which allows full and proper examination of the facts'.

When Lord Butler reported in July 2004, the media made much of the many differences between his conclusions and Lord Hutton's. Butler was unequivocal in condemning both the way the agencies had gathered and assessed the pre-war intelligence and the way Downing Street had used it. He did not share Hutton's conclusion that Dr Kelly's allegations were 'unfounded'.

A 'high proportion' of the human intelligence sources prior to the Iraq war were dubious, Butler found. And so was the quality of the intelligence and assessments sent up to the Prime Minister and his officials. Some intelligence was third hand, a sub-source reporting to a main source. That was the case with the 45-minute intelligence. Some sources were authoritative, others little more than gossips. Some were 'new' and 'on trial' and had yielded intelligence which was subsequently withdrawn. None of it was the raw material of conviction. All of it questionable and some of it 'probably wrong' and known to be.

Butler found that, contrary to the September dossier's bold and unqualified assertions, Saddam did not have significant, if any, stocks of chemical or biological weapons in a state fit for use. Nor were plans for using them 'well developed'. Nor was there any 'recent intelligence' to justify the Prime Minister's belief that Iraq was a greater threat than the other rogue states. He was 'surprised' that no one in the agencies, the JIC or Downing Street had looked again at the intelligence in January and February 2003 when UN weapons inspectors were reporting their failure to find WMD where the intelligence said it should be.

As to the 45-minute claim, Butler determined that it shouldn't have been in the dossier without making it clear what it referred to – essentially agreeing with the intelligence analysts in the DIS and endorsing Dr Kelly's allegation. He also found that it was the only piece of intelligence that hadn't been correctly reported in JIC assessments. It had been questionable from the very start. And while he didn't speculate why questionable intelligence, strongly believed to be wrong in some parts of the intelligence community, was included in the dossier the answer seemed obvious.

By the time Butler reported, the analysts' concerns had been fully vindicated in other ways, too. MI6 finally conceded that the 45-minute intelligence had 'come into question' – though they'd known the limitations of the reporting chain from the moment it came in. Lord Butler concluded the analysts were right to voice their concerns over it and that they should also have been allowed to see and analyse the 'mystery' intelligence that the JIC chairman John Scarlett had used to overrule their concerns. He also found that it was 'a serious weakness' that the dossier didn't make clear intelligence chiefs' warnings about the limitations of the sparse intelligence they had. The September dossier's judgements 'went to (although not beyond) the outer limits of the intelligence available' and the Prime Minister gave the impression that the intelligence was 'firmer and fuller' than he knew it to be when he told MPs that the picture the intelligence agencies had painted was 'extensive, detailed and authoritative'.

The media made much of Butler's criticisms of the casual and secretive way business had been done in Downing Street in the run-up to a war. The 'informality' or 'sofa government' reduced the 'scope for informed collective political judgement'. And, just as Lord Hutton had done, Butler hinted very strongly that the JIC chairman, John Scarlett, had gone native, becoming more keen than was proper for an official in his position to deliver what his political masters required. Lord Butler concluded bluntly that future JIC chairmen should be people with experience of dealing with ministers, 'demonstrably beyond influence'.

Taken together, his findings couldn't have been more clear nor a greater condemnation of Hutton's work. The September dossier was not the carefully judged, carefully written, honest assessment of sound intelligence that Blair, Campbell and Scarlett argued and that Hutton believed it to be.

• • •

It's the conventional wisdom that the BBC became more cautious, more risk-averse, less ready to challenge government and authority after Hutton. Richard Ryder's and Mark Byford's apologies and 'The Process' certainly made it seem that way.

And, as ever, the more the BBC's critics in the press said there was a new atmosphere of caution, the more 'true' it became.

One of those critics was former *Today* journalist John Kampfner. He wrote in the *New Statesman* that, after Hutton, BBC stood for 'broken, beaten and cowed'. It had become 'excessively risk averse' and was 'deliberately avoiding giving offence to the government and the establishment'. BBC journalists had lost their backbone 'on the day Lord Hutton delivered his verdict', he opined.

It just wasn't true. It certainly wasn't true of me and I replied angrily. His notion of 'risk-taking' was warped, I wrote. 'There are real risks in journalism. Hundreds have died practising the trade…' But Kampfner's idea of 'risk' was 'the kind of journalism that sees causing trouble or getting up people's noses as ends in themselves … I won't be judged by that standard or accept those terms of debate … Is that risk averse? Frankly, I don't care. It's what I've always believed journalism to be – at *PM*, *World at One* and now at *Today*.'

Kampfner and others only had a point if all they were reading were the signs and signals coming from the office of the Deputy DG, Mark Byford. Greg Dyke's resignation had thrust him briefly centre stage but many believed his panicked responses to Hutton cost him the top job. Once Mark Thompson had arrived, Byford became Deputy DG and Head of BBC Journalism – a colossal brief, taking in not just News but any and every department that had a journalistic function. And he became responsible for 'standards'.

Byford was cautious by instinct, corporate by choice. He was BBC through and through and without doubt believed he had the best interests of the corporation at heart. But he'd spent most of his career in boardrooms or in the BBC regions and had little first-hand experience of New Labour's and Campbell's 'truth creation' nor of the grinding, wearying, daily hassle of dealing with the most sophisticated and relentless spin operation ever known in the UK. As well as 'The

Process', intended to 'learn the lessons of Hutton', he also set up a committee of the BBC's great and good to do the same. Former TV News executive Ron Neil chaired it and it took Hutton's conclusions at face value, as it was bound to. But that meant it was also bound to look in the wrong places and learn the wrong lessons.

Its recommendations were little more than a restatement of BBC Editorial Guidelines and good journalistic practice. It advised that 'accuracy and precision ... is paramount' and evidence should be 'robust and tested'. No one could argue with that – but they weren't the lessons of Hutton. The real lesson was that when you write a script and get it passed by your editor, it's a good idea to use it.

Similarly 'accurate note-taking'. Again, no one could argue with the importance of accurate notes. But the issue with Gilligan's 'notes' wasn't whether, when or how he'd made them. Or how accurate they were. It was whether the transcript he presented to me and my day editor was exactly what he said it was.

And so it went on: 'granting anonymity to a source should never be done casually or automatically'. Absolutely – but there'd been nothing casual or automatic about my decision to report Dr Kelly's allegations anonymously.

Where Neil did add to existing guidelines, it was with recommendations that were as unrealistic as they were excessively cautious. 'The BBC should not normally break stories making serious allegations in live two-ways' was one. Again, it missed the point. Because of his loose use of language, the allegations Gilligan actually reported in that 6.07 two-way weren't those he intended, the allegations he'd scripted. In any event, the recommendation, if interpreted literally, would have made the life of every BBC political correspondent impossible and taken News 24, now the News Channel, off the air.

Neil also echoed Hutton's misunderstanding of media law: 'allegations made by a third party will often be regarded by many viewers and listeners as also being made by the BBC itself.' Anyone who cared to could read that as a warning to editors not to assume the BBC would let them rely on a 'Reynolds Defence'. And the committee reminded us all that 'editors and executive producers must take the day to day responsibility' for their reporters and presenters. That went without saying – but written down in black and white, it read like a finger-wagging warning that editors would be expected to account for any unforeseeable moment of madness from a presenter or reporter. Neil's most lasting effect, though, was its recommendation that the BBC should set up a new College of Journalism. A good idea that would almost certainly have happened in due course anyway. It was a pity it was in the shadow of Hutton.

In the end, Hutton's impact on the BBC was dramatic but short-term. There were momentary wobbles and everyone wore more serious faces for a while. But the fact was, BBC journalism had always been safer, more sound than most of the competition. It had always been more restrained, its standard of proof higher than the press. And so it continued. At the same time, the idea that *Panorama* or *File on 4* or *Newsnight* backed away from investigations and exclusives or that John Humphrys or Jeremy Paxman became Hutton-fearing pussy-cats is nonsense.

• • •

I stayed at *Today* for two more years. But it was wearying.

Lord Hutton cast a long shadow and even those who'd dismissed his conclusions as a 'whitewash' still took them and the evidence he'd heard as the starting point for anything they wrote or said about me, *Today* and the BBC. Even after Lord Butler had so comprehensively torn Hutton to shreds. Critics built fanciful theories about 'what was wrong with the BBC' on the flimsy foundation that was Hutton. One of the most prominent came from the veteran *Financial Times* journalist John Lloyd.

I had a lot of time for Lloyd and we're still friends. But his long essay, 'What the Media Are Doing to Our Politics', was seriously flawed – not because his arguments and scholarship were poor but because his starting point was Hutton's discredited inquiry. Lloyd argued that Gilligan's 6.07 two-way was clinching evidence that media were over-powerful to the detriment of our self-government and had become 'increasingly destructive of their environment'. It was 'carelessly done' and fed on the 'cynical assumption that politicians are born liars and rogues'. He took it as read – from Hutton – that 'the editors didn't know [Gilligan's story] was well founded' and that 'they didn't check that it was before it was broadcast'. 'And', he continued, 'quite soon after it went out they discovered it wasn't [well founded]'. It was way off. And though I knew Lloyd's description of what happened was wrong, it was there in black and white and it got me down – partly because I shared his view that our media had got into habits that damaged our politics. But the way we reported Dr Kelly's allegations wasn't part of that.

By the time it was all over, I'd been editing BBC programmes for over twenty years. Very little now seemed new. Very little was. Same stories, same angles, same faces. And the rites and rituals of political journalism seemed empty and pointless. Worse, I was finding the relentless negativity of 'devil's advocacy' interviewing – *Today*'s staple – as pointless as it was damaging to sensible debate and discussion.

One moment should have lifted the weariness, but it didn't. At the end of September 2004, we finally got Blair and Humphrys in the same studio after a three-year hiatus. The last time they'd done verbal combat on *Today* was at the start of the 2001 election campaign in what I thought was the worst political interview I'd ever heard. It spent most of the available time on Blair's honesty and that of one of his junior ministers

– no bad thing in a different interview on a different occasion. But the wrong interview for the start of an election campaign. It sounded snarky, felt like the settling of scores, got nowhere and did nothing for the audience. As it happens, Campbell hated the interview too, though for different reasons. In a fit of pique fed by a public, priapic row with the then editor Rod Liddle, he refused to field Blair for any more interviews with *Today*. The myth took hold that Blair was snubbing or even afraid of Humphrys. He wasn't, but it did reputations no harm to pretend he was.

Three years on, the best chance of getting Blair back in the studio with Humphrys was at that year's Labour Party conference. If Humphrys was sitting in a studio in Brighton and Blair refused to walk along the corridor to talk to him, it would be a big story and the headline would be 'FRIT'. We prepped for four or five days. I had a researcher doing nothing else, digging into everything Blair had ever said on the war and on the other questions we planned to cover. And Humphrys and I played out every scenario we could think of and practised confronting Blair with all his contradictions, all his shifting arguments.

It was a brilliant interview, the best Humphrys did in my time at *Today* and by far the most penetrative that anyone did with Blair on WMD and the Iraq war. He began it in typical blunt style: 'we'd been taken to war on a false prospectus'. Blair was immediately uncomfortable. He could 'apologise for the fact that the information we gave has turned out to be wrong' but he couldn't 'apologise for saying that we got rid of Saddam Hussein, or that the basis on which we went to war was wrong, because we took the action as a result of Saddam's failure to comply with UN resolutions'.

I smiled. We'd expected him to shift the focus away from the intelligence and his unjustified beliefs and towards the UN. Humphrys wasn't having it: 'we weren't told we were going to war to get rid of Saddam Hussein.' Blair had to agree: 'That's absolutely right. Regime change was not the cause for it.'

One-nil to Humphrys. It didn't end there. Humphrys fired a salvo of legal and diplomatic arguments that Blair couldn't dodge. The UN Secretary General himself had said the resolutions didn't justify war … 'it was illegal.' Blair was cornered, and showed it: 'I totally understand that, and I'm not disputing it…' Wow – not disputing the war was illegal. 'I'm simply saying that we don't accept that.'

Two-nil. Then the dossier. Hadn't he accepted the more alarming intelligence – intelligence that turned out to be wrong – in 'a very naïve, in fact gullible, way?' And wasn't that because 'you had already decided with President Bush that you would go to war? So you were not looking for information that would prove the case for war. You were looking for information that would justify a decision you had already reached.' Blair's response was untenable: 'There was no doubt in respect of the intelligence about Saddam and weapons of mass destruction … I believe that any sensible, reasonable Prime Minister would say that's clear evidence there is a WMD threat here.' That was never more than debatable and by the time of the interview, we had Lord Butler's report telling us it was wrong.

Again, Humphrys's riposte: 'there was considerable doubt about it. I spoke myself, and others did too, to very senior figures in intelligence who said, and I quote on the basis of one particular conversation, on any Cartesian analysis "Iraq does not emerge as the priority" … there were questions about the 45 minutes' warning.'

Three … four … five-nil. Blair struggled and was unconvincing. Humphrys was back on the offensive. What about the confusion over the 45-minute claim, whether it referred to battlefield munitions or WMD. 'Why didn't you ask the questions?' There was, Blair countered, 'a mass of evidence'. Humphrys quoted President Putin: 'Russia does not have in its possession any trustworthy data that would support the existence of nuclear weapons or any weapons of mass destruction in Iraq.'

'I'm as fallible as anyone else. I may be wrong in it. But I don't believe I'm wrong.' Blair tried to argue again that it had all been about compliance with UN resolutions, but we all remembered it hadn't.

All the preparation had paid off. Humphrys had let nothing go. Everything was precisely aimed and in a different league from the matutinal bleary-eyed brawls he enjoyed and I loathed. But he was on a high and so should I have been. Instead, I thought 'so what?' It changed nothing. Not the past and almost certainly not the future. Everyone who cared had already made up their minds about Blair and the war. It was all just words.

My mood never improved. The 2005 election was a soulless trot around a well-worn track, its outcome never in doubt and by the end I knew I couldn't face another. But there was no other job in the BBC that I wanted to do. I certainly didn't fancy the corporate boardroom, nor was I ever likely to be invited in.

By the winter of 2006, I was on the point of jacking it all in and leaving the BBC when Vin Ray, the Director of the embryonic College of Journalism, asked if I'd like to write some articles for him. I said 'yes'. A couple of weeks later, he asked whether I'd like to join him full-time as the college's executive editor. He didn't expect the answer 'yes' but it seemed to me an exciting new thing to do. The only reason to say 'no' was the certainty that some witless oaf would write in the press that I'd 'been moved to training'. And, sure enough, they did.

• • •

Now, we all know that Dr Kelly was right when he spoke about the way the dossier was 'transformed'. The dossier was 'sexed up'. *Today* was right to report it.

It's worth recalling one last time what the allegations actually were and what they weren't. The allegations in the script I passed for broadcast and expected to hear on air. In that script,

Gilligan wrote that Dr Kelly had told him that, amongst other things:

> ... until the week before it was published, the draft dossier produced by the Intelligence Services, added little to what was already publicly known ... It was transformed in the week before it was published, to make it sexier. The classic example was the statement that weapons of mass destruction were ready for use within 45 minutes. That information was not in the original draft. It was included in the dossier against our wishes, because it wasn't reliable. Most things in the dossier were double source, but that was single source, and we believed that the source was wrong.'
>
> Now this official told us that the transformation of the dossier took place at the behest of Downing Street, and he added: 'Most people in intelligence weren't happy with the dossier because it didn't reflect the considered view they were putting forward.'

We now know that except for the claim that 'most people in intelligence weren't happy with the dossier' Dr Kelly's allegations were accurate. Nowhere did the BBC accuse the government, the Prime Minister, of 'lying' – it was Campbell who decided that's what the allegation amounted to.[†] Nowhere did the BBC accuse Campbell of 'inserting' false intelligence into the dossier – again, it was Campbell who decided that was the allegation and repeated it again and again until most people thought that's what had actually been said.

From its inception in early 2002, 'the dossier' had always

---

† Campbell's diary entry for Sunday 29 June 2003 reads: 'Birt [John Birt, the former BBC DG] drafted my letter to Sambrook, which we got out by 4 p.m. By then, Sambrook [was] digging in deeper saying that they never said TB [Tony Blair] lied – what the fuck do they think saying something whilst knowing it to be untrue means?'

been a Downing Street inspired production to serve Downing
Street's purposes. A political document intended to persuade
by 'creating the truth'. From Sir David Manning's March 2002
paper on, the idea of a dossier was to justify a course of action.
It was never intended to be a dispassionate account of the
intelligence passing across the Prime Minister's desk. Such an
account would have argued strongly, as one insider put it, for
doing nothing.

Much of the published dossier was produced under John
Scarlett's ownership, that's true – the executive summary and
main body. But its wording and content were changed significantly at Downing Street's behest to 'sex up' its message, to
'transform' it, in the week prior to its publication. The downbeat conclusion the JIC team had written was cut, an alarming
foreword drafted by Campbell was added, a foreword that
John Scarlett did not consider part of the dossier. And the decision was made to include the 45-minute claim – single sourced,
via an unreliable reporting line – shorn of qualifications some
in intelligence thought essential.

Gilligan didn't go to the Charing Cross Hotel to meet Dr
Kelly with the intention of uncovering this 'truth' of the dossier.
He stumbled on it. And once he'd told my day editor about
it, everything I knew told me we had a duty to report it. At
the same time, everything I knew about Gilligan's limitations
and loose language told me we had to try to ensure he didn't
stumble over his words, too. Scripting the allegations should
have been enough. It turned out not to be.

Once we'd had time to reflect, we shouldn't have defended
that first broadcast as resolutely as we did. And had Gilligan
been as frank with us as he was in due course with Lord
Hutton, I think we would have conceded his mistakes in that
one broadcast while standing by the allegations themselves,
allegations he reported accurately in nineteen or so other
broadcasts that day. Campbell would still have complained and
there's no guarantee that his determination to 'fuck' Gilligan

by 'outing' his source and divert attention from the February 2003 'dodgy' dossier would have led to any different outcome.

Once Dr Kelly's body had been found, Campbell realised 'it had all gone too far'. Until then, it had been business as usual. A game of words and headlines. The September dossier was just another passage of play in that game.

That's the 'truth' of the dossier, the truth Gilligan stumbled on and stumbled over. It was routine New Labour business, the business of 'creating the truth'. Nothing special.

Tony Blair didn't take us to war on a lie. He took us on a shrug.

APPENDIX

John Humphrys (J. H.): The government is facing more questions this morning over its claims about weapons of mass destruction in Iraq. Our defence correspondent is Andrew Gilligan. This in particular, Andy is Tony Blair saying, they'd be ready to go within forty-five minutes.

Andrew Gilligan (A. G.): That's right, that was the central claim in his dossier which he published in September, the main ... erm ... case if you like against ... erm ... against Iraq and the main statement of the British government's belief of what it thought Iraq was up to and what we've been told by one of the senior officials in charge of drawing up that dossier was that ... actually the government probably ... erm ... knew that that 45-minute figure was wrong, even before it decided to put it in.

What this person says, is that a week before the publication date of the dossier, it was actually rather ... erm ... a bland production. It didn't ... the ... the draft prepared for Mr Blair by the intelligence agencies actually didn't say very much more than was public knowledge already and ... erm ... Downing Street, our source says, ordered a week before publication, ordered it to be sexed up, to be made more exciting and ordered more facts to be ... erm... to be discovered.

J. H.: When you say 'more facts to be discovered', does that suggest that they may not have been facts?

A. G.: Well ... erm ... our source says that the dossier, as it was finally published, made the intelligence services unhappy ... erm ... because, to quote ... erm ... the source he said, there was basically ... that there was ... there was ... there was unhappiness because it didn't reflect the considered view they were putting forward ... that's a quote from our source and essentially ... erm ... the 45-minute point ... erm ... was ... was probably the most important thing that was added ... erm ... and the reason it hadn't been in the original draft was that it was, it was only ... erm ... it only came from one source and most of the other claims were from two, and the intelligence agencies say they don't really believe it was necessarily true because they thought the person making the claim had actually made a mistake, it got, had got mixed up.

J. H.: Does any of this matter now, all this, all these months later? The war's been fought and won.

A. G.: Well the forty-five minutes isn't just a detail, it did go to the heart of the government's case that Saddam was an imminent threat and it was repeated four times in the dossier, including by the Prime Minister himself, in the foreword; so I think it probably does matter. Clearly, you know, if ... erm ... if it ... if it was ... if it was wrong, things do, things are, got wrong in good faith but if they knew it was wrong before they actually made the claim, that's perhaps a bit more serious.

• • •

ANDREW GILLIGAN'S SCRIPT FOR *TODAY*, 29 MAY 2003

This is the dossier that was published in September last year, probably the most substantial statement of the government's case against Iraq. You'll remember that the Commons was recalled to debate it, Tony Blair made the opening speech.

It is not the same as the famous 'dodgy' dossier, the one that was copied off the internet. That came later. This is quite a serious document. It dominated the news that day and you open up the dossier and the first thing you see is a preface written by Tony Blair that includes the following words:

'Saddam's military planning allows for some weapons of mass destruction to be ready within forty-five minutes of an order to deploy them.'

Now that claim has come back to haunt Mr Blair because if the weapons had been that readily to hand, they probably would have been found by now.

But you know, it could have been an honest mistake, but what I have been told is that the government knew that claim was questionable, even before the war, even before they wrote it in their dossier.

I have spoken to a British official who was involved in the preparation of the dossier, and he told me that until the week before it was published, the draft dossier produced by the Intelligence Services, added little to what was already publicly known.

He said: 'It was transformed in the week before it was published, to make it sexier. The classic example was the statement that weapons of mass destruction were ready for use within forty-five minutes. That information was not in the original draft. It was included in the dossier against our wishes, because it wasn't reliable. Most things in the dossier were double source, but that was single source, and we believed that the source was wrong.'

Now this official told us that the transformation of the

dossier took place at the behest of Downing Street, and he added: 'Most people in intelligence weren't happy with the dossier because it didn't reflect the considered view they were putting forward.'

Now I want to stress that this official and others I've spoken to do still believe that Iraq did have some sort of weapons of mass destruction programme: 'I believe it is about 30 per cent likely there was a chemical weapons programme in the six months before the war and considerably more likely, that there was a biological weapons programme. We think Hans Blix down-played a couple of potentially interesting pieces of evidence, but the weapons programmes were small. Sanctions did limit the programmes.

The official also added quite an interesting note about what has happened as a result since the war, of the capture of some Iraqi WMD scientists: 'We don't have a great deal more information yet than we had before. We have not got very much out of the detainees yet.'

Now the forty-five minutes really is not just a detail, it did go to the heart of the government's case that Saddam was an imminent threat, and it was repeated a further three times in the body of the dossier, and I understand that the parliamentary Intelligence and Security Committee is going to conduct an inquiry into the claims made by the British Government about Iraq, and it is obviously exactly this kind of issue that will be at the heart of their investigation.

INDEX

FOR POLITICS, CURRENT AFFAIRS, INTERNATIONAL RELATIONS, HISTORY, BIOGRAPHY & MEMOIR AND MUCH MORE, VISIT:

WWW.POLITICOS.CO.UK
@POLITICOS_CO_UK

THE UK'S ONLY SPECIALIST POLITICAL ONLINE BOOKSHOP.